OUT OF
RUSSIA

OUT OF
RUSSIA

Based on the True Story of
Brian Grover and Ileana Petrovna

Brian Grover with Jim Rickards

JOHN BLAKE

Published by John Blake Publishing Ltd,
3 Bramber Court, 2 Bramber Road,
London W14 9PB, England

www.johnblakepublishing.co.uk

First published as *Field of Light* in 1995
This hardback edition published in 2009

ISBN: 978 1 85782 606 7

British Library Cataloguing-in-Publication Data:

A catalogue record for this book is available from the British Library.

Design by www.envydesign.co.uk

Printed in the UK by CPI William Clowes Beccles NR34 7TL

1 3 5 7 9 10 8 6 4 2

Papers used by John Blake Publishing are natural, recyclable products made from
wood grown in sustainable forests. The manufacturing processes conform to the
environmental regulations of the country of origin.

NOTES ON THE
NEW EDITION

Out of Russia is based on a true story. However, certain characters and events have been fictionalised by the authors for dramatic purposes.

PUBLISHER'S NOTE

You can thank Lavrenty Beria for the exquisite love story you are about to read. Beria was born in 1899, and rose to become chief of Stalin's notorious secret police before he was executed by Khrushchev in 1953. It is fair to say he was rather a nasty piece of work.

However, he did do one decent thing in his horrible life, and that was to reunite a romantic English engineer called Brian Grover with his beautiful Russian bride, Ileana Petrovna. I read about this uncharacteristic act of kindness in a biography of Beria, and became fascinated by the story.

I eventually managed to track Brian Grover down to his remote farm in the Transvaal, South Africa. He was then 90 years old, but he was lucid and charming when we spoke on the phone, and he invited me to come to visit, so he could tell me his wonderful story. His farm was at the end of a 30 mile long muddy track and my hire car was bogged down repeatedly in the deep red slop, with monkeys and wild animals all around, before I managed to splutter to the gate of his perfect, little farm-house.

'You must be hungry,' he chuckled, as he rustled up a frontier breakfast consisting of six eggs and half a loaf of home-baked bread each, plus a mountain of wild mushrooms he has picked that morning.

Our feast was interrupted twice as he pulled out the six-gun he wore on his belt to fire in the direction of baboons that were moving in on his fruit crop. Later, he proudly showed me the ancient motor-cycle he still used to ride into town for supplies. He was also hugely proud of the wonderful collection of photographs he had taken with his splendid Hasselblad professional's camera.

Ileana had died a few months earlier, shortly after their blissfully happy fifty-eighth wedding anniversary. As we sat talking in his beautiful garden, surrounded by a rainbow of meadow flowers, a tear occasionally trickled down his cheek when he told me of their extraordinary romance. His tale of a love between two people, which melted the hearts of dictators and tyrants, was the most life-affirming story I had ever heard.

Finally, after days of talking, I asked him if he had not been afraid of dying when he made his terrifying flight behind the iron curtain.

'No, not at all, Mr Blake,' he replied. 'You see, without Ileana I was as good as dead. I would rather have really been killed than face the thought of a life without her. In the end, it was all worth it.'

John Blake, February 2008

PRELUDE

The bentwood chair creaks as I rock to and fro. In the distance the Soutpansberg mountains are bathed in late afternoon sun. But one of nature's most spectacular displays is of less interest to me these days than the small silver case with its tatty ribbon, which I have in my hand. The intricate swirls at its corners are blackened by years of handling, microscopic reminders of the generations of Lena's family who treasured it then lovingly passed it down from mother to daughter. I have also played my part, proudly showing it to my friends or simply, as now, feeling its smoothness and remembering the remarkable woman who gave it to me.

Inside, the tiny portrait is fading but it still has the power to move me. It's a simple watercolour, no more than thirty deft strokes, but the likeness is there. The unknown artist on the streets of Grozny has caught her perfectly, the few wisps of russet brown hair across her forehead, the creases at the corner of her mouth, the dimple just above her chin and a hint of the small mole on her cheek. Like me, he seems to have become entranced by her in just a few moments. His fleeting admiration is captured in this charming portrait. Then, no doubt, he turned to the next person with a few roubles to spend on a love token. But for me the enchantment continued to grow. It took over my life, forced me to do things that still surprise me. They caused me pain and at times despair, but nevertheless left me a truly contented man.

I rub my nipple and smile.

CHAPTER ONE

Mother had only ever given me one piece of advice: 'Brian, never, repeat never, marry a woman who has no money. You will only live to regret it.'

Little did she know as she intoned the mantra once more over the Christmas lunch table, that I was already married. And she was right, I did regret my marriage. Not, however, because Maddy had little money but because the free spirit who had bowled me over when we first met turned out to want nothing more than to tie me down to a routine office job in the hope I might become a bank manager.

No one from the outside would have suspected a thing but, in truth, behind the walls of our 'modest' mansion in the Home Counties, every member of the comfortably middle-class Grover family lived with regrets. For my parents, the greatest of them was the way I had turned out. Born in the first year of the twentieth century, I had enjoyed all the advantages that went with this lifestyle. I had been educated by a governess until the age of nine and then at public school, and while Mother and Father were never close to me, they had given me what they deemed necessary and had every reason to believe I would grow up in their image, a son they could be proud of.

The change came during my time at university. Cambridge allowed room for nagging doubts to worm their way into my mind. I didn't *have* to join the army to fulfil the ambition my father had nursed for me ever since dropping me off for my first day at Charterhouse. I didn't *have* to marry the daughter of a wealthy, society family to make my mother happy. I had a degree in engineering and that could be my passport to a much more attractive life. The reality came with a jolt. But the greater shock was that I had not thought of it before. Suddenly it seemed obvious, and easy.

The week after graduation I deliberately missed the long-planned interview that would have opened the doors to officer training. Instead I spent the day at Shell's headquarters and managed to talk my way into a post in their oilfields in Sarawak. On the train home I rolled the vowels round in my mouth. They tasted exotic, worth suffering the icy reception I was going to receive when I broke the news to my parents.

But now the job in Sarawak had been shut down by the depression, and as 1930 came to an end, I was 'enjoying' my first Christmas at home for some time. I'd gone back mainly out of duty and while my parents were pleased to see me, they could not refrain from regularly pointing out 'what a mess you have made of your life' and expressing the hope that now that I had come to my senses I would get a proper job and become part of the smart set in the West End rather than squandering my time with those roughnecks I had been associating with.

'Your trouble, young man, is that you have never listened,' Father said as he carved the duck, each slice punctuated by a word of rebuke.

I felt little connection with these two people who seemed to exist in a different world from the one I knew, the one that continually tempted me to new experiences and new places. I was aware that I was a disappointment to them but on Boxing Day I realised just how deep that ran. One of their old friends came for lunch. He was completely in tune with them, agreeing with Mother that 'great deeds were being done for the poor by the Rotary Club', and also nodding vigorously when Father blustered that 'the blighters are never grateful, no matter what you do.' Over coffee, the conversation turned to me and what I'd been doing all these years that I'd been away. Before I could answer, Mother said: 'Brian has been exploring. He's been on an expedition in Sarawak.'

I was ready to correct her when I caught Father's eye and realised that admitting I had been pumping oil among a horde of uncouth roustabouts with grubby hands was taboo. What they felt was beyond disappointment. It was shame.

With the ease of many years in polite society, Mother soon guided the conversation on to safer ground and after a short while I excused myself, claiming I had an important letter to write. In fact it was only a brief note, explaining to my parents that I was sorry they felt the way they did but I had to live my life the way I thought best. I expressed the hope that the next time we met, we would be able to accept each other's differences and with a certain childish satisfaction, I finished off: 'Please don't worry about me. I can look after myself. I always have.'

I gathered my things together and slipped quietly out the door. Almost all I had to show for my years of independence was stuffed into two bags. In addition I had three-months' severance pay, a failed marriage, deeply disappointed parents and a list of addresses provided by our family lawyer of people who might give me work. Oh yes, and my optimism and the friendship of an American named Frank.

CHAPTER 2

My parents would certainly have disapproved of Frank Brown. Apart from his obvious failing of having been born in Texas, he was rough-edged, bluntly spoken and not always to be trusted in polite company. There were even times when my Cambridge-honed sensibilities cringed at his antics. But he was my most reliable friend and support.

We met in Sarawak. My first few months there had not been easy. My accent marked me out as different from the rest of the riggers, my inexperience and my mistakes didn't exactly endear me, and I was starting to wonder if this was the life I was cut out for. Then Frank arrived. Even among oil men he was big. He'd been working the wells for 20 years from Dallas to the Middle East. The business was in his blood and more obviously in his body. His hands were calloused where endless blisters had burst and healed over until the skin had lost the elasticity to blister ever again. His forearms were flecked with ingrained tar and scarred by blasts of scalding steam. Even at 40 he was powerful enough to match any man on site, still fearless and agile enough to be quick and safe around the 100-foot-high platforms, and with still enough energy to relish staying in a bar long into the night after a day spent in the heat and the dirt.

His experience immediately commanded respect among the whole crew and his easy-going nature meant he soon became popular. To my surprise, he singled me out for attention. When I got to know him better, I asked him why and he said: 'You looked like you needed help.'

He'd been right about that but what had started for him, I suspect, as a vaguely interesting time filler, getting to know about this strange, out-of-place Englishman, quickly developed into something more. We became a good team. I had the theory and the latest ideas from around the world that had found their way to Cambridge, he knew the practice and could show me how to keep on the right side of the people who mattered without becoming a stooge. Befriended by Frank, I was accepted by everyone and by the end of the year we were overseeing a successful team and responsible for the main well on the field.

He enjoyed teasing me, calling me 'the professor', accusing me of having my head in the clouds. He was constantly amused when he could do the physical tasks more deftly than me. But I knew he respected me and the two of us spent many hours together after work. After a while we used our spare time to build a raft from local cane, sometimes talking quietly, sometimes comfortably silent. And once it was complete, we enjoyed nothing more than taking it out into midstream of the Rejang river, anchoring it with a stone on a rope, and gently drifting while we swapped stories and drank a few bottles of the beer especially imported for the riggers.

I learned to respect his advice. I didn't always take it and then usually regretted not listening to him. I definitely should have taken more notice when he told me not to take the job I'd been offered drilling for oil in California. He pointed out it was the same relentless sun just in a different time zone, and that one oil rig was much like another, adding what he saw as the killer argument - he wouldn't be there to hold my hand. But I was restless and went anyway. In fact, I had no problem with the job; it was the journey out there that caused the trouble.

The ship was packed with emigrating families and old couples who had settled into a life of full-time cruising. Content to have every whim provided by solicitous waiters, they were no longer even interested in disembarking when they arrived in a new port. I was bored. There was little to do except read or lean over the railings and watch the ship frothing up the sea. Some nights I played cards with a few off-duty sailors. Then, over dinner one evening, I met a woman from Alabama who introduced me to her daughter.

'Brian, this is Madeleine. She's been on the Grand European tour,' Mrs Jacobs informed me with more than a hint of satisfaction. Madeleine was very pretty, petite with short blonde hair cut in a flick across her face. She had large, green, arresting eyes. I noticed they didn't smile with the rest of her face but I let it pass. I was just relieved to have someone young and lively to talk to. Like me, she seemed to be desperately trying not to become a replica of her parents. Whereas her mother toured Europe because it was the thing to do, Madeleine was genuinely captivated by the sights she had seen in Rome, Paris and London.

From then on, we ate together regularly. Looking back I can see that the formidable Mrs Jacobs manipulated it, managing to 'bump into me' on the deck just before the gong sounded for dinner. But I didn't mind. I was relatively inexperienced with women and enjoyed the attention. Suddenly the trip was transformed. My first thought every morning became to seek out Maddy and she was clearly pleased to see me. We played deck games, strolled from bow to stern, and ducked giggling into nooks and crannies as we tried to avoid her formidable mother. At night we would hide in the shady, smoky corners of the casino and if I'm honest I suppose I was impressed by this worldly young woman who knew her way around the gaming tables, would win hundreds of dollars and then carelessly blow the money on a single bet or in buying lavish cocktails.

We had fun together and when we anchored in America, I was delighted that she agreed to keep in touch. I went to Long Beach and she went back home, and for eighteen months we wrote to each other regularly. Her letters were warm, amusing and filled with her apparent longing to experience more of the world, to shake off the dust of Alabama and the life her parents had planned for her. The further apart we were, the closer we became. I only saw her once. I had a week's leave and went to stay at her parents' house. Everything was very proper. We went dancing, took in a movie. On the last night, I kissed her. It felt what I imagined love must be like. Somewhere along the way I got it into my head that the inevitable next step should be marriage.

I didn't have much time to think about it. When I returned to California, I found out I was to be posted to Trinidad so I wrote to Madeleine and proposed, asking her to move to the West Indies with me. She accepted and her parents were thrilled - 'Our Madeleine is marrying a wealthy Englishman, you know.' There was a hasty but quiet wedding in New York. There was no time for a honeymoon, but I thought life in Trinidad would be holiday enough.

When our ship docked in Port of Spain to the sound of a steel band, I felt I'd been washed up on the shores of paradise. Miles of untouched white sand beckoned wherever we looked. Small boys stood by, ready to scamper up the palm trees that lined the coast and chop down a refreshing cocoanut. I was in love, had my bride by my side and a job I enjoyed. I thought life was perfect. But it was soon apparent that this was not the kind of adventure Madeleine had envisaged. Over the next few months I realised that she had more in common with my parents than with me. It was not her family lifestyle she disliked, it was simply that her mother was in charge and that she was surrounded by people from an older generation. She wanted to be the leading lady rather than the decorative daughter. Marriage, she had hoped, would allow her to have her own salon with her own friends. She loathed Trinidad. She hated the long hours I worked and despised the people I worked with. From day one she complained about the humidity, about the food, about the locals.

It wasn't what I had expected from marriage. I still loved Madeleine but I longed to find again the spirited woman I had known on the boat or the writer of those wonderful letters. It seemed that had all been a ploy, the bait to attract a man she thought she could mould into the ideal husband. She thought I was demeaning myself by doing the work I did and told me so, pointing out that I would be better off joining the bank where her father worked. 'Why, in a few years you would be a manager,' she said, amazed that I didn't find the idea attractive.

I tried to see things from her point of view. I realised she was probably homesick, and while I met plenty of people at work she was alone for hours on end. I clung to the hope that as she made new friends, she would settle and enjoy Trinidad as much as I did but one day in the middle of a fierce row, she threw a local Alabama paper at me and yelled: 'That's what I think of you and this benighted place.' Inside was an article she had written ridiculing oilmen for their uncouth ways and sneering at the 'primitive' Trinidadian way of life.

Soon we were sleeping in separate beds and a few weeks later

I returned home to find her standing in the lounge, suitcase by her feet and dressed to travel.

'I'm going back home,' she said. 'If you come with me now, I will forgive you.'

I didn't feel I needed forgiveness. 'I have a job, Maddy. I can't just up and leave.'

'Then, it's over, until you see sense.'

'Then it's over,' I replied.

She returned to America and I stayed put. I thought of following her, of trying to make it work. Perhaps I was being selfish; perhaps I should have made an effort to be the kind of husband she wanted. But I knew it was as impossible for me to be happy in a bank in Alabama as it was for Maddy to enjoy being an oilman's wife in the Caribbean. After a while, I asked her for a divorce. She refused and I was taken aback by the bitterness in her letter. She wrote that she was humiliated daily by the absence of her husband and if I thought I could swan off to a new life without paying the price, I had better think again. It ended with the sentence scrawled in capital letters: 'YOU WILL PAY ONE DAY!'

That was the last I heard from her for some time and surprisingly quickly it was as though Madeleine had never happened. I remained in Trinidad for a year or so then went back to Sarawak and joined up with Frank again. The revelation of my failed marriage was something new for him to tease me about, to say, 'I told you not to go, you should have listened to me.'

He was the one who warned me that the job in Sarawak was about to finish. It took a while for the newspapers from late October 1929 to reach us but as soon as he read them, Frank grasped that the waves engulfing Wall Street would soon be lapping at our shores thousands of miles away and they would still have enough force to be overpowering. As usual he was right.

'What will you do?' he asked, as we sat on our raft, drinking cold beer.

'I'll probably go back to London and see what happens. Something will turn up. You should come with me. We can find a job in some faraway part of the world and forget all this hassle.'

Instinctively he knew my concerns weren't only about finding work. 'Maybe,' he said. 'You can't keep running away forever you know. She'll come after you one day and screw up your life.'

'No,' I replied, unconvincingly. 'She's not that vindictive and I certainly won't let any other woman have that much power over me ever again.'

Frank roared with genuine laughter. 'Brian, you have no choice. You are a starry-eyed Englishman. Whatever you may say, you believe in love. You need it. One day you will meet a woman who will melt your bones when you see her. You will want to be with her every minute of the day. You will want to own her.' He took another swig from the bottle. 'You, my old son, will be jelly.'

'Never in a million years,' I retorted. 'Only a fool gets bitten by the same dog twice.'

He smiled. 'I tell you what. I'll have a bet with you that you'll be completely hooked within five years.'

'And if I win, what do I get?'

'Lunch at Simpson's in the Strand and enough champagne to fill a bath.'

'Done.'

I smiled at the memory as I walked away from my parents' house. It had been six months since Frank and I had made the bet and the odds were even more in my favour because there was scarcely time to think about women. I needed a job.

CHAPTER 3

As soon as I found bed-and-breakfast lodgings in London, I sent Frank a telegram: 'COME OVER NOW. OPPORTUNITIES GALORE.' The reply was swift and to the point: 'LIAR. SEE YOU 28th JANUARY, WATERLOO STATION 7.30 AM.'

Of course he was right.

I met him off the train from Southampton. He was grey and tired after a rough Atlantic crossing so when I took him for a slap-up breakfast in Lyons, I didn't bother to tell him I only had one name left on the list that the lawyer had given me. And I made light of the fact that when I'd been to the others, and to many that weren't on the list, I'd been told there were no engineering jobs to be had. 'But that's only so far,' I added, hoping he would be encouraged. We still had this one last hope which read: 'If all else fails try Stephen Talbot, 104c The Strand. He normally has something up his sleeve. He can be tricky, so be a bit careful what that something is.' I decided Frank probably wouldn't be interested in these finer details and walked him across Waterloo Bridge to the Strand.

'So this is the heart of the Empire?' Frank said. 'No wonder it's crumbling.'

I could see what he meant. London was a sad place, almost devoid of colour except for the buses which were running half empty as people tried to save every penny they could. Those lucky enough to have a job were in constant fear of being called in to be told they were being let go. It showed in their faces as they scurried towards their offices. Others walked much more slowly, on another fruitless trip to the Labour Exchange, or just whiling away the day window-shopping for things they could no longer afford. Even that was made more dispiriting by the number of boarded up shops and having to step over the tramps curled up in doorways clutching a bottle containing a little something they had managed to beg but were now saving to fight the night chill.

'It's bad,' I admitted. 'But I guess it can't be much better in the Land of the Free, or you wouldn't be here.'

He grunted, but didn't dispute my logic.

At first we went straight past the cubbyhole entrance of 104c. It wasn't hard to do. The letter T on 'Talbot Enterprises Unlimited' had slipped upside down and the sign had clearly not been cleaned since the day it was put up. When we retraced our steps and went in, the small square hallway at the bottom of the stairs was strewn with old newspapers and there was the distinctive smell of stale urine. The stairs were unlit.

'So this is why I have been churning my guts up for the last few days,' Frank said. 'I must be crazy. I could be on holiday in Florida or I could be in Borneo with a beer and a beautiful woman. Look at this place. What kind of job are we going to get here? I'm booking on the next ship back.'

I didn't want to tell him that I'd been turned away from worse places than this in the last few weeks. 'Come on,' I said as cheerfully as I could. 'Let's go in and see what he says. If you don't like it, you can still get the boat home. At least you will have seen something of London.'

He snorted but allowed me to drag him upstairs and into the office on the first floor landing.

Stephen Talbot was best described as Dickensian. His hair was slicked across his head thanks to copious amounts of Brylcreem. His body was oval - his trousers tucked some inches below his waist while above, his cream and gold paisley waistcoat did its best to hold everything in place, the points manfully stretching down in an effort to cover the wedge of shirt gaping between belly and belt. There were sharp lines at the corners of his eyes but it was impossible to tell if these were created by laughter or stress.

His greeting was effusive. I detected a slight Irish lilt beneath his impeccable gentleman's accent as he said: 'Grover, my dear fellow. Thank you so much for your letter. It's really good to see you. And who is this?'

I introduced Frank who was hovering near the door, ready to make a quick getaway.

'Come in, dear boy. Here, sit down, sit down.'

Easier said than done. Along with dust, there were boxes, papers and files on every available surface, including most of the threadbare carpet. The shelves groaned with books, most of which looked as though they had never been read. Talbot shuffled out from behind his desk and dumped an in-tray from the only chair on to the floor, motioning me to sit, then looked around in vain for another seat.

'Don't worry,' Frank said laconically. 'I don't mind standing.'

'Nonsense, dear boy. Here perch on this,' and he dragged across an upturned tea-chest. 'Be careful, the edges are sharp.'

Frank delicately eased his big frame on to one corner of the chest and raised a sceptical eyebrow at me.

Talbot resumed his place behind his desk, clasped his hands together around his belly and addressed himself to the room in general.

'You are most welcome. These are terrible times. You are so well qualified, intelligent and experienced yet these dreadful conditions have thrown you, and so many others like you, on the scrapheap. Terrible times indeed.

'But don't despair. There is always a demand for people like you. It's just a question of finding it. Find the gap and fill it - that's what I've been doing all my working life. Now let me see.'

'What gaps are there, if you don't mind me asking?' Frank interrupted. 'My friend here has traipsed all over London and visited every firm that needs people like us and has turned up exactly nothing.'

Talbot bristled slightly but smiled. 'If I may say so, you should have tried me first. I'm well known for finding a way.'

He started to riffle through the papers on his desk and not finding what he was looking for, turned his attention to one of the drawers. Frank glanced across at me, shook his head and drew his hand across his throat as if to say 'I've had enough, let's get out of here'. I pretended I didn't understand. At the very least I wanted to hear what the man had to say. After all, there was nothing to lose.

Talbot stopped ferreting around in the drawer, obviously deciding he didn't need whatever it was he was searching for.

'Now I think you are going to like what I'm going to offer you,' he said.

'Which is?' Frank replied.

'All in good time, all in good time. If we are to do business, we need to know each other a little first.'

With that, Talbot proceeded to tell us virtually his whole life history. He was a natural storyteller. Even though he had obviously narrated these events many times and his speech was spattered with truisms and slogans - 'life is easy if you know how' and 'I always say don't find objections, find solutions' - he had a zest about him that made the whole thing sound fresh and I couldn't help but warm to him. He told us that he had vowed when he left school never to have any boss but himself and claimed that sticking to that philosophy was the secret of his success. His eyes brightened with each triumph recalled. Initially he had set himself up as a tea merchant selling into the major Russian cities until 'the Revolution rather scuppered a handsome source of income'. But he had managed to spot the changes that were coming and switched his attention to the right people at the right time and was still doing a lucrative business with the Soviet Union as well as those people in England who had sold their stocks before the crash and were now busy buying up bargains from people who had not been so far-sighted or fortunate.

'So, now you know about me. What about you? Are you good with languages?'

'I can get by in French, German and Spanish,' I said.

'And you?' he turned to Frank.

'I get problems trying to understand you English.'

'Ah. Right. So what would you say were your special talents?'

A little edge was creeping into the exchanges and Frank wasn't one to back down.

'Sorry, could you rephrase the question, please?' he said.

'What are you good at?'

'You've got my résumé.'

'Would you say you are good at communicating?'

Even I didn't know if this was a genuine question or a barbed comment.

'Depends who I'm communicating with.'

Talbot sighed. 'Evidently.'

Frank stood up. 'Where's the john, I'm busting for a pee.'

We both stared at him, neither able to work out what was bugging him.

'Out the door, first on the right.' our bemused host waved a hand in the general direction.

Talbot and I both knew he wasn't coming back.

'Your friend could use some work on his interview technique,' Talbot said.

'Yes, I'm sorry. He doesn't always give a good first impression.'

'Pity. They can be so very important.'

He shuffled some papers together, put them in a neat pile on the corner of the desk and stood up to let me know the interview was over.

I was livid with Frank. This man was about to offer us a job and for some reason he'd got his stupid American hackles up and walked out, blowing the whole deal. I had to try and rescue it.

'Look, please, take no notice. He's just got off the boat from New York this morning. He's whacked. I promise you he's not normally like this and he's a damned fine worker, the best I've ever met.'

Talbot shook his head. 'I'll be straight with you. I'm doing some business in Moscow for the next few months and I need a couple of people with your kind of experience to give me a hand. I have no problem with you but your friend could...'

'Please, he'll be OK. We'll take it.'

'Mr Brown doesn't seem so keen.'

'We won't let you down, I promise.'

'Look, I want to be fair. Why don't you both come back in a couple of days when he is rested and we'll see what we can do.'

I'd been on enough job interviews to know this was just another brush off, that if we came back the job would 'sadly' have been filled.

'No. Let's sort it out now.'

Talbot looked surprised. Then he smiled. 'OK. I like a man who says No for an answer but won't take it. Go and get your hot-headed friend and we'll discuss terms.'

I took the stairs at a gallop and found Frank outside smoking a cigarette.

I shoved him in the chest. 'What the hell are you playing at?' I yelled.

'Brian, he's a waste of time. I wouldn't trust him with my enemy's future let alone mine.'

'The feeling's mutual, believe me. But the man has offered us a job in Russia. Remember jobs? Those things where you work and people pay you money?'

'Why would we want to go to Russia? It's cold and it's full of Bolshies.'

'Do you know anyone who has ever been?' I was getting exasperated.

'No and that's my point. No one wants to go.'

I wanted to yell at him again but I knew that would make him even more stubborn. I tried coaxing. 'Please, Frank. This could be our last hope of a job. People are working in Russia and there are massive oilfields over there where we might be taken on.'

'I'm telling you, I don't trust him.'

'Why not? He seems all right to me.'

'So did Madeleine.'

That hurt. We both stood in silence and didn't notice the old woman approach us. She was only about five feet tall, dark rings round her eyes and sunken cheeks. She had a headscarf tied so tightly that the folds of baggy skin under her chin hid the knot. She reached up to Frank and put something in his buttonhole.

'There you are, ducks,' she said. 'A bit of white heather to bring you luck.' She turned and did the same to me. I rummaged in my pocket for some change but she said: 'No, dearie. No charge. We are all in this together and two such fine looking gentlemen should never go out without a buttonhole.' Then she slowly moved away, muttering to herself.

Her simple generosity had obviously touched Frank and changed his mood. He smiled ruefully at me. 'Sorry,' he said. 'Come on, let's go and see what the old twister has to say for himself.'

Talbot welcomed us back casually as though nothing unusual had happened. 'Here's the plan,' he said. 'I'm putting together contracts between British firms and Soviet government agencies. I need people who understand machinery to act as runners, intermediaries, vital links in a chain of high-level business negotiations.'

'Packhorses,' said Frank, but shut up when I threw him an icy stare.

Talbot chatted on for another half hour or so but I realised later that he hadn't really told us anything concrete about what we were expected to do. Nevertheless, the money wasn't bad, all our expenses were covered and we would at least be getting out of London and hopefully leaving the depression behind us.

We sealed the deal over lunch in a little place in Villiers Street. Talbot took great delight in showing us a string of business cards that tumbled out of his wallet. 'Every one of these is a contact and it is contacts that make business go round,' he said. 'I think I can honestly say that between Britain and the Soviet Union, I have more of these cards than anyone else. Believe me, chaps, the important thing in life is not to make friends but to make lists, lists of people who you can put together and take your commission off the top. I have plenty of clout in Moscow and I can do you two a lot of good. I can introduce you to the right people who are looking for workers with your skills and experience. You will do all right, trust me.'

'And what's in it for you?' Frank asked. 'You are paying our expenses and a good wage and now you are promising to fix us up with the top people in the oil business. What's the catch?'

'No catch. I need your expertise and I need you to be my legs while I put together my deals. I can't do it all myself. I'll get my money's worth don't worry.' He smiled. 'And, Frank, you can pay for lunch. I don't want you to worry that you are getting something for nothing. Now I've got to go. I'll see you at the station next week. Bring plenty of warm clothes.'

The two days on the train passed very pleasantly. The steady clack of the wheels on the rails and the gentle swaying of the compartment became a comfortable rhythm that insulated us from all the world's cares. Hours stretched ahead of us with no responsibilities, no demands and no interruptions apart from taking meals. Talbot was the perfect travelling companion, spinning yarns, sharing jokes but also willing to listen when I had something to say and making telling observations that made me realise he was no fool. He spent some time giving us information about Moscow. He clearly loved the city and its people and while he emphasised repeatedly that he was going there to make money - 'the Soviets get our expertise and contacts, we get the cash' - Moscow was also a second home, perhaps his preferred home. Even Frank's scepticism faded a little and the two of them began to communicate in whole sentences. I had a suspicion they started to like each other.

As we crossed the Elbe, Talbot looked out at the winter sky darkening on the horizon and took in the scene with the small boats moored to rocks on the banks of the river, the odd fisherman casting his line and a modest row of cottages, windows already shuttered against the cold of the night.

'Picture book,' he said. 'But also so much more. I love trains. You can look out and glimpse places whose names you don't even know but with the realisation that if you stopped off and visited a local bar you could soon strike up a conversation with people you had never met before. It always reminds me that the world is full of endless possibilities, potential friendships, possible deals.'

When we stopped in Berlin to take on more fuel, he disappeared for a while to wheel and deal. Frank was asleep in one corner of the compartment. I looked out and caught sight of my reflection in the carriage window. All in all I didn't think I looked too bad. Maybe the face was a little thin, but it had always been so. The blue eyes were perhaps a bit deep set but still quite bright. My hair was still thick and unlike Frank, I didn't have the first signs of grey at the temples. I looked older than I thought of myself but certainly not old. 'Handsome in a craggy way' was how my friends described me. I didn't know what they meant, but I felt they were being kind. The years in Sarawak had toughened me up and broadened my shoulders. I was still fit and felt ready to face whatever the next few months had to offer. At least I wouldn't have to concern myself about what my parents thought and even Madeleine wouldn't be able to trouble me in the Soviet Union.

I sat back and studied the 100 useful Russian phrases Talbot had prepared for us. I was starting to get the hang of the language. I'd always had a good ear and thought I would soon be able to pick up enough to get by in conversation even if reading and writing the unfamiliar characters might take a little longer. Tomorrow we would cross the border and soon we would be in Moscow, so I would quickly find out.

CHAPTER 4

In Russian, Moscow is a feminine word, *Moskva*. It is the mother of the people. Even though it wasn't always the capital city, travellers have made their way there for hundreds of years and when we arrived it was at the heart of a Union that stretched for over 6,000 miles from the Ukraine to the Bering Straits, looking across to the former Russian-owned Alaska. North to south it ran for more than 3,000 miles from the Arctic Ocean to near the Afghan border and within that vast space the climate varied from arctic to sub-tropical. The people - around 160 million of them - were an extraordinary variety of ethnic groups but all looked towards and were controlled from Moscow, at this time often a somewhat harsh mother.

'Just remember,' Talbot told us as the train steamed through the last few hours of our trip, 'Moscow is the everything city. Everything is legal and everything is possible. It is all a matter of *blat*.'

Blat was the Russian word that covered the informal network of connections and agreements that allowed the system to function reasonably efficiently. If you were part of it, there was nothing you could not do. It was a bit like the old boy network in England but more open to outsiders who were willing to obey the rules and see the right people got what they wanted. Talbot, we learned later, had *blat* in excess.

He had warned us that we would be arriving when the Moscow winter was at its fiercest but nothing could have prepared us for the shock as we stepped off the train. Our eyelashes stuck together and as we stood gathering our luggage our shoes became fixed to the ground.

'Put me on the next train back to civilization,' Frank moaned, vainly pulling a scarf further over his face.

Talbot ordered a cab to take us to our hotel. As we passed through the streets, we only saw a few Muscovites trundling along beneath a weight of furs that seemed to leave no part of their skin exposed. It looked like brutal conditions yet it was also beautiful. We'd arrived at dawn on a clear morning with a thin sun that sparkled off the snow and ice covering the buildings. The light was perfect and the details of the old churches were razor sharp. There were dark alleys, down which I glimpsed what looked like alluring shops and restaurants; parks with skeleton trees appeared from nowhere amid great concrete office blocks; and as we crossed the river, we could see a handful of children braving the early morning cold to skate around the stanchions of the bridge.

When we reached the north bank, Talbot pointed towards a massive fortress with sheer walls, fifty feet high. 'That, my friends, is the Kremlin. Nearly a mile wide in all, including four cathedrals and four palaces. That is where the money is. That is where the deals are done.'

'Sod the money,' Frank grumbled. 'I'll just settle for somewhere warm.'

Talbot laughed. 'Don't worry, Frank. All buildings in Moscow are warm. The Soviets are experts in heating, it's one of their strengths. Besides, you are staying in the Metropol, probably the best hotel in the city. It has wonderful views, fabulous food and it's close to my office. I will pick you up from there tomorrow and show you round.'

'If the hotel's that good,' asked Frank, still determined to be suspicious, 'how come you are not staying there?'

'I have my own flat. We may be friends, Frank, but we don't know each other well enough to live together.'

Talbot's description of the Metropol was no exaggeration. It was staggering in its opulence. Marble staircases sprang from massive hallways, their walls covered in paintings and mosaics. Priceless Persian rugs stretched from wall to wall in the dining room. It was a relic of the past, built towards the end of the 19th century by an eccentric millionaire, the manager informed us, then taken over by Lenin during the revolution. In some ways it reminded me of a Victorian folly: a giant mismatch of styles and influences from baroque to modern. When you looked a little closer it was possible to detect that the Metropol was an institution struggling to live up to its former glories. Dust had gathered on the gold chandeliers, the mosaics in the restaurant were fading and, in the lobby, like an alien from a more primitive world, there was a huge stuffed bear, reared up on its hind legs as though ready to pounce on anyone stupid enough to pass its way.

The manager fluttered around us as though we were VIPs. 'We don't have so many foreign visitors these days,' he explained in English, 'and this is a quiet time of year.' He showed us to our rooms, cavernous chambers with four-poster beds and balconies overlooking Prospeckt Marksa and Red Square. And beautifully warm.

'If you require anything,' he informed us, 'pull the bell

handle by the wardrobe, we'll attend as soon as we can.' We tried it later that evening. 'As soon as we can' meant an hour and 'attend' meant the arrival of a sullen and distracted waiter in a crumpled suit. He looked old enough to be my grandfather's grandfather.

Talbot turned up the next morning as Frank and I gorged ourselves on a breakfast of black bread and sour cream cheese. He was laden down with parcels.

'Just to show I take care of my associates,' he said and spilled an array of fur hats, woollen coats and fishermen's jumpers on to the table. From one package he removed two pairs of boots that looked as though they had been chopped straight off the leg of a yeti and hollowed out. We tried the clothes on there and then. The other residents carried on eating and ignored us. Nothing was unusual in Moscow and anyway it was best not to get involved or pass comment.

'What do you think?' Talbot asked.

'I feel like that stuffed bear in reception,' I replied.

Frank pulled on his new footwear and stomped around the room.

'What are these things?' he asked.

'They are *sapagi*. The best that dollars can buy and invaluable in this weather.'

'Why can't they call them boots, like everyone else?'

Talbot sighed. Like a frustrated but resolute teacher he said: 'Frank, you are in Russia and believe it or not, most people here speak Russian so they use a Russian word. You would do well to get used to the idea and learn to play along. Here, this might help.' Out of yet another bag he took a couple of English-Russian dictionaries and step-by-step Russian courses.

'Russian for simpletons,' Talbot said. 'I believe even some

26

Americans have become fluent using these.'

Frank grunted. Inevitably he preferred to pick up the language without too much studying and was soon telling me how valuable the Russian word *drygoi* was. 'It means another,' he explained. 'I use it all the time - another vodka, another brandy, another jar of caviar.' My own foray into Russian was a bit more methodical. I spent most of my evenings and spare time going through the course book then trying out my new phrases on the hotel staff.

For the first couple of weeks Talbot allowed us plenty of spare time. He took us to his office on the Bulvar and pointed out the main routes around the city but on the whole he left us alone while he started to negotiate his contracts. I grabbed the opportunity to explore and quickly realised that my first impressions of a quiet, thinly populated city were completely wrong. We'd seen it very early, before the place burst into a frenzy of activity. Beneath posters that proclaimed THE FIVE-YEAR PLAN IN FOUR, people scurried around like ants. Roads were being ripped up and rebuilt ready for heavy vehicles; old buildings razed to the ground and replaced with severe blocks of flats to house the workers; piles of rubble appeared overnight but were carted away by the end of the day. Frank was quietly impressed by the industry of the Muscovites but occasionally wondered aloud if anyone had thought through what they were doing. He was also sceptical about my desire to drag him along to view the stunning collection at the Pushkin museum, or the five golden domes of the Cathedral of Assumption, or the Novodevichy Convent, which stretches along the banks of the Moskva and had been turned into a Museum of Women's Emancipation by the Soviets.

'Brian, I'd really rather stay in the warmth of the hotel,' he said. 'I'm here to make money not be educated in fine art or 15th century architecture. If I must tramp around in arctic conditions,

I'd rather it was in the cause of commerce than culture.'

He soon got his way. We would turn up at Talbot's office at eight every morning and each day his smile seemed to get broader. Towards the end of February he said: 'There's a lot of money to be made, chaps. Time to start earning your keep.'

He told us we would be delivering packages to his contacts across the city and from time to time, picking up a contract from one address and taking it to another. 'Keeping the cogs running smoothly,' he beamed.

First we had to come to terms with his system, which seemed designed to make life easy for him but much more complicated for us. He gave each of us a list of addresses which we were told must never leave the office in case they were lost. Each address had a corresponding lettered code which was what appeared on the package. We had to learn the codes so we knew where to make the delivery.

'Why don't you just address each package?' Frank asked. 'It would be much easier.'

'Maybe for you, but it takes hours to write in Cyrillic. This way I have done it once and don't have to bother again. You'll soon get the hang of it. It's a bit like cabbies finding their way around London, after a while they don't even have to think about it.'

Frank was clearly unimpressed. 'I'm an engineer not a cabbie,' he snorted. 'I thought we were here to advise you with our expertise, to help with your deals, not act as glorified packhorses.'

'You are not ready yet,' Talbot said. 'I've spent years building up contacts, winning their trust, so I can do business in a system that is deeply suspicious of foreigners. A wrong word here or there from you could wreck everything I've done. Don't forget who sorted out your visas, put you in the best hotel and is paying the bill without querying your somewhat excessive spending in the bar. All I'm asking in return is some co-operation. Believe me, it will stand you in good stead.'

It sounded reasonable enough but, as ever, Frank still had something to say. 'You said you would fix us up with introductions in the oil business. What about that?'

'All in good time. First you need to get to know the city better and how it operates. Now there's a pile of packages for each of you, one labelled Brian, the other Frank. Simple enough for you?'

I decided I'd better step in before it got really ugly. 'C'mon, Frank. The sooner we start, the sooner you can treat me to vodka on Stephen's bill.'

As we reached the door, Talbot said, 'If you are stopped and asked for your papers, just smile, show your cards and look simple.' He looked at Frank and savouring having the last word, added, 'That shouldn't be too difficult, should it?'

For the next couple of weeks, we crisscrossed the city, mainly on foot, seeking out offices and apartments, fetching and carrying. It was arduous in the biting cold but as Talbot had predicted it did become easier and it was a wonderful way to get to know Moscow. We soon started to recognise landmarks and learn which little alleyways would save us five or ten minutes on our journey. Having to ask the way to obscure addresses made even Frank more fluent in Russian and we both found the local people friendly and eager to be helpful. As Talbot had warned, we were regularly stopped by uniformed officials wanting to see our permits (city and suburbs only) but the few phrases of explanation our mentor had made us learn by rote seemed to do the trick and even the most officious of the security men changed his attitude when he saw the ministerial authorisation Talbot had managed to obtain for us. One guy became so effusive that he offered to drive me to my destination but I recalled the advice that things may not always be as they seem and reluctantly declined despite the protests from my tired legs.

February turned into March and the relationship between Frank and Talbot became edgier because there was no sign that we were ever going to be anything more than delivery boys. I was increasingly starting to side with Frank. Whatever Talbot's motives, he didn't need trained engineers to do what we were doing.

One afternoon we were summoned back to the office for what we were assured was going to be good news. 'This must be it,' Frank said. 'At last he's going to come across.'

He was, but not in the way Frank or I hoped.

'Chaps, you have done such a superb job, I have a treat for you. Tonight you will drop all your plans, don your best bib and tucker and come with me to the most famous theatre in the world. We are going to the Bolshoi.'

I thought Frank was going to hit him. Not only no new job, but a night at the ballet! Talbot was equally put out, shocked and hurt that we were not falling over ourselves to recognise his brilliance at getting hold of tickets that the elite of Moscow would trade several dinners for, not to mention his generosity, which included a horse and cab to and from the hotel. It took all my, by now weary, diplomatic skills to calm them down and several more hours to persuade Frank to make the effort and come with me.

'I know how you feel about Talbot and to an extent I agree,' I said. 'But right now we need him. If we upset him, we'll be kicked out of the country in hours or worse, locked up and forgotten with no one in the world aware we had a problem. Just play along a bit longer and let me work on him. I'm sure I can persuade him to come up with a better job.'

'But the ballet,' groaned Frank.

'Have you ever seen one? You might enjoy it!'

Frank downed his brandy in one gulp, uttered a Russian word I hadn't yet learned and went off to change.

CHAPTER 5

Moscow at night was magical. The dark descended like a balm, easing the sores that had been chaffed by the demands of the collective. The streets were quiet again and the lights picked out the flakes of snow as they silently drifted down, giving the whole place a fairy-tale atmosphere. The illusion was heightened by the fact that at night you seldom saw anyone but those who had the means to dress in their finest clothes and go seeking the pre-revolution pleasures of fine food and artistic excellence.

By the time we emerged from our cab, full evening dress hidden under thick furs, I had forgotten the hassles of the afternoon and was looking forward to an experience I'd read about but never expected to have. My anticipation grew when I caught my first sight of the Bolshoi Theatre, like a palace on the edge of Sverdlova Square, glistening in the blue lamps shining up from the base of the eight huge columns that supported the grand entrance. Above, Peter Clodt von Jürgensburg's iconic horses and chariot reared up stark against their ornate, illuminated background. To one side there was a fountain, trapped in a frozen pond.

In the lobby, champagne imported from France flowed as the Moscow elite made small talk before the performance. There was a special buzz because it was to be *The Rite of Spring*, a privilege and welcome relief for those who regularly had to sit through modern operas extolling the virtues of concrete, and two-hour long pastorals to the glory of the tractor and the agrarian revolution. There was an air of self-satisfaction as if to murmur 'See, we communists still know how to enjoy ourselves'. I spotted Talbot flitting from influential group to influential group, constantly looking past the shoulder of the person he was greeting to see if there was anyone more important he should be moving on to. As soon as he saw Frank and me he came over and ushered us into our box, careful to avoid any unnecessary introductions. I seethed quietly but decided to ignore the slight and enjoy the evening.

If anything the interior of the theatre was even more spectacular than the approach. The many tiers of boxes curved around the auditorium, all directed towards the stage which was hidden behind a heavy curtain. Our box was decked in plush red velvet and the seats were soft, cushioned leather. Everywhere you looked there were crystal chandeliers and below them a sea of dress suits, fashionable gowns and glittering jewellery.

As the house lights dimmed and the chatter faded, I realised that the only two empty seats I could see were next to me. I leant over to Talbot. 'Are you expecting friends?' I asked.

He shook his head. 'I only managed to get these three tickets at the last minute. They are like gold dust. Whoever squandered theirs doesn't know what they are missing.'

The vast orchestra started the dissonant but haunting opening bars and just as the strings started to slash out a tribal rhythm, the door behind us opened. A woman came in. She hesitated when she saw the two empty seats but then unwrapped her fur cape from her shoulders, revealing a simple Venetian red dress subtly decorated with black flowers. It was nothing extravagant but she carried it well, a slim elegant figure not at all out of place in this setting. Frank and Talbot shuffled to their feet, pushing back their chairs. She smiled, murmuring *'Izvinitye, Izvinitye'* as she squeezed along the narrow aisle. I stood up and let her pass, noticing the sleek line of her chin, the single wisp of hair that fell across her pale cheek and a tiny mole, like a beauty spot. As she took her seat I caught a hint of rose-water - more like a sensual memory than the presence of real perfume but it made me catch my breath. I glanced across at her and wondered who her lucky partner was and why he wasn't there.

I turned back to look at the stage but the strident music was now out of time with my mood which had changed since she had arrived. I told myself not to look but I couldn't help it. She was clutching a small evening bag, her fingers twisting the strap. Her eyes were on the stage but they were not following the action. Her mind was elsewhere. I guessed on the empty seat between us and for some irrational reason I felt angry at this careless, unknown person who had stood her up. He must be mad.

I ordered myself to look away but soon glanced back. She pulled out a programme that shook in her hand so she used the other to try and steady it, then gave up and flattened it on her knee. She pretended to be absorbed in the contents though I doubted she could read much in the gloom. She realised I was looking at her and turned towards me. In the fleeting seconds that our eyes met before I turned away embarrassed to have been caught staring, I saw her emotion flick between surprise, defiance then alarm. I could feel heat rise in my cheeks and was glad Frank and Talbot were watching the stage.

She stood and brushed past me towards the door. I wanted to grab her and apologise for upsetting her, assure her she was safe to watch the ballet, that I wasn't some crank about to leap on her. But she was gone. I hesitated for a moment then went after her, ignoring the questioning glances of my companions. I looked left and right along the elegant passageway but there was no sign of her. I ran down the stairs but the lobby that had been heaving only a few minutes before was now empty apart from a surly looking attendant.

'Did you see a young woman come past here?' I asked. 'She was small, wearing a red dress.'

'There are many women in Moscow,' he replied.

I fished a couple of pound notes out of my pocket - always a more welcome bribe than roubles - and stuffed them into his top pocket. 'Please, it's important.'

'She left.'

'Which way?'

He shrugged. I put another note in his pocket and he smiled. 'That's the only exit.'

I ran out into the square and was hit by the cold against which my jacket wasn't too much help. I scanned the darkness. There weren't many people about and none of them was the woman I was looking for. I'd almost given up when I was attracted by a movement by the fountain. I squinted against the light and could just make out a figure through the flurries of snow.

I didn't want to make her anxious again so I called out as I made my way towards her. She turned and started to walk away.

'Please, wait a minute. I'm not going to hurt you. I want to apologise for embarrassing you in the theatre. Please come back in and see the end of the performance.'

She slowed and I caught up with her. She was shivering. I took off my jacket and put it round her shoulders.

'Please. I'm sorry. The last thing I wanted to do was to upset you.'

Her face relaxed a little. 'You are English.' It was half a statement, half a question.

'It's that obvious, huh? I'm still learning to speak Russian
properly. Come on, we should go in, you will freeze out here.'

'No, I can't,' she replied, but I could see she was hesitating.

'But you've left your coat inside. And I could really do with
mine back - I'm not used to this climate of yours.'

She nodded slightly and let me put my arm gently across her back
and guide her towards the theatre. I was shocked at how light she felt,
as fragile as a bird. As we came back into the light, I could see her face
clearly for the first time. My first impressions had been right, she was
quite beautiful in an understated way. She had a slender face with
high cheekbones and wide brown eyes that didn't turn away when
they met my gaze. She wore hardly any make-up but it was carefully
applied and did the job for which it was intended. Her hair was tied
loosely and fell gently around her neck. I suddenly felt awkward and
could hardly think what I wanted to say in English let alone Russian.

When we reached the entrance she slipped free of my arm,
looking about her apprehensively. There was no one around and
she seemed to relax.

'I'm all right now,' she said. 'You can go back to your friends.'

'Who were you expecting?'

'It doesn't matter,' she said defensively.

'I'm not trying to pry. It's just that you seem nervous.'

She didn't reply and I realised that I had gone too far. She and I
were strangers and you didn't tell strangers too much in Moscow.

I persuaded her to come back to the box. We arrived just as the
interval was starting. Frank looked disappointed to see us. 'I was
just going to come and find you,' he said. 'Anything to get away
from this.'

Talbot raised an eyebrow archly and said in English: 'Ah there you are, Sir Galahad. And without his jacket. My, my.' Then switching into Russian: 'Now introductions, dear boy, introductions.'

The woman ignored them both and went and gathered her coat.

'I must be going,' she said.

At that moment a waiter swished in balancing a silver tray of hors d'oeuvres and vodka in iced glasses. I saw her eyes follow the food,

Talbot stretched past us to pluck a *bliny* from the tray. He stuffed it in his mouth, theatrically closed his eyes and said: 'The music is a joy but the food is even better. It's the best in town. And all for a dollar tip!' A dollop of sour cream dribbled down his chin. A fat tongue snaked out and scooped it up.

'Now are you going to tell me the lady's name, or do I have to be forward?'

While he bantered she edged to the door, her fur hanging over one arm.

'Please, stay for the rest of the show,' I said.

'I should not be here.'

'Why?'

'My friend did not come.'

'Then join us instead. We're staying at the Metropol, you could have dinner with us later.'

She hesitated, but she had already made up her mind. 'This is not for the general public. Everyone here is Party. A friend got me good seats, you know how I mean? I could lose my job if they caught me here.'

I nodded, thinking, 'I don't care what the reason is, just stay a little longer.' A silence followed. It hung between us, willing me to break it, but I couldn't find the right words.

'What do you do then?' I asked eventually.

She gave me an unblinking but guarded look. 'You ask a lot of questions.'

'I – '

'He didn't come,' she interrupted me, 'so I should go.' She moved towards the door. Talbot was too busy cramming caviar into his mouth to notice, but I saw Frank watching the proceedings with an amused expression. I didn't care what they thought. I needed to find a way to make her stay.

'Thank you, you were very kind,' she said.

'I was very rude.'

'No, I don't think so.'

She opened the door and was halfway through when I said, 'Wait. I don't even know your name.'

'Ileana Petrovna.'

'Brian Grover.'

I offered my hand. She took it gently. I felt foolishly pleased.

'Enjoy your stay,' she said and disappeared down the stairs.

I returned to find Talbot trying to persuade Frank of Stravinsky's genius. 'What a mind to be able to conceive those sounds in his head then orchestrate them and put them down on paper. Don't you think?'

'Incredible,' Frank said, but I feared the irony was lost on Talbot. Frank turned to me. 'Here, I managed to save you a cream roll.'

'No, no, no, Frank. This is Russia. It's a *bliny*,' Talbot insisted. '*Bliny, bliny, bliny*.'

'I'd prefer a vodka.' I said

'Looks like you need it,' Frank said.

'You could say that.'

'Well?' Talbot slapped his stomach. 'What was she like?'

He beamed at me, all 'boys together' innuendo. I felt my temper starting to rise and snapped: 'We talked, that's all. And for your information I followed her.'

Talbot knocked back another short and swayed slightly from the effort. 'So where's your jacket then?'

I looked down at my shirt and bow tie. 'Christ!' I'd forgotten all about it.

Talbot sneered, 'Oh I'm sure she wouldn't have robbed you. She was probably so touched by your gallantry that she took it as a keepsake, a little something to remember the nice Englishman.'

I realised my wallet and, more importantly, my papers were in the jacket pocket. For a moment I doubted her but then reasoned it couldn't be true. She couldn't have taken it deliberately. After all, I had put the jacket on her. She didn't ask. Besides, the whole thing didn't seem to fit. The way she'd been shivering out by the pond, her discomfort in our box without her friend. It couldn't have been planned.

'Hope she was worth it.' Talbot winked at Frank, who thankfully wasn't sharing the joke. 'I think we'd better contact the police,' he added, suddenly serious.

'No.'

'She's robbed you, old boy. Can't you see that?'

'It's a misunderstanding I tell you.'

He sighed. 'Whatever you say. All the same, you can't go far without your permits. They will lock you up in no time.'

'She'll return it. I'll stay in my room tomorrow.'

'No you damn well won't. You've got important deliveries to do.'

'Dock my wages then! Better still, do them your bloody self. You need the exercise!' I grabbed my overcoat and hat and stormed off leaving Frank for once to play the role of peacemaker. I trudged back to the hotel, fighting my doubts, and wondering if I had been duped by a pretty face.

CHAPTER 6

For the first time since we'd arrived in Moscow, Frank left the hotel bar for bed before me. As he went he slapped me on the back and said, 'OK, lovelorn, I'll do your deliveries tomorrow. But you owe me. Understand?'

'Thanks,' I said. 'I'll make it up to you. I'm sure she'll come. She knows where we are staying. She's not a thief.'

'Let's hope not.'

I downed another brandy and made my way to my room. My confidence wasn't at its highest during those dreadful hours around three and four o'clock when even the greatest optimist can foresee little but problems. I tossed and turned, unable to sleep despite counting sheep in both English and Russian. But by breakfast both my heart and my brain told me there was nothing to worry about. She would soon turn up with my jacket and maybe I'd even be able to persuade her to let me see her again.

I started to read a thriller I had bought in America. It was called *Red Harvest* and it had seemed an apt title when I stuffed it into my luggage back in London. My Russian studies meant I'd never got round to reading it. I liked the hard-bitten style but I was distracted and struggled to concentrate on the intrigues of the Continental Op and put the book aside when I found it difficult to keep up with the number of murders being committed. I decided to tidy up my things instead but that was quickly done, so I paced around the hotel foyer, reckoning I would see her sooner if I was there. The stuffed bear appeared to mock me every time I walked past. I ordered some food but even fine beef stew held no appeal for me and I pushed more of it around my plate than I put into my mouth.

I went back to my room and sat on the balcony, looking to see if she was coming down the street. There were plenty of people and a few made me peer harder just to check but they never turned out to be her. For a while I distracted myself by watching the building of the first Metro line along *Prospekt Marksa*. Groups of heavily clothed men toiled around the drilling site, while dump trucks carted away the debris then returned for another load. Even though it had stopped snowing for a while, conditions were still grim for that kind of work and I admired their resilience, their determination to keep the city moving. If that represented the new Russia, across Red Square I could pick out the old in the form of the distinctive outline of St Basil's Cathedral, its domes capped white like icebergs against a darkening sky, a reminder of a former regime when the church held more sway.

As I looked around the city skyline I wondered where she lived, what she was doing, why she hadn't come. I still couldn't believe that she had deliberately taken my jacket. That defied logic but perhaps having found it, the temptation to keep the contents was too great. I pushed the thought to the back of my mind. 'She probably just had to work and wasn't able to come,' I told myself out loud. 'She'll come tomorrow.'

While I chose to believe that, it was harder to persuade Frank that she was at all likely to turn up. When we sat down to dinner he didn't even bother to tease me. Instead he said: 'Wake up, Brian. You gave her a chance to put things right and she didn't take it. You have no alternative, you've got to report her to the police. You are putting yourself at risk, you've upset Talbot and to be honest, I'm not too thrilled to have double the workload.'

'I know. I'm sorry and I promise I'll take the weight next week and you can have a break. It's just that...' I sought an explanation that might satisfy him but could only manage to add, 'I like her.'

'You like her. God sometimes... Listen, Brian, we've enough problems as it is without you pining for a woman you've known for ten minutes.'

'I'm not pining. I'm concerned.'

'Well save a bit of concern for yourself. And for me. You are always telling me not to upset Talbot in case he gets rid of us, then you annoy him more than I ever have. And what happens if the police do a check? Considered that?'

'They won't.'

'And if they do?'

'Trust me.'

'Name one reason why I should.'

'She'll come. I'm sure she'll come.'

He pulled his napkin from his neck and scrunched it into a ball.

'OK, I'll be messenger boy for you tomorrow but that's it. No more. Agreed?'

'Agreed.' I smiled weakly. I was in no position to haggle. He'd done enough for me already, and his reasoning was indisputable, but logic played no part in my thoughts. I didn't care how many times I'd been wrong before - and if I was honest there had been plenty - I'd be right this time.

'I mean it,' he said.

'I know you do.'

She came late the following afternoon.

I got a call from the hotel manager: 'There's a woman down here with something for you. I've asked her to leave it but she insists on seeing you.' I could tell from his tone that he didn't approve of my choice of friend - they may have all been comrades now but some were clearly more equal than others.

I raced down to reception and let him know I didn't appreciate his attitude. 'I'll decide who I want to see, not you. Next time get her a drink,' I said.

They had shown her to a draughty seat beside the entrance. She looked like a small child, sent to the corner of a classroom. She was wearing the same dress she had worn to the Bolshoi. When she saw me she got up apprehensively, half-smiling, unsure of how I would react. She had the jacket over her arm.

Her words tumbled over each other in her anxiety to explain. She spoke so quickly I struggled to take it in and translate what she was saying: 'I meant to come sooner, yesterday morning, but I couldn't be late for work. I came last night but the porter wouldn't let me in. That's why I wore this dress again, to look more proper. You must believe me, it was an accident. I wouldn't steal. I only realised I still had it when I got home and it was too late to go back. Your papers are here. You didn't report it, did you? It was a mistake, I didn't mean...'

'It's all right, it's all right. Slow down. I knew you'd return it. The police don't know. It's my own fault for not noticing in the first place.'

She handed the jacket over, relieved to be shot of it. 'I thought you would be angry so I pressed it.'

'It seems I owe you a drink then.'

44

'In here?'

'Why not?'

She glanced at the manager. 'He won't like it.'

'It has nothing to do with him.'

We went to the bar, Ileana looking over her shoulder to see if the manager would try to stop her. Then, relieved, she looked around her. 'I've only seen the Metropol from the outside. It's beautiful.'

We took seats by the bay windows overlooking the street. I tried to catch the attention of the elderly waiter who stood by the bar polishing a glass. I couldn't tell if he hadn't seen us or if he was deliberately ignoring us. Eventually, he came over. I ordered a brandy, but when I asked her what she wanted she hesitated. 'Perhaps I shouldn't. Perhaps I should go.'

'Stop worrying. You're my guest. After all the trouble you've been to, the least I can do is buy you a drink.'

She glanced out of the window while the waiter hovered. A couple of workmen in overalls walked past, hugging themselves against the wind. 'I'm also normally out there looking in,' she said.

'Not today. Please, choose anything on the list.'

'They're very expensive.'

'It goes on my room bill. My colleague pays. He can afford it. Order whatever you want.'

She chose the cheapest vodka, with soda. The waiter raised his eyebrows and made his way back to the bar.

'He thinks I shouldn't be here.'

'You're not breaking any laws are you?'

She hesitated before answering. 'That depends on who's watching.'

We talked of small things or in truth I did most of the talking,

45

explaining how Frank and I had come to be in Moscow and what we were doing. The afternoon turned into evening and as the bar started to fill up with regulars and visiting businessmen, we became less conspicuous and slowly Ileana relaxed. She'd told me little about herself other than the fact that she was a nurse and lived in a small flat in the suburbs. But she accepted another drink and to my surprise and delight when I asked her to stay for dinner, she said, 'Thank you, that would be nice.'

Frank arrived and I introduced him to Ileana properly. He shook her hand and said to me: 'See, I told you she was OK. You should have more faith in people!' I punched him on the arm and he laughed.

When I spotted Talbot, I went over to him. He didn't look pleased to see me. I said, 'Stephen, good news, Ileana's here, she's brought my jacket back, I'm sorry about the other night. I was rude and I shouldn't have been. Please accept my apologies.'

He switched on the charm as I'd seen him do so often. 'Don't even think about it, old chap. It looks as though I was wrong too. I'm delighted for you. Now let's all celebrate.'

He led us through to the dining room, extravagantly tipped the head waiter and said: 'I want you to take especial care of my young friends tonight. I would deem it a personal favour if their glasses were never allowed to be empty.' Once we were seated, he insisted on ordering for everyone and the food never seemed to stop coming.

Ileana ate as though she feared someone might notice her and ask her to leave before she had time to finish. Finally, she rested her silver spoon delicately on the side of her plate. 'I have never eaten so well,' she said. 'It is very good of you.'

By this time, we had one end of the table to ourselves, which suited me fine. Frank had moved over to the bar and Talbot was down the other end trying to impress some new acquaintances, telling stories, dropping names and exchanging business cards. You could see why the man was so successful, he never let a single opportunity pass and while his boastful tales became a bit boring to those who had heard them a dozen times before, you had to admire his stamina and his determination to impress.

I suppose I was also working quite hard to make a good impression but in a different way. I tried not to be as egotistical as Talbot but a lot of the conversation did seemed to revolve around me as I told Ileana stories about the countries I'd visited and the jobs I had done. She was a wonderful listener, apparently fascinated, laughing in the right places and asking an occasional question. She forgave me my imperfect Russian and when I came to the end of a story, she would prompt me to tell her more.

'What about your childhood?' she asked. 'What were you like as a little boy?'

I told her about my governess and Charterhouse, and described the house where I had lived in Monmouth.

'Eight bedrooms!' she cried. 'And you really had maids to do your washing and make your food!'

'It seemed the normal thing to me. I was only a child. I knew nothing else.'

'Don't apologise. Tell me more. What was it like living there?'

'It was quite lonely actually. My parents rarely spoke to me and there were no other children of my age for several miles. I made my own entertainment. I used to pretend I was the people I had read about - an explorer in the Amazon or a hunter in Africa or a merchant along the Silk Road through China, India, the Hindu Kush and Afghanistan. I loved the sound of the names and I felt I was destined to be someone that people would one day write stories about.

'There were three massive yew trees at the bottom of the valley just near a little hotel. I built a tree house there from planks of wood and watched the people going in and out. Sometimes I'd stay there all day making up stories in my head, pretending guests were spies sent by the Kaiser and I had to keep an eye on them in case they were involved in some dastardly deed.'

'You were a happy child. You had everything you wanted. When I have children, they will grow up with smiles on their faces too.'

I hesitated. 'No, I didn't have everything. I had things, but I didn't have hugs from my mother or play-fights with my father. They thought that kind of thing was silly. They were typically middle-class English in many ways, just like you'll find in your school books.'

Ileana waved a finger at me playfully. 'No, no. In our books you are all fat like your friend. And they all wear bowler hats.' She cocked her head to one side. 'Why don't you wear a bowler hat?'

'Oh, I've got it safely tucked away. It only comes out on special occasions.'

'Like when?'

'Well, if I'm posing for a photograph for a Russian school book about strange Englishmen. Or going to see my, uhm, stockbroker.' I didn't know the word in Russian so I said it in English.

'What's that?'

'A vile capitalist bureaucrat.'

'It can't be so bad. Do they lock you up?'

I laughed. 'I think we may have a language problem here.'

A waitress staggered up to us bearing a massive tray of coffees with biscuits, cream-filled chocolates and flavoured vodkas to wash it all down. She was struggling under the weight but she kept going from table to table, knowing that it would only take a

few westerners to feel sorry for her and she would pick up
enough hard currency in tips to fund a few treats for her family at
the weekend.

Ileana's eyes widened at the sight of sweets. This oasis of
affluence and plenty was clearly new to her and she still wasn't
quite certain that she belonged or if she was allowed to join in.
She took a wafer mint and nibbled at it like a squirrel. I realised
she was restraining herself so I pushed the plate towards her. 'Take
as many as you want, nobody's counting.' And she did, the tempo
of her munching increasing with each biscuit until she stopped
abruptly with the realisation that she was very full indeed. She
looked embarrassed, as if she had done something wrong.

'Enjoy things while you can.' I filled our glasses with more
champagne. 'All this time I've talked about myself, but I know
nothing about you,' I said.

'There is nothing much to know, compared to your life.' There
was no bitterness in her voice, no self-pity. It was just a statement
of fact. Acceptance was something I was to come across many
times in Russia. If someone complained, 'What is to be done?' it
was usually met with a shrug, another glass of vodka, and the
reply, 'About what?'

'I have never left my country,' Ileana said. 'I would like to see
other places. When I was a girl I loved maps. My mother used to
say I would go on great journeys and marry a foreigner. She
warned me against Germans, "They are full of beer", and the
French, "Too unreliable", but she liked the English. She would
have liked you.' She blushed slightly, then changed the subject.
'But now we can't go anywhere without permission so I don't
know if I will ever see all the places I dreamed of.'

She took a large gulp from her glass. 'It is no matter. Anyway
you don't want to hear about me, it is nothing interesting.'

'I promise you, you are not boring me at all. I want to hear all about you.' I had seldom been more honest.

She blushed again. 'You flatter me.'

I pressed her and 'nothing interesting' turned out to be fascinating. She had been a teenager through the chaos of the revolution, seen the looting, the riots and the massacres at first hand. She started to tell me about her family and once she started, it poured out in a stream, her eyes reflecting the memories, shining at one moment, clouding over and distant when she recalled past pain.

'We had a baby brother who died young of heart disease. The rest of us were girls. It changed Mother and she became very strict. One time when she was upset with us, she brought us all together and told us she would happily trade her four daughters for the life of her son. It made a deep impression on me, made me want to prove myself.

'When the troubles hit St Petersburg, we were forced out of our house. My father, Petr, was a postmaster. A simple man but he made us a little home that we loved. The mob came in and requisitioned it for the people. They wrecked it. Eventually, we left with many others as the famine hit. All the food was going to the army to fight the civil war. I wanted to do something to help the suffering. Not the cause. That's how I became a nurse. I trained on the front line. It was terrible. They only saw things in terms of right and wrong. There was no middle. They never took White Russians into our hospital. Whites were considered traitors and left in the mud to die. I saw them just as people screaming in pain. But I was forbidden to go to them.

'When it was all over I came to Moscow and found my present job. In the summer the sky is blue and I go swimming with friends in the baths. In the winter, people stay indoors unless they have to go out, eating their jars of pickle and barely surviving.' She lowered her voice, more out of habit, I thought, than necessity. 'Occasionally, there is a knock on a neighbour's door in the middle of the night and the next morning they are gone. I've never had that knock, thank God... I make it sound gloomy, don't I? It isn't. Really, I'm quite happy. The hospital is a good place to work, I have some friends, I have enough money to live.'

She stopped.

'Then why were you so hungry tonight?' I asked.

Ileana looked down at her fingers, started picking at them. 'I traded a week's food coupons for my dress and now there isn't much in the cupboard.' There was an embarrassed smile on her face. 'It was stupid, wasn't it?'

'It's good to treat yourself sometimes, it makes things seem brighter. And the dress suits you. But when was the last time you ate properly?'

'I have soup, and my friends share, but most days they have hardly enough for themselves. They understand though, they don't begrudge me.'

The lights dimmed slightly and from the corner of the room music started playing. It was a Gipsy band, all stringed instruments and drums. Soon, couples were dancing in the clearing between the tables. One of the band members left the stage and came round selling poppies. I bought one and threaded it into her hair.

'You look beautiful.'

A song started up again. She pulled me up. 'For that, I will let you dance with me.'

'I'm not very good. Especially after all this wine,' I said.

'Don't worry, nobody's watching.'

She moved smoothly and I tried to follow, anxious not to tread on her feet and cursing that I had never bothered to learn to dance. It would have been perfect if I could have swept her round the floor, everyone standing aside to watch this couple in perfect harmony. Instead I just felt awkward, uncoordinated and embarrassed. But she smiled encouragingly and when the tempo slowed, whispered in my ear , 'Pretend it's a waltz. Everyone can waltz.'

'Everyone except me.'

We moved around the room, sometimes bumping into other couples, collapsing into each other's arms when the song stopped.

'What do you wish for more than anything else?' I asked in a lull between songs.

She looked at me directly, answering immediately as though it was something that she had thought about many times before. 'I have met some nice people, foreigners I would like to have known better but always they are just passing through. I would like to meet someone who is not just passing through.'

I squeezed her hand. 'Maybe you will,' I said.

It was getting late. The customers dwindled until all the tables had been cleared and we were the last group left. Talbot called for one final brandy all round, 'Just to celebrate a spectacular night' but the weary-looking waiter regretted they had run out until another delivery arrived tomorrow morning. We got the message.

I led Ileana down the marble steps to where Talbot had ordered a horse-drawn cab to take her home. The driver was scowling and muttering to himself as we came out. I offered to accompany her but she declined.

'People might get the wrong impression.'

'And what impression might that be?' I asked, teasing.

The driver shook his reins, made a display of clapping his hands together. 'You want to turn me to stone? Get in woman, or I'll find another fare.'

'Another at this time of night?' I called back. 'Not a chance. Here's the money in full, plus something for yourself.' I gave him a note. 'Can we talk for a few minutes? Uninterrupted?'

He grinned through his beard. 'You can talk all you want on a fine, warm night like this.'

I returned to Ileana. 'Well?'

She bowed her head. 'I don't know what you mean.'

'Ileana, I haven't enjoyed myself this much in years,' I said. 'It was lovely when we danced, or rather when you danced and I stumbled.'

'You're not so bad. You just need practice.'

'Will you teach me?'

Hair blew over her face. She pulled it away with a flick of her hand and laughed. 'I'm a nurse,' she said as though that explained everything.

'I'd like to see you again,' I said. 'Teach me to dance.'

'When?'

'Tomorrow.'

'I can't. I work double shifts, right through.'

'In the morning. Six o'clock. We can dance along the river.'

She shook her head. 'You're mad, Mr Grover. If your blood weren't so hot you would surely freeze.'

'But will you, Ileana?'

She was silent for a moment then she said. 'If I have to take you to hospital afterwards as my first patient of the day, don't blame me.'

'Taganka Square,' I called out as she got into the carriage.

She leaned out of the window and beckoned me forward.

'Don't forget the Russian farewell.' She took my head in her hands and kissed me on both cheeks. 'Thank you,' she said. 'And you can call me Lena. My friends do.'

CHAPTER 7

I was up at four-thirty, dressed quickly and tiptoed past the bear and out through the door so as not to wake the porter who was snoring gently in his chair by the desk. I pulled my fur hat lower over my ears and my scarf tighter round my face. I looked down at my clomping *sapagi* and smiled - such elegance, such style, the perfect gentleman, a veritable Noel Coward perfectly turned out for a dancing lesson. Back in the real world, every other street light was switched off, another part of the efficiency drive to safeguard Stalin's Five-Year Plan, and there was hardly any sign of life. It was a little forbidding but nothing could dampen my mood. I reflected that the moon and June clichés of popular songs which seemed so trite at times were, in the right circumstances, so apt. I hummed a few bars of a love song I'd heard in the States.

I swung myself round a lamp standard. I felt a little giddy with anticipation, foolishly happy. Time really did seem to slow down. The hour I waited in Taganka Square for the clock to strike six seemed interminable. I tried to rehearse some appropriate words that would let Ileana - no, Lena - know how I felt about her, but for a moment couldn't think of a single phrase in Russian. Hell! What if I couldn't speak to her when she came? What if she thought I was boring? We'd told each other so much the night before, what would we speak about? I smiled at myself, grateful Frank wasn't there to read my mind and laugh at a grown man having such adolescent emotions.

When the clock marked half-past six, I wasn't too concerned. Seven came and went and I checked the sign to make sure I was in the right square, walking around the square to see if there was a hidden corner where she was waiting. Seven-thirty and eight. Eight-thirty. Perhaps she was ill. Perhaps she'd been in an accident on the way home last night. How could I find out? I checked the sign again, carefully sounding out the Cyrillic letters. It was definitely Taganka Square. Wait. Perhaps she'd misunderstood. Perhaps she'd gone to the hotel and was waiting there, cursing me for not turning up just like her friend at the Bolshoi. I wonder who he was? We hadn't talked about him. I made a mental note to ask her. Should I go to the hotel and check? But if I did and she turned up here a minute after I'd left, what would happen then?

Just after nine I reluctantly returned to the Metropol. My last faint hope disappeared when I entered the lobby and there was no sign of her. I decided I must have been too drunk to notice that she had really been bored last night and had never entertained any intention of meeting me. But the kisses on the cheek, I couldn't have misread them could I?

Frank appeared. 'At last, my fellow workhorse ready to be harnessed up again,' he said. 'Good time last night?'

'Fine.'

'When are you seeing her again?'

'I doubt if I will. You know, easy come, easy go.'

I'm not sure if he believed me but he didn't comment and to his eternal credit he was the epitome of friendship as I withdrew into myself, hurt, confused, saddened. Even if he'd asked for an explanation, I doubt I could have provided one. I didn't understand why I felt such loss for someone I hardly knew. It felt as though I had been led to the brink of a wonderful place, glimpsed the rich possibilities there and been able to sample its delights for a few hours only then to be turned away with no word of explanation. What made it worse was that the image of what might have been grew stronger than the memory of what had actually been, so that I became convinced I had suffered a loss that would remain with me like a scar for the rest of my life.

Over the next few days I contacted all the hospitals but was told they could not give out any information about staff. I went to the Bolshoi to see if they had an address where they had sent the tickets. They told me they didn't and even if they had, they would not be able to tell me.

Mostly I worked, picking up parcels and delivering them until I was tired enough to go back to my room and try to sleep. The city no longer held any charm for me. The frantic rebuilding seemed now to be no more than the destruction of all that was elegant and stylish and its replacement no more than harsh, concrete utility. I became less tolerant of surly service from waiters and shop assistants, less willing to excuse the third rate bitter concoction that passed for coffee. Spring was slowly turning the crisp and sparkling snow into a dull grey slush. The cold may have been lifting, but it was being replaced by an insidious damp that seeped in everywhere and, while it was possible to dress up against the bitter chill, there was no escaping this; it seemed to permeate right into your soul. Frank had been right, this was a terrible place.

'Are you OK, old chap? You seem a bit down in the mouth,' Talbot asked.

'No, I'm fine. Just a bit tired.'

'Good. Good. Now I just have a couple of extra parcels that need to get there tonight if you don't mind.'

'Sure. No problem. I have no plans.'

I got into the habit of going into a little café on the corner of Taganka Square. It was nothing much but it was clean and the coffee was less sour than in the other places I'd tried. One afternoon, I ducked in there to get out of the rain that had been relentless most of the day, and took my by now customary seat facing the window. I started to read a copy of *The Times* that had recently arrived in the post. Apparently at home there was talk of a national government to cope with the financial crisis but it all seemed so far removed from me that I turned to the crossword which was as impenetrable as ever. As I chewed the end of my pen, pondering a particularly tricky anagram, a figure went past the window. It was only seconds later that my brain registered that it had been her. I threw a few roubles on the counter and dashed into the street. It was unmistakably her, walking away from me, laden down with two heavy bags of shopping.

'You owe me a dancing lesson,' I called out. She slowed but didn't turn. Then she hastened away again.

I went after her shouting. 'I could have frozen to death - why didn't you come?'

'Go away.' Her voice was frail against the pounding of the rain.

'I waited and waited.'

'Go away!'

'I waited for you all morning. Ten policemen asked me what I was doing,' I lied, hoping my exaggeration would make her stop.

'Then you are stupid. You should have stayed in your nice hotel.'

We came to the end of the square and she turned sharply down a narrow alley I hadn't seen before.

'Why won't you talk to me?'

She walked on, battling against the heavy bags and the rain that was matting her hair against the back of her neck. I followed her down one street, then another into the old part of the city where rows of houses and small shops opened straight on to the narrow roadway.

'Let me take one of your bags,' I said, trying to say or do something that would make her take notice of me.

'No!' She yanked the bags away from me. Then she said quietly, 'Please, leave me alone. I can't see you.'

'Why not?'

Finally, she stopped. 'Brian. Look, thank you for the other week. It was a wonderful evening. You were very thoughtful and I'm sorry if I disappointed you by not turning up the next morning.' She searched for the words that would end this hassle. 'You have to understand - that was then, today is different. Today is today.'

'What about tomorrow? Can I see you then?'

'Tomorrow is another today. Don't you understand?'

I didn't. 'And next week?'

'The same.'

'And that's it?'

She nodded.

'Why?'

'Because . . .' She was about to say more but changed her mind. Her face became closed, no expression. 'I'm going now, don't follow me.'

'You can't leave me here.' I waved an arm at the empty streets, the crumbling old brick walls, the turnings that led nowhere. 'I don't know where I am.'

'You know Moscow well enough. You'll find your way home.'

'I don't have my papers. What if I'm picked up?'

There was a momentary flash of concern in her eyes then it quickly turned to anger. 'And what if we are both picked up? You are all right, you're English, you are just passing through. They will ask you a few questions then let you go. But what about me?'

I could think of no reply that made any sense but as she set off I kept pace with her. I couldn't let her disappear again but I didn't seem to be able to get through to her. She had grown weary of the whole thing and just walked on, ignoring me but no longer protesting. Soon, the dingy alleyways widened into roads and then into a main thoroughfare. I recognised an office block at the far end. We were about half a mile from the Bulvar ring.

'Go left here, it will take you all the way back to your hotel,' she said.

'I don't want to.'

'I want you to.' She looked close to tears but I had to try just once more.

'Lena, for the last two weeks all I've done is think about you, wanted to see you, talk to you, have you teach me how to dance. Tell me why you didn't come. Surely, I deserve that much. At least I'll know then. Tell me, and I'll go. I promise.'

'You don't understand. People talk.'

'Is that it? You're scared of gossip?'

She looked around warily. 'It's not safe. You and me. It was different in the Metropol.'

'It can be different anywhere you want it to be.'

'Not here. If you run, you can catch the tram.'

'I'm not going anywhere.'

'I explained! You promised.'

'I lied. Lena, I like you very much and that night when we

60

danced I felt that you liked me. I want to get to know you better, to spend time with you. You can't worry about what might happen. Life's too short.'

'It will be if I keep seeing you. Leave me or I'll call the police.'

'Call them, let them cart me away.'

She picked up her shopping and began to leave.

'If you leave me I'll sit on the line and wait for the next tram to run over me.'

She ignored my threat.

'Look, I'm doing it,' I called.

I lay across the lines, waving my arms. A group of people standing under the canopy of a vegetable shop selling mainly carrots turned to see what the noise was. They didn't laugh.

Her face appeared above me, upside down and stern. 'Get up!'

'Not 'til you promise me you'll teach me to dance.'

'People are staring.'

'That's because they're bored. Do you promise?'

'Why are you doing this?'

'Because I like you.'

She looked at the crowd nervously.

'Someone's coming over. Pretend you've hurt your leg.'

'What?'

'Just do it!'

I clutched my knee and contorted my face in mock pain. She knelt down beside me. 'Put your arm around my shoulder.'

'With pleasure.'

'Hobble when you get up.'

'Huh?'

'I'm not joking.' She cursed under her breath and lifted me with surprising strength. 'We'll get the tram.'

Upright again, I saw the man she was talking about. He was striding towards us, looking intent on giving us a hard time. 'Perhaps you're right.'

Lena grabbed her shopping with her free hand. 'Come on.'

A tram arrived on the opposite side of the street. As we passed the man Lena snapped, 'Space please, Comrade. I'm a nurse. This man is extremely ill.' He hesitated at the authority in her voice and we squeezed through the tram doors as they were closing. Lena pulled me to the back seats and plonked me in a corner. 'Say nothing,' she whispered.

That was fine by me. For ten minutes, the tram rattled towards the suburbs. Every time it rounded a corner, Lena's body pressed against mine and I felt her warmth. I noticed she did nothing to prevent it.

We got off at a square of four red-brick apartment blocks surrounding a tree-less patch of mud. *Ploschad 1905,* declared a bent metal sign on rusty railings. I limped beside her and she said in a level voice, 'You can drop the pretence now. And you can take a bag.'

'You're angry.'

'If I was angry, Brian, I wouldn't be inviting you in for tea.'

Her flat was small and dark but she had lavished attention on it and made it her own, covering the walls with multicoloured hangings she said her uncle had brought back from the south when she was a child. A square oak table with two bare chairs stood by the window. On it was a photograph of a young man in full army uniform, smiling broadly. I picked it up.

'My father,' she said. 'Before the World War.'

I nodded. 'He looks confident.'

'He was always full of hope.'

We chatted into the evening. She made some tea which was

sweet and strong. I apologised for embarrassing her in the street. 'It was the only way to convince you,' I said, unsure if I really believed that to be true.

She apologised for leaving me alone that morning in Taganka Square. 'It was cruel, after such a lovely evening,' she said. 'But I came home and the flat was dark and I had to face work the next day. I decided this isn't possible. I have my life and you have yours. Soon you will be on your way. I had the memory and I didn't want to risk spoiling it. But it was very rude. I should have contacted you.'

'Well, we both have something to apologise for.'

She smiled. 'It's not a good start.'

I felt my heart thump. She'd said start. I wanted to hug her but I didn't want to overpower her and spoil the moment.

'It looks like I'll be here for quite some time,' I said. 'My friend promised me work but it hasn't materialised. I'm stuck in Moscow. We could always meet up again.'

'I would like that,' she replied. 'Very much.'

CHAPTER 8

The next day was Saturday and when I woke I discovered the mild south-west wind that had started the thaw had been forced to give way as cold air swept in once more from Siberia, the sting in winter's tail, mocking those who had started to hang their furs at the back of the wardrobe. The grey slush froze once more and was covered by a clean white blanket of snow, sparkling in the sun.

Lena was excited when I met her at a café for breakfast. 'Isn't it wonderful? Now we can go skating,' she said.

'Except I can't skate.'

'Don't worry, I'll teach you. First skating, then dancing.'

I liked the sound of a series of lessons stretching into the future that would give me an excuse to hold on to her. I was confident that my lack of co-ordination alone could see us well into the summer. But I was less sure that I wanted to risk my limbs and dignity trying to master a tricky new skill surrounded by hundreds of Muscovites who had skated almost as soon as they could walk. But I wasn't going to argue.

'Good. We'll start this morning.'

It is strange how precarious you can feel when elevated on two slender inches of steel. I hovered by the edge, reluctant to move in case I fell over. 'Show me what you can do,' I said, buying time. She pushed off and within seconds was moving effortlessly and smoothly, arcing her body as she swooped first this way then that. She came to within ten yards of me, spun in a blur, stopped and in a single motion pushed off on one leg, the other straight out behind her, her arms spread wide. She skated to the centre of the river, turned and raced back straight towards me at top speed, her hair flowing out behind her. Just before the edge she leaned back, turned her body sideways, dug in her skates and showered me with ice. She stood there, out of breath, cheeks pink with exertion, eyes glowing.

'God, you are so beautiful,' I thought.

'Come on,' she said. 'You can't stay on the edge like that. You look silly.'

'I'll look silly if I come out there.'

A boy, no more than five years old, sped past.

'Look,' she said. 'It's easy.'

'The confidence of youth.'

'Oh, you're not too old to learn. Hold on to me and do what I do. Now, push out with your right, lean to your left, push out with your left, lean to the right.' 1 followed her steps and soon I started to feel my confidence growing. It reminded me of when as a child I learned to ride a bike and later to swim. It was all about relaxation, trusting your body and reasoning that if everyone else didn't fall off or sink, then you probably wouldn't.

'That's it, that's it!' she cried. 'Stop looking at your feet.' I realised her voice was coming from ten feet behind me. She had let go. I was my own.

I fell.

She skated over, laughing, offered me her hand and pulled me up. 'You've got it. Now try again.' This time I kept going, concentrating on the rhythm. The air rushed at my face and my ears burned. I felt ridiculously proud of myself.

We skated along the Moskva most of the afternoon until my limbs ached with the effort. Lena laughed and chattered as we took off our skates and as we made our way to find a hot drink, she slipped her hand into mine and squeezed it. I wasn't sure what I was feeling. I'd had good times with Maddy but I couldn't ever remember being so content, so comfortable. I wondered if this might be love.

Lena and I spent every spare moment together for the next few days. We skated some more, ran through the parks, walked through the streets of the old city, slipped into the back seats of the state cinemas and held hands while the newsreels recorded the rapid progress of Stalin's vision. At times we just sat in her flat talking. I loved the way she would curl up at my feet in front of the fire, leaning against my legs, her head on my lap. She didn't speak much about herself but she had an endless curiosity about my life,

'Tell me more about your childhood,' she said. 'Who was this governess? Was she very strict? Did she beat you when you were naughty? Make you study when you wanted to play?'

'No, she was my best friend when I was a boy.' I said, smiling at the memory. 'Her name was Miss Roberts. She was the opposite of everything that my parents were - she was lively, warm and open-minded. She taught me to be curious, to ask questions and not to accept the first thing I was told. She didn't just teach me from books. When it was fine, we would go outside and she would tell me the names of trees and clouds and where to look for birds' nests and animal tracks.

'I remember early one spring she took me to see the pond at the far end of our garden, looking for frogspawn. It was dry but windy and Miss Roberts took my hand as we walked through the orchard into the grove where the air was damp and smelled of moss. The ground was spongy underfoot and I imagined we were the first people who had ever walked there, intruders in an enchanted land. It was one of my favourite spots, perhaps I'll take you there one day.

'Miss Roberts talked to me all the time. Her voice was soft and melodic. "This is an oak... and that is a sycamore, see the leaves are like the palm of a hand and in the autumn its seeds spin to the ground like little helicopters. That one over there with the silver bark is a birch tree. Do you know how you can tell the age of a tree?"'

I stopped the story, suddenly recalling what came next.

'What's the matter?' Lena said. 'You look sad.'

'Yes, I just remembered that was one of the only times that Miss Roberts got angry with me. I haven't thought about it for years.'

She squeezed my hand. 'Why? What happened?'

'Oh, it's silly really. She explained to me that to tell the age of trees you count the rings and she showed me the broad stump of an old oak and let me count. I reached over a hundred before I stopped counting and was amazed how something could grow that old.'

'But why did that make her angry?' Lena asked, confused.

'It wasn't that. But then I asked her if trees died of old age and she said, "They can, like everything else that lives, but this one was chopped down by Alex, the man who helps your father in the garden." I'd always been frightened of Alex. He was a big, burly man and I remembered that the previous summer when he had been heaving huge rocks into the stream to make stepping stones, he had taken off his shirt and he had a hairy back. I thought he might be a monster pretending to be a gardener.'

'Did he hurt you?'

'No, he never even spoke to me. I just found him scary. Anyway, I was shocked that someone should chop down a beautiful tree and I think I called him a murderer at which Miss Roberts slapped me across the face. It's the only time I can remember her hitting me. She said I was a wicked little boy to say something so cruel and that Alex was a good man, a gentle man, and I should be grateful that he provided enough wood to keep the fires burning in the winter. "The world would be a much poorer place without Alex," she said.'

Lena looked up at me. 'What happened?'

'I ran off crying. She caught up with me when we got to the pond, wiped the tears from my cheeks and said, "You must remember that gentlemen don't say harsh things like that. The tree was meant to be chopped down and be used to keep you warm so it was the right thing to do. People who do hard, physical work like that are to be respected. Without Alex pruning and tidying we would not be able to enjoy this garden nearly as much."'

Lena got up, kissed me on the forehead. 'She was in love with him,' she said. I was startled. It had never occurred to me. Miss Roberts in love. But now I understood. I reached out to catch her hand. 'It's late. Now you must go,' she said. 'I am working extra shifts for the next two days but then I will take you for a walk and show you one of my favourite places.'

I walked back to the hotel, wondering if I had ever been happier.

CHAPTER 9

We arranged to meet at the café in Taganka Square at two but before that, Talbot had said he wanted to see Frank and me in his office.

When we arrived, he looked even more pleased with himself than usual. 'Come in, come in,' he said. He waved a document at us and chortled, 'Here it is, signed and sealed, the biggest deal I have ever done in Russia. And I have to thank you chaps, you have been most helpful. Unfortunately, it means I won't be needing your services again for a while.'

I felt Frank bristle beside me. I didn't know whether to grab hold of him, or jump in and thump Talbot before he got the chance.

'But,' Talbot added hastily, sensing a frosting of the atmosphere, 'I have found someone who wants to employ you and you'll be pleased to know it's in the oil business.' He handed us each an envelope. 'All the details are in there, permits, train tickets, and a little extra cash as a thank-you from me. You start tomorrow and the contract runs until the end of the year. It's much more money than I could ever afford so I'm sure it will suit you down to the ground.'

Frank let out a long whoop. 'At last. That's just fantastic. You old son of a gun, you came through.'

I reached for Talbot's hand and shook it warmly. This was great news. Then the words 'train tickets' reached my consciousness.

'Where is this job?' I asked.

'Grozny, dear boy. Never been myself but I'm told they've got the best wine, the best women and the best weather in the whole of the Union.'

'Sun? Am I going to see the sun again?' Frank was ecstatic and started to waltz Talbot round the office. 'Stephen, I take it all back. You are a genius.'

Grozny. It was a thousand miles away to the south. My brain was churning. I couldn't focus. Talbot's laugh cut through the confusion. 'Is he always like this when he gets his own way, Brian? ...Brian?'

I was already on my way out of the door. What the hell was I going to tell Lena?

I made two decisions as I sat in the café waiting for her: I must tell her straight away and I must figure out a way of persuading her to come with me. I went back on the first the moment she arrived. She was bubbling over with excitement. 'I've been looking forward to this so much,' she said. 'I had a terrible shift at work and it was only the thought of seeing you and taking you to my special place that kept me going.' My news would have to wait, I decided. Maybe a suitable time would present itself as we walked.

As we made our way along the banks of the Moskva, Lena took off one of her gloves and slipped her hand inside mine. 'The river is very mysterious in the winter,' she said. 'It looks as though it has stopped but beneath the ice, it continues its journey, it is always flowing away from Moscow even when you think it's not.'

After a while we came to a loop in the river and suddenly the city ended and the countryside began. Where before there had been building sites and cranes just the other side of the tree line, now there were open fields, stretching for miles. The embankment gave way to a narrow path overgrown with bushes. Lena brushed her hand across the top of a bush and then stood and watched as the snow rose into the air before gently cascading to the path, sparkling in the pale sun. She ran ahead, repeating the action further down the path, then scooped up a large ball of snow and ran back towards me, not releasing it until she was sure it was going to hit me full on. I chased after her. She seemed to have no problem with the icy surface whereas I was slipping and sliding, struggling to keep my feet. She eventually sat on a bench and let me catch up with her. I threatened to shower her with snow but she pleaded and I couldn't resist her, so I turned and flung the snow as hard as I could towards the centre of the river.

The bench was enclosed by a grove of trees and it was easy to imagine what a special place this would be when the leaves started to bud and birdsong filled the air.

'Come, sit down beside me. I love this spot. In the summer I come here and pick *Klyukva*. It's my favourite fruit of all. The berries keep for months and are delicious when you roll them in sugar powder - you get the sour juice mixed with the sweetness. When I feel trapped in the city, I like to remember that this place is here and that if I wanted I could keep walking to new lands. Do you see those two trees? They are over 100 years old and local people say that if you walk along a straight line between them and keep going, you wouldn't meet another town until you reached the Sea of Okhotsk.'

'Is it true?'

'No, not now anyway. And the people who originally said it

probably never left Moscow and certainly never saw the sea. They were just dreaming of new places just as I did when I was a child.'

This seemed like the perfect time to suggest she came to Grozny with me but before I could say anything, she leaned towards me.

'Kiss me, Brian.'

I took her face in my hands and gently brushed my lips against hers. Her lips were cold but her breath was warm and sweet. Her eyes looked straight into mine. There was no ambiguity, no doubt. I pulled her towards me and kissed her again, this time longer and harder. Then again, and again, more and more passionately. I felt her body mould itself to me and we clung on to each other, neither speaking. This was new. I had never felt like this with Maddy even in our most intimate moments. I wanted time to stand still. I lifted her up and swung her round. I threw off my gloves, discarded her fur hat and wrapped my fingers in her hair, holding her face close. I kissed her again and she kissed me back. I was hers and she was mine.

'I was going to teach you to dance,' she said after a while, pulling away and taking up her position as if she was at the edge of the dance floor and could hear the music playing.

'My partner never turned up,' I chided gently.

'Perhaps you assumed too much.'

'Perhaps I hoped too much. But now...' I searched for the word in Russian, 'Now I can celebrate because what was just hope is very, very real.'

She started to gently hum a tune I had never heard before and led me as we slowly shuffled around in the snow. The steps didn't matter because we hardly moved. We were just locked together. Everything felt right. Everything fitted perfectly. I kept telling myself that I had to remember this moment, capture forever exactly how it felt. I kissed her again and we stopped dancing, clinging to each other as though our bodies were trying to become one.

She smiled. 'If we don't move, our feet will stick to the ice and we will have to stand here until it melts. We would either starve or freeze to death.'

I could think of worse ways of dying.

'Lena, I want you to come with me.'

Her body tensed. She stepped away.

'What do you mean? Where are you going?'

'Grozny. Talbot has found a job for Frank and me in the oilfields. I have to leave tonight. I want you to come with me. They are bound to need nurses there.'

'You knew you were leaving all the time and you never said. How could you?'

'It wasn't like that. I wanted to find the right moment.'

'You lied. You said there was no job. You said you were staying in Moscow.'

Tears had appeared on her cheeks. She turned and started to stumble away from me.

'I didn't lie. I only found out this morning. Lena, come with me.'

'You are like the rest. You say "Come with me" but you know it is impossible. You know I will not be given permission. You were just leading me on. I thought you were different.'

I tried to hold her but she shrugged me off and kept moving away from me. She was more deft than me and the faster I tried to chase after her the more I slipped. I fell several times and she started to leave me behind. By the time I got round the bend in the river she had disappeared, taken another route, slipped back into the city. I went to her flat but she wasn't there. Her neighbours said they had not seen her. There was no sign of her anywhere, just the memory of her hurt and anger.

CHAPTER 10

At least in Moscow there were parts of the old city as yet untouched by the new Russia, areas where you could still find delightful old houses not yet destroyed by Stalin's sweeping changes. With a covering of snow lending the city enchantment it was possible to imagine that the upheaval wasn't all encompassing, laying waste much of what was treasured and beautiful. But here on the plains of Grozny with the snow melted there was no such illusion.

It was all in the name of progress. Over millions of years, before man ever set foot there, this vast plain had silently witnessed the vegetation from forests the size of the Amazon grow, topple, decay and then be crushed by the weight of rocks and sands blown from great deserts. Layer after layer - each few inches marking the passing of centuries - had done its work until the whole plain now floated on an ocean of thick, black oil. It had taken aeons to create but having discovered its value man had decided he wanted to suck it back out of the earth as quickly as possible. Wherever you looked oil derricks broke the skyline like a massive bed of nails. The translation of Grozny is 'terrible'. It lived up to its name.

It had been two months since Frank and I had left Moscow and if we thought that Talbot had at times been a hard taskmaster he was a novice compared to those who now controlled our lives. It seemed a week never went by without one of them summoning us to the office to pass on the news that the quotas had been increased and demanding that we hit them. No amount of reasoning or explaining that it was impossible did any good. These men understood nothing of the industry and cared even less. They only knew that if they failed to deliver, the people above them would make their life hell, so it made sense for them to make our lives hell in order to prevent that. Without the luxury of time, the modern pressure that produced oil was just layers of bureaucracy bearing down on the level below until it reached us and those who worked with us. Those foolish enough to complain too loudly or dare to point out that the equipment was not up to the job would soon find themselves working somewhere even less congenial, somewhere their muscles rather than their expertise would be called upon.

What we didn't learn until later was that in many respects we were the fortunate ones. We didn't realise that as we slaved away in the oilfields, blank-eyed soldiers were descending on villages, rounding up farmers and their families and carting them off to the collectives where they toiled until the exhausted soil turned to desert. The men grew emaciated, fed just enough to keep them working, while the rich harvest they produced was despatched to fill the bellies of people like us, 'the real workers'. We did occasionally glimpse a bone-thin peasant wearily making his way through the streets of Grozny but we didn't understand the harshness behind his stumbling gait. We were more concerned with our own problems: the delays when machinery collapsed from neglect, the chaos when much needed trucks stalled because the wrong grade of petrol had clogged the engine, the incompetence that demanded the impossible then blamed everyone else when it failed to materialise.

Our daily journeys between Talbot's well-heeled establishment figures had cut us off from the reality for most ordinary Russians who were bombarded in the newspapers, on the radio and from giant posters with messages instructing them that no matter how hard they were working, they should be contributing more. Here in Grozny I began to get an understanding of the persistent anxiety of their everyday life, of knowing that any suggestion of personal happiness at the expense of the collective effort was seen as a betrayal of their country. I started to appreciate why Lena had been so nervous about allowing me to get close. She had managed to survive the upheaval that followed 1917 and found a niche for herself, a life that while not exciting or in any way glamorous, gave her a job she enjoyed doing, money to eat well enough most of the time, and a handful of friends she trusted and with whom she could enjoy her few leisure hours. No wonder she had resisted me, knowing that by associating with a foreigner she risked losing her precious anonymity. Then having made the momentous decision to let me in, she had to face up to me moving on, leaving her with her old life but now possibly exposed to the gaze of the authorities. Too late, I fully understood the risks she had run. Understanding brought no comfort and only added to my concern when my stream of letters went unanswered.

I tried to bury my fears in work and, God knows, there was enough to ensure I didn't have hours to sit around brooding. The ridiculous edicts from my bosses turned the guilt I was feeling at leaving Lena into anger. Several times I spoke out, complaining that they were driving the men too hard, asking too much, cutting too many corners and putting lives at risk. Each time I was told to be quiet and just get on with my job. And then I was warned: 'Mr Grover, do not think that because you are English you are immune from the discipline that everyone else is subject to in Russia. It does not pay to be so outspoken.' I resolved to bite my tongue more in future but didn't always succeed. I was impressed by the fortitude and resilience of the Russian men who worked alongside me. But I was appalled by those who commanded them.

As I sat in the refectory forcing down breakfast before my next shift, I looked out of the window and watched as bunches of clean-faced workers climbed into the back of open-topped trucks to be driven off to the well where they were working that day. The lorries returned with grey-faced men, lined with the fatigue of a twelve-hour shift, wanting nothing more than a meal, a shower and then the luxury of collapsing into a clean enough bed until their next call to duty.

Frank slumped down beside me and groaned at his plate of black bread and fried eggs. I guessed he was grappling with yet another hangover after spending too much time drinking vodka at Lily's and not nearly enough in bed. He stuck a knife into the yolks, added a dollop of caviar and mixed the concoction in the grease around the eggs. He shuddered, turned a bleary eye to me and said: 'You look terrible.'

'Thanks,' I said. 'You too. Do you want me to get you some coffee?'

'Gallons. Thick and black.'

We sat in silence for a while and I only realised that I had drifted off thinking of Lena when I felt the rap of a spoon on my head.

'Hey, dreamer, Andrei is talking to you,' Frank said.

I looked up and sure enough Andrei was standing there, smiling apologetically. He was barely out of his teens, a minor official who was probably destined for great things. He was a hard worker and very intelligent. He had studied engineering but was also fluent in English, German and French. His only flaw was that he was attracted to foreigners, fascinated to learn as much as he could about their countries and their way of life. He'd taken to talking to Frank and me ever since he'd shown us to our 'special rooms' on our first day in Grozny and explained how and at what hour it was possible to persuade at least a tepid flow of water from the shower. It suited his bosses to ignore the fact that he was friendly with us because he was able to translate any instructions we didn't understand and we seemed to respond to him, reluctant to tell him that our orders were crazy and unmanageable. But they had certainly taken note and he was vigilant not to give them cause for concern.

'Will you join us for the projection tonight? I understand it is very special film,' he said.

I knew it was important for his credibility that Frank and I went along to the weekly bout of propaganda extolling the virtues of the unparalleled achievements of the first two years of the Five-Year Plan but it was a hell of a price to pay. Last week's epic had consisted of a formidably large man, apparently in a laboratory, staring straight into the camera and delivering an hour-long speech on the importance of personal hygiene to the revolution.

'We'll try,' I said not very convincingly, 'but we may be too tired after our shift. We have a big quota to meet today.'

'It would be good if you could,' he said and made his way off to twist a few other arms.

Frank pushed his plate away. He had wiped it clean with his bread and chased the whole lot down with yet another cup of strong, bitter coffee. I was in awe of his constitution. Whenever I had a hangover, I was unable to face food for hours. Frank on the other hand seemed to be able to swallow anything and everything without his stomach even murmuring a complaint.

'I don't know about you,' he said, 'but I'm going to Lily's tonight. She's throwing a party. Why don't you come? Meet a few people, have some fun for a change. Let your hair down. You never know, you might find you enjoy it!'

'Thanks, but...'

'No buts. I'm sick of you moping around the place. I know you miss Lena and feel guilty about walking out on her but there's nothing you can do about it. You have to get on with your life.'

'You don't understand...'

'I understand perfectly. It's you that doesn't understand. Lena is beautiful and you want to be with her but she is not here and she can't be here. That's the way life is in Russia. You have to accept the reality. Take Lily and me. We are having a fantastic time, I think she is an incredible woman, funny, smart and very sexy, but we both know that in a few weeks or months I will have to move on and she won't be able to come with me. We live for today. What's the sense of wasting your life pining for what you can't have? It's not a rehearsal, you know, this is it. You are so busy wanting perfection, wanting more, that you aren't having any life at all.'

I tried to protest but Frank ploughed on: 'Brian, Lena knows the score. All Russian women know the trade-off of getting involved with foreigners. She has her place in this society but you don't belong here. You are just passing through, working for a few months before you go back to England where you will meet someone else and settle down in your cottage in the country or whatever you Brits do.

'It's time you snapped out of it. It's starting to affect your work - look at that cock-up with the charts last month. We lost days because you misread the figures. They are already unhappy because you argue so much. Many more mistakes like that and you'll be called in and told that they have a nice new job for you involving salt mines. And there won't be any appeal to the British ambassador.'

'Frank, I can't just ignore how I feel about Lena.'

'You are going to have to. For God's sake, haven't you got enough problems already with Madeleine? Have you forgotten you have a vengeful wife who as we speak is sitting in Alabama wondering how she can give you most grief? You are a married man and until you get that sorted out, I suggest that avoid any other serious relationships and just have some fun.'

I didn't answer. If only it were that easy.

'Am I right or — '

His sentence was interrupted by a dull thump, like thunder in a valley some distance off. It was just loud enough to make you realise that at its source, it was deafening and terrifying.

Instinctively everyone turned towards the window. Then we scrambled to see what had caused the explosion. Outside everyone else had frozen where they stood and was looking in the same direction. We were all focused on one thing - a giant plume of fire, oil and gas surging up into the sky and at its peak a black cloud, spreading like a tumour. A mile away Number Three had blown.

It was mesmerising. Nearly fifteen years later I read how those far away enough not to be in immediate danger had been unable to resist looking on as the fallout from the bomb that evaporated eighty thousand lives in an instant rose above Nagasaki. Some of them stared too closely or too long until they were blinded, the hell of the moment scorched on the back of their retinas, the last thing they saw on earth. I understood why they couldn't look away. We had been the same. Every man on site had experienced the damage that could be done by just a small accident on the wells. Many carried the scars and the burn marks; many more had helped friends who would never be fit enough to work again. They knew that for those at the heart of this it would be a holocaust.

The awed silence was broken by a wail. 'Misha! My little Misha!'

A dumpy woman on stout legs, a port wine stain down one side of her face, pushed her way through the crowd to the window. I recognised her as one of the kitchen staff who spent her whole day chopping vegetables. I had never heard her voice before. It was frail and filled with pain.

'My son! They have killed my son! The bastards.'

Andrei went to her, put his arm round her shoulders and gently led her away. 'Ssh, you don't know he was working on that well. He may not have been,' he said.

She shrugged off his arm and turned to us. 'Look at you, all of you, just standing there watching my son die, watching your friends die, just as you stood by and watched the vermin take over our country.'

A voice from the crowd said, 'That's loose talk, Oksana Ivanova.'

'Loose talk,' she spat. 'What care I of loose talk. Before the revolution I had two sons, a farm and a man. After today, I have nothing. My husband died of exhaustion, my other son was killed in the army fighting for *this*! And now my Misha has been blown up in the name of progress. We never wanted this. We always supported the Whites. For all their faults, they didn't kill boys to make fat men fatter. At least the Tsar cared about his people. This lot care for nothing but themselves.' Andrei led her away, sobbing.

I turned to Frank. 'We'd better go and see if there is anything we can do.'

When we got outside, the wailing of a siren had cut through the shock and everyone was now on the move, racing this way and that, some yelling orders, others shouting back questions. It was a scene of adrenaline-fuelled panic.

'They don't know what the hell they are doing,' Frank shouted above the hubbub. It was true. Nothing was actually being done. It was just a noisy crowd, their faces etched with concern about the physical danger ahead of them and perhaps worse, the risk of being blamed for a major disaster.

A lorry pulled up beside us. 'Get in,' the driver yelled. 'We can use all the help we can get.'

We clambered aboard. 'What happened?' Frank asked.

'Gas pocket. They drilled down too quickly and it blew.'

As we careered round a corner, something bumped against my feet. I leaned down to move it and my fingers came in contact with a sticky mess. When I looked closer, there were four makeshift stretchers piled on top of each other. The driver was on his second trip. What I had felt was blood.

'How many hurt?' I said.

'Too many.'

The lorry came to a halt. We were still some way from the burning well but unable to get any closer for the chaos of people and trucks. It was close enough. We were already deep inside a hell. It looked as though nature had surrendered, unable to withstand a force far greater than itself. As we clambered down I noticed there was no sky. A column of pure white heat rose where the tower had once been, one thousand feet from top to bottom. At ground level the air was thin, the fire burning the oxygen out of the atmosphere. When I opened my mouth to breathe, the heat dried my tongue and burned the back of my throat.

Sixty-one tons of high tensile steel had crumpled under the strain. Foot-long bolts, two inches thick, had shot into the air like primitive artillery. Girders that had taken ten men to fix in position had kinked and snapped as though they were no stronger than bits of a child's Meccano outfit. The main structure of the derrick was twisted to one side, like a mangled monster desperately trying to crawl from the heat. Sections of pipe which had been forced out of the drill hole by an ancient pressure of gas lay scattered on the steaming ground around the base, where the last few blades of grass burned orange. Several men lay around us, their bodies scorched, waiting for help. Some groaned with the pain. At least we knew they were alive. Others lay still and silent.

Near the site office a group of men were arguing frantically. I heard one voice above the others. 'You do as I say, or we all die.' There were shouts of protest and the voice rose again. 'You get your orders and you follow them!' This seemed to calm them down. As we approached, Edvuard Nikitich, chief driller for .the south section and one of the few experienced oil men pushed his way out of the throng.

He came towards us. He was not welcoming. 'Come to gloat, huh?'

'We've come to help,' I said.

'You touch nothing. You're not authorised.'

'Who cares about authorisation? Look at it!'

'Get back to your soft beds and read a book. You shouldn't be here.'

'We've got the experience. We've handled this sort of thing before,' I lied.

'Really?' he raised a sceptical eyebrow. 'And what do you

suggest? Mr Brown here can plant his great arse over the pipe while you paw over the wrong charts?'

At this Frank stepped in. 'Do you think that rabble know what they're doing? I've seen wells blow from Texas to Borneo but I've never seen a sonovabitch this big. You need all the help you can get.'

Nikitich raised his arms in frustration. 'Yes,' he said, simply. He must have seen the logic of recruiting our hands and heads. He glanced back at the crowd. 'They're just boys. They should be in school. What can you do?'

'Whatever you want.' I looked up at the fire licking the sky. 'What's the plan?'

Without a trace of irony, Nikitich replied: 'The plan is to confer with Comrade Sirienko and follow his advice. Follow me.'

Sirienko? The Party man, the bureaucrat of bureaucrats? He ate production figures for breakfast but didn't know one end of a derrick from the other.

'Surely it will be you who advises him,' I prompted.

'I do as he says and you do as I say. That's how it works.'

'But – '

'Leave it Brian,' Frank warned.

As we walked, acrid smoke from the fire enveloped us. It stung our eyes and, with each breath, took hold in our lungs. Frank bent over, spitting a black gobbet on to the ground. 'I'm too old for this,' he spluttered.

Lights from the office appeared through the gloom. The door was shut firmly. Nikitich knocked. There was no reply. He knocked again. Still no reply. He stood to one side patiently. Millions of gallons of oil were spewing into the stratosphere, an unknown number of men were dead, many more gravely injured and here he was following protocol.

'What are you waiting for? Go in!' I shouted.

Nikitich gave me a withering look. 'It's all in hand. Comrade Sirienko will see us in his own time.'

'I don't believe it! I just — '

'Shut up!' Frank hissed. 'There's nothing we can do. We go in, we give 'em some advice and they follow it or they don't. That's all.'

'There are people burning out there. And we are waiting to be invited in by some petty bureaucrat.'

'I know, I know.'

We heard a faint 'Come!' and we entered the Party lair. Sirienko was at his desk. Behind him, a portrait of Stalin gazed down benignly on proceedings. Long lists of quota figures and graphs were pinned on the remaining wall space, yet more covered the desk, some of them held down by a small bust of Lenin. There was silence as the man rearranged his desk. Edvuard shuffled his feet uncomfortably, uncertain whether to speak before being addressed.

'Well?' Sirienko said finally. He looked up and there was no mistaking the fear in his eyes. He leant back in his chair trying to look self-assured. 'You've come to tell me what to do. Isn't that right, drillerman? But why do you bring these capitalists. Do we really need their help to solve this temporary problem? Mr Grover is always so critical, I doubt he can add anything constructive.'

'With respect,' began Edvuard, 'we come to seek your advice. The men are ready but we must act quickly. What do you suggest?'

'Concrete.'

Frank grimaced openly at me. This was simply unbelievable.

'After all, we have a lot of it. Snuff out the flame. Just like that,' he said, snapping his fingers.

'How old is the well?' Frank asked.

'This is the new field. Why do you ask?'

Frank ignored the questions. 'How deep?'

'Deep enough to get oil and the occasional pocket of gas.'

I'd had enough of his flippant remarks. 'Look out there!' I demanded of him. 'What can you see?'

Sirienko smiled condescendingly. 'On a good day I can see the mountains. Today is not so good.'

Now I exploded. 'This isn't a bloody game!'

Frank pulled me back, saying rapidly, 'Please excuse my friend, he's upset.'

'Mr Grover gets upset very easily. He doesn't appear to understand the Soviet way,' Sirienko said, a glint of malice under his apparent concern. 'Perhaps he should go home?'

'He is very knowledgeable, I think he should stay.'

'Very well.' Sirienko turned languidly to Nikitich. 'What – '

'Please listen,' I interrupted. 'You must take out the fire first. Concrete's no good. If there's another gas pocket there could be a second explosion. With steam we can put it out quickly, then work on halting the flow and capping the pipe.'

Sirienko went silent. I think he realised it was the only way but did not want to admit it. He was scared. If he made the wrong decision, his whole career was on the line, but if it were ever discovered he had listened to foreigners... He turned back to Nikitich. 'And, with all your knowledge, what do you think?'

This was the litmus test. Frank and I turned to the driller. His face was set, his eyes blank.

'I think you are correct, Comrade. We should try concrete first,' he said without hesitation.

We worked into the evening, and then into the night. There were at least fifty of us in tandem, shirts pulled off our backs, handkerchiefs or rags wrapped over our mouths, sweat pouring from every pore. We bolted makeshift ramps around the well, using winches and pulleys to carry great sheets of steel. All the while, the oil streamed out of the ground, igniting some fifty feet up. From a distance it must have looked like a massive blowtorch with us just moths fluttering to the light.

Dump trucks came, laden with the quick-setting concrete they used for the bases of the towers. They reversed up, getting as close as they dared. The concrete poured down the ramps, inching towards the source.

By about nine o'clock it looked like we were making real progress, so Frank and I took a breather for a drink. We were standing by the water urn filling up our glasses when Frank grabbed me by the arm. 'Look!' The urn was trembling on the table.

The ground juddered underneath my feet and I felt myself falling. Then the world turned over. And everything went black.

CHAPTER 11

I came to, aware I was being dragged along the ground, the back of my throbbing head bumping against the rough earth. Frank spotted my eyes open, dropped my legs and yelled: 'Get up! Run!'

I hauled myself into a kneeling position and somehow scrambled to my feet, not sure where I was or what I was doing. My brain and body were a fraction of a second out of step, the messages garbled between leaving my head and reaching my limbs so that I was stumbling over debris rather than avoiding it, running into people who seemed not to notice me in their desperation to be somewhere else, anywhere else. As I looked back towards the roaring well and screaming men all I could see was an inferno against which the black, stumbling figures looked so vulnerable. It was like a medieval painting of hell. I forced myself to turn and run. I summoned every ounce of strength I had and ordered my body to obey, yet I seemed to make no progress, my legs pumping pointlessly as though I was on a treadmill.

Behind me the ground trembled and the furnace roared again, a ravenous monster determined to devour everything in its path. I tensed myself, expecting to feel its fiery claws drag me into its flaming maw but somehow I just managed to keep ahead of it and eventually felt cooler air on my cheek. Only then did I stop, gasping for air, trembling like a horse that has sensed danger. I looked back again. Men were emerging, coughing, spluttering, screaming with agony as scalding oil peeled the skin from their backs. Others clutched arms smashed by lumps of flying concrete or dragged legs that would never be straight again. They were too terrified to heed the pain that yelled at them to stop. Further back other men fell to the ground, exhausted, beaten, unable to move out of the way of danger.

Nikitich stumbled towards me, then sank to his knees as if in desperate prayer. Despite the din, I heard him say to no one in particular, 'I had no choice.' I despised his wallowing self-pity while men burned to death but then I saw the bubbling black patch on the crown of his head. I went to help him but my body wouldn't let me. I turned my head away and emptied the contents of my guts on the scorched grass then passed out.

I don't know how long passed before I came to. Nikitich had gone. I forced myself to my feet again and made my way back towards the site office. Those who had not been caught in the inferno were carrying men on stretchers towards waiting trucks, each movement accompanied by agonised yelps of pain as stripped backs chaffed against rough canvas. Those with no strength left to scream, whimpered like beaten dogs. The air was thick with the smell of scorched flesh.

I kicked open the office door. Sirienko was slumped over his desk. He hardly looked up as I yelled: 'Are you satisfied? Have you seen what you have done? Why won't you people ever listen?'

He was a defeated man, unable to summon any authority. He just whispered: 'The apparatus is ready. Do what is necessary.'

Within an hour we had connected six boilers like carriages so that we could force steam through a long elbow-shaped pipe. Frank picked out a gang of the toughest roughnecks and cajoled them into pointing the high pressure jet fifty feet up towards the base of the fire, then working it up and around. As it started to take effect, we inched forward. I could feel the heat blister my arms but we kept going, aware that we had to act fast. Another explosion would kill us all and might burn for years. High pressure steam beat back the flames. Then, with a sigh, the furnace collapsed into nothing.

It had taken a little over two minutes.

Everyone cheered, not concerned that they were being splattered by oil that was still gushing out erratically from the severed pipe duct. Unless it was cut clean so it could be capped it would continue to spew into the air. With Nikitich injured and Sirienko nowhere to be seen, all eyes were on Frank and me.

He grinned at me. 'Fancy a long oily shower?'

'You don't think I'd let a drunken Texan tackle that on his own, do you?'

'Believe me, I'm stone cold sober.'

'I'm glad to hear it.'

Frank organised some men to go in and set up arc lights focused on the centre of the well, then he and I went in armed with a two-man hacksaw and wearing goggles to try to keep the oil out of our eyes. We were followed by three of the strongest men in the group, dragging a huge hose pipe that uncurled along the ground like a giant boa constrictor. The roar of the oil was deafening. Frank yelled something inches from my ear but I couldn't hear a word. He took some rag from his pocket, ripped it into small pieces which he balled up and stuffed in his ears. I followed suit but there was no way of shutting out the dull rumble completely. Oil tried to drown us. It was in our mouths and in our noses and there was no way of getting rid of it.

We climbed in among the girders that had twisted away from the centre, some of them so hot that they welded together to form nightmarish sculptures fit only for the galleries of hell. Frank signalled and a jet of water hit us with the force of a punch. It was another obstacle to overcome but absolutely necessary. The smallest spark would see us all blown to pieces. I braced myself against it and, on Frank's nod, started to saw.

For two hours, on and off, we concentrated every drop of energy into our work, ignoring screaming muscles and throbbing hands. Each thrust of the saw took a bare millimetre off the pipe. At times it seemed we were making no progress at all. We tried to keep a regular rhythm, leaning back, pushing forward, leaning back, pushing forward. Beneath my breath I went through all the sea shanties I'd learned at school. Sweat mixed with oil slid down my face and tried to seep under the goggles. From time to time we had to stop, borrow some clean rag and wipe our faces. It was pointless but it was a break. Water slammed cold into the tension of my back and sprayed in a hazy cloud off the hacksaw blade. My legs ached, my neck felt ready to snap, my fingers locked round the saw until I began to worry I would never be able to unwrap them. The second hour was achieved on pure instinct, the mind numb, the body working automatically. The only thing that existed in the world was that lump of metal and the cut that was edging from one side to the other. Push forward, lean back. Push forward, lean back.

When the final resisting piece of metal came free, we collapsed backwards on the concrete table, nothing left to offer. I looked up at the clean column of oil, finally controllable but felt nothing. For minutes I could not move. Then I got to my knees. Frank was still lying on the other side, completely motionless. I crawled over and shook his leg. 'Time to go,' I shouted though I knew it would be impossible for him to hear me. No response. I got right up to him and slapped his face. He was out cold. I shoved my arms under his, heaving his great weight away from the centre, grunting: 'You can't stay here, old man,' and, 'You're on a diet, as from tomorrow.' I'd gone about a foot when I felt something catch. I looked over and saw that his foot was stuck under one of the girders, a nail jabbed into his ankle. 'Jesus,' I said. He must have blacked out from the pain. I crawled back, got my fingers between metal and concrete and, summoning reserves I didn't know I had, heaved it off him. The nail gouged at his flesh as it tore clear of the wound. The shock brought him round with a scream so loud it was audible against the roar.

Bit by bit, we made it to the edge of the table, Frank gripping my shoulder, his nails digging in with each painful step. In the distance the whooping and cheering started. Taking heart, Frank broke free and hobbled ahead waving his arms in the air like a maniac. I went after him. Suddenly the cheering stopped, replaced by urgent cries. I couldn't make out the words and didn't know what was happening. Then I heard a hissing sound behind me followed by a thud. I turned and less than two feet from where I was standing a lump of metal had dropped from the derrick and embedded itself into the ground like a tombstone. One step less and it would have been my grave that it marked.

As the crowd gathered round, cheering and slapping us on the back, I suddenly became aware of my own mortality. Too many times in the last few hours, I had been within a whisker of death and for what? This was crazy. I had to get away, leave the wells behind me. I needed to find Lena. Dozens of letters had been unanswered but I would try again. I pushed through the crowd. I needed to get cleaned up and to write again. I had to tell her what had happened, to ask her forgiveness one more time and beg her to take me back.

I posted it the next morning and made my way to get some breakfast, people waving and calling my name as they passed.

I bumped into Andrei. 'Brian,' he said. 'You and Frank are heroes. You are in the papers. *Pravda, Isvestia* - all of them.'

'I saw. What a night.'

'We are all very grateful to you.'

'I'll make a good comrade yet. Did the team arrive and cap the well?'

'Yes, it's done. Everything is secure again.'

In the refectory I asked a group of men about Oksana. There was a lot of shrugging of the shoulders. One man muttered: 'She's gone away.'

'Where?' I asked.

'She's gone to the sanctuary. When it was confirmed that her son had been killed she went mad. She was disturbing everyone so they took her to the sanctuary.'

'What's that? A hospital?'

'Kind of. It's an asylum. She will be well cared for there.'

I turned away. Suddenly I had lost my appetite. I just wanted to crawl back into my bed and sleep.

CHAPTER 12

The old courthouse in Grozny nestled incongruously between the municipal swimming baths and a construction site for a new heavy-duty bridge over the river. A leftover from Tsarist days, it was elaborately decorated inside and out, with masses of fine detail that suggested the architect had been enjoying himself so much, he found it impossible to stop once he had started. The gold leaf was peeling from years of neglect but this only added to the charm, amid the new, depressingly drab concrete that was starting to hem it in.

The building overlooked a central market square lined with poplars that leaned slightly to one side, yielding to the prevailing storms from the south which shook the town every year. Once a place to be feared by locals, who only entered in a crisis, the courthouse was now a general meeting place. Old men stood rubbing rough tobacco and stuffing it in pipes; large women rested their weary legs, dumping down bags of food while they gossiped on the bottom steps of the entrance; gangs of boys hoofed their tattered footballs repeatedly against the side wall. It was now used as the local Party meeting hall, where protests against American imperialism were staged by men from the factories, although most would rather have spent the time at home with their families. It was also the venue for lectures as varied in interest and usefulness as the power of the proletariat and how to spot the first signs of potato blight. Commemorations of Lenin's death were solemnly observed there, enthusiastic celebrations of Stalin's birthday staged; and here the local municipal officials met to pass unanimously resolutions they had received from above.

Today it was our turn, Frank's and mine. After a month in which we had been feted, interviewed and found ourselves unable to pay for a single drink, today we were to receive the official thanks of the town. As we sat on the stage waiting for the ceremony to begin, I scanned the rows for familiar faces. Nikitich was on the front row looking slightly ridiculous with a bandage swathed round his head. Sirienko was alongside him, his confidence and poise restored though I'm sure still smarting that I had seen him looking so vulnerable. Andrei, who had enjoyed the reflected glory of being able to claim us as friends, was chatting excitedly to his neighbour. And around them, sat many of the local people who had cautiously steered clear of us before the disaster but were now happy to be seen exchanging the time of day. In one corner there was a handful of other ex-pat workers who had found acceptance easier to come by since Frank and I had risked our necks.

Alongside us on the platform were the town's three most senior Party officials. Each sported the bushy moustache made fashionable by their leader but somehow it failed to give them the authority enjoyed by Stalin. Perhaps it was the fact that peeking through gaps of their uniforms that stretched over well-fed bellies you could glimpse their yellowing vests. They reminded me of characters from Gilbert and Sullivan, more comic because they took themselves so seriously.

They perched pompously beneath a beautifully printed, highly stylised poster of three lean, handsome men toiling for the national good, happy to labour so that Russian families could look forward with optimism. One held a scythe swung back with vigour; the second was bringing a hammer down on an anvil until sparks flew; the third, with arched back, shovelled coal into roaring furnace. In the distance, factories rose proudly, black against a blood-red sky on which was written in heavy type: FORWARD! WITH THE CHILDREN OF THE REVOLUTION!

Frank followed my gaze and grinned. 'The dream . . .' he nodded his head at the poster '. . .and the reality.' He glanced at the party officials.

The most senior of them stood up, smiled in our direction and looked down at his notes ready to address the audience. He was halted by the sound of the double doors creaking open. All heads turned to the figure framed against the light streaming in behind him. He strode into the hall, a commanding presence. He was immaculate. His hair was parted sharply from the right, dark eyes stared out from behind gold-rimmed spectacles and his chin was shaved so close as to give the impression that he saw that chore as a patriotic duty. His tunic was folded precisely into pleats and held by a belt buffed to a shine. But even it could not outshine his boots which positively sparkled as his heels clicked across the wooden floor.

The party officials knew their place and rapidly cleared a space at the centre of events. They looked flustered and were clearly not expecting such a visit.

'Who's he?' Frank whispered.

'NKVD, GRU, *Cheka,* whatever they call security these days. Come to rally the troops and flush out the doubters.'

'How do you know?'

'Just watch… '

The officials lined up to greet him, each shaking his hand as if they were touching royalty. He spared them each a brief, thin smile giving the impression that any more would have been a wasted effort. With all the confidence of power, he strode in front of them and turned to the crowd, who now sat rigid with attention.

'Today is a great day,' he began. 'That is why I am here. To celebrate with you an achievement that proves to the world that the proletariat's march of progress is unstoppable. Why, you may wonder, should we have cause to applaud the rectifying of something which should never have happened in the first place?' He paused for effect, scanning the people in the front row, lingering just a shade too long on Sirienko.

'Indeed those blood-sucking leeches, those self-congratulatory fat-cats of the imperialist West, always quick to laugh at us, will ask the same question. Well, I shall answer them simply… They are right.'

A murmur rippled through the audience. Heresy from a top man? Maybe a test? Whoever agrees first, is noticed first.

'It is true that such accidents would have been unthinkable under the Tsar.' The officials on the stage looked very uncomfortable, not sure how to react. If this turned out to be a renegade speaking out of turn, they should stop him. But…

Fortunately he came to their rescue. 'It would have been unthinkable because before the revolution we had no oil fields. Only a small trickle, a little boy taking a leak.' The tension left the hall. The trio of officials led the laughter and everyone looked relieved. The natural order had been restored and they could all relax again. The man raised a hand and the laughter stopped instantly.

'There are those, however, who still look back on the old days with bourgeois affection. "The good old days." It was Marx who said people always thought the world was better when they were children...'

I whispered in Frank's ear, 'It was Socrates actually.' He looked at me puzzled, as if to say, 'Who the hell's he?'

'...Nostalgia is a dangerous affliction. It blurs the sharp edge of reality. Where were we twenty years ago, comrades? A nation on the verge of greatness? A people content at work and play? No! I'll tell you where we were. In the dark ages! Nicholas and his *kulak* cronies licked the cream in Leningrad, while honest workers, you! and you! and you!' he stabbed his finger towards the crowd in time to the words, 'with not a crumb in your stomachs, could only eat the mud. And if you protested, the capitalist boot pressed against the back of your neck, pushed your face further into that mud. Did our country thrive? Did we lead the way in industry? Did we walk with our heads held high, our faces smiling as we went to work? The answer is no, comrades. A thousand times no...'

'Is he talking to us?' Frank sniggered.

'...So let the West mock. I say, let them! Behind their superior smiles lies the tight grimace of fear. For they know they are beaten. Their system is crumbling. Inexorably, the tide is turning our way. In London, affluent, bloated London, workers queue up in their thousands for a bowl of soup no thicker than water. In Munich they riot for bread because the money they are paid might as well be used to light a fire for all it is worth. And across the United States of America whole families travel in search of work that isn't there. They are forced to scrabble in the earth like pigs, trying to nose out scraps but they find none. The American dream has become a nightmare.'

It was a rousing stuff, but even this great orator hadn't learned that you can only inspire for so long before the effect starts to subside. One peasant, whether deliberately or from naivety I never worked out, stood and started to applaud as though the speech was over. He received a chilling glance from the stage and was dragged back into his seat by an embarrassed wife who would later remind him that rule number one is never voluntarily stand out from the crowd.

The speaker hardly missed a beat. 'Comrades, we are fighting together for a better future and we are secure in the knowledge that our cause is just. Each and every one of you is at the heart of the fight. We must modernise our machinery and our factories, build up our industrial strength until we are the envy of the world. We must work all the hours necessary, make the breaking of quotas a matter of personal pride, until we have achieved our aim. You above all understand that we cannot fulfil the glorious destiny of the Soviet Union without oil. Oil is the lifeblood of the nation. When a well blows, it is like a bullet shot at the Motherland; when it is put out, it is like a healing hand.'

He turned to us with a dead-eyed smile that made me shudder. I realised how much he hated having to thank two westerners, people he saw simply as the enemy. But ignoring us would not have looked good so he was determined to use the occasion for positive propaganda. That was why he was here - he couldn't trust local officials to get it right.

'These men are converts to our cause. They could not find work in England or America so they came to us. They know we are right, that is why they joined us,' he said, his look warning us not to contradict him. 'They are examples to us all. Without

102

thought to their own safety they risked everything to ensure the aims of the First Five-Year Plan are met. They did not think of reward, heroically putting their lives on the line for the greater good.

'Comrades, we are here today to hold out our arms in welcome and thanks. Brian Grover, Frank Brown, it is the wish of the Communist Party of the Soviet Union and the working people of Grozny that you are awarded the highest honour for your selfless act, Heroes of the Soviet Union.'

The courtroom erupted with applause as he pinned a simple red star on to our lapels.

He pressed an envelope and a black box into my hand.

'In the box there's something for a real celebration, Mr Grover,' he said, in unfaltering English. 'Good lemon vodka, you won't find it anywhere else.'

'Thank you so much, Comrade - ?'

'Beria, Lavrenty Pavlovich.'

The name meant nothing to me. Frank and I stood either side of Comrade Beria clutching our money and displaying our medals, looking like schoolchildren who had just won a form prize. Press photographers came forward, and we blinked into the flash bulbs. Beria took one final opportunity to get his message across. He stretched his long arms across our shoulders and squeezed us into his sides. Shouting above the hubbub, he said: 'Admire them, comrades. Emulate them. *Beat* them!'

With that he shook the hands of the local officials and disappeared as quickly as he had arrived. The crowd started to disperse, each group deep in discussion about the significance of the visit of such a man, Frank slapped me on the back. 'Well, what did you make of that?' he chortled. 'I reckon we are Grozny's favourite sons, maybe even Russia's. And here is my Lily to help me celebrate. Look at her, isn't she beautiful? And all mine. See you later.'

He curled a possessive arm round Lily's waist, and whispered something in her ear. They both burst out laughing. Then he looked back and added: 'Do you want to come with us? We're going to have a few drinks.'

I shook my head. Despite the excitement of the past couple of weeks I was still not feeling very sociable. I had finally received a reply to my last letter to Lena but it wasn't what I'd hoped for. She had simply written 'Please don't write any more' and not even signed it. I stood with my back to the door, staring up at the poster, wondering why I had never felt as satisfied or committed as the men depicted there. I knew they didn't exist, that it was just idealised propaganda, but I had always believed that work should be more than just about earning money and somehow I had never quite felt the fulfilment I'd desired. I couldn't help wondering if it was because I'd never sorted out the other side of my life, never given myself a reason to work beyond work itself.

I heard someone come into the courthouse. I turned, half expecting Andrei but it was Lena. I couldn't register what I was seeing. I couldn't find any words. I stood there like an idiot, staring, terrified she might disappear.

Only when she started to walk towards me did I dare move. We met in the centre aisle. We embraced. Her fingers dug into my back and I knew she was real. She buried her face in my chest and clung to me with animal strength. I prised her away, cupped her face in my hands, wiping the tears from her cheeks with my thumbs. My head was still spinning. Finally I managed to speak. 'What are you doing here? How did you get here? God, it's so good to see you. You don't know how much I've missed you. How did you...'

She put a finger over my lips. 'Not now,' she whispered, and kissed me deeply. 'There's something we have to do.'

CHAPTER 13

The room was very familiar. The simple dresser, the basin in the corner, the black iron bed, wallpaper starting to peel off the walls, a stain on the ceiling shaped like Africa. I had come to know every inch of it over the last few months. But now it looked different. It wasn't just that Lena's suitcase lay open on the floor, her clothes spilling out. Suddenly it was no longer just a place where I slumped exhausted after work, or sat quietly avoiding people. It had come to life because she was there.

She had forbidden me to speak all the way back. When we reached the apartment she led me into the bedroom, unselfconsciously undressed herself and then me. The evening light slanting through the window cast a golden glow over her body. I thought she was the most beautiful thing I had ever seen. My body wanted to throw itself at her, devour her. But my mind and my heart wanted to savour every second to make this such a special memory that it would survive forever. I lay down beside her and traced a finger along her shoulder, round her breast and then down her side and her thigh, relishing the satin softness of her skin. I gently kissed her triangle of hair, the flat of her stomach, then moved up and kissed her warmly on the lips, slowly, tentatively giving myself to her at the same time. She took me inside, wrapped her arms around my neck and looked deep into my eyes, totally trusting. At that moment I knew that she was completely mine and my body ached to show her the depth of my feeling for her, to express physically the things that no words could adequately say.

It felt as though our bodies had become one as we moved easily together as though we knew each other's desires without needing to be told. Then more urgently, more passionately. Wanting it to last forever, I tried to withdraw for a while but she curled her legs around me, her heels pressing against my back, and kept me inside her. 'Don't leave me,' she said. I lost myself in her body.

For some time afterwards there was nothing but the sound of our breathing and the warmth of our bodies clinging on to each other as though they would never let go. Eventually she lifted herself up on to an elbow, smiled down at me and said: 'Now we can talk.'

'I don't know if I can after that,' I laughed.

'You don't have any questions?'

'Millions. What on earth are you doing here?'

She tossed her head in mock petulance. 'Ha! A fine thing. For months he bombards me with begging letters – "Come be with me", "I miss you", "I can't live without you". Then when I arrive he asks, "What are you doing here?" Men! OK, I'll go.'

'Don't you dare. I'm not letting you out of my sight again. What I meant was how did you get away from Moscow?'

'Your friend Talbot. And your persistence. You hurt me badly Brian, and your first letters went straight in the bin.'

'I know. I tried to explain....'

'Ssh. I know what you're going to say. Wait. After a while I cooled down a little so when the next one came, I kept it. I didn't know whether to open it or not. I wasn't sure I wanted to know you any more but all the same I couldn't bring myself to throw it away. It sat on the mantelpiece gathering dust, mocking me every day because I was too scared to read it and too weak to put it in the bin. Others joined it there.

'Then I received your last letter. That decided it. I was being stupid. I told myself, "You either face it or forget." I chose to face it and opened them all. I read your words and believed you. I found myself wanting you beside me. I remembered what you said when you lay down on the tram lines. "Life can be different anywhere you want it to be." And I thought, what do I have, what do I really have?

'Next day, I went to Talbot's office. You told me he knew everybody so I thought why not? He was surprised to see me, he hardly remembered me in fact. He was even more surprised when I asked him to get me transfer papers. At first he wasn't very helpful. He was very loyal to you. He thought we'd only met a couple of times and that I was some spurned Russian girl looking to make trouble. I explained to him how we'd wanted to keep it discreet. I showed him one of your letters as proof. I hope you don't mind.'

I winced, remembering how intimate some of my letters had been, but I was not in a position to argue.

'He told me that you'd had no choice about leaving. You had to take the job, once it was offered, if you wanted to stay in the country. The head of *Soyuz-Nyeft* is a very powerful man, he said, and wouldn't take kindly to a rejection, especially from a foreigner. That settled it for me. I knew I was doing the right thing. Talbot said he would see what he could do, no promises. Two days later my transfer papers arrived.'

'And now,' she leaned across me, resting her chin on my chest, 'I'm here.'

'I love you,' I said. The words came out abruptly as though they had spoken themselves. I let them hang there. I didn't want to retract them. Lena laughed. 'Prove it. Tell me what you love about me.'

'I love the way my nose fits into your belly button.' I pushed my face into her stomach. She rolled over onto her back.

'That's not enough,' she said.

'I love your dimple and the little mole on your cheek. I love the way you smile - when you are naked your body smiles with you, everything curls up in a grin.'

'More.'

I placed my hand around her ribcage. 'And the way you pretend you're not ticklish. You go rigid, your face tightens and you try to fight it but if I count to ten...' I wiggled my finger. 'One... two... three...'

'That's not love,' she screamed, 'it's torture. You're no gentleman.'

'Whoever said I was a gentleman?'

Her eyes opened wide and her mouth dropped. 'Puh! You did.'

'You're mistaken,' I said loftily. 'That must have been some other man you have been seeing.'

She went quiet then and looked away.

'Lena?'

It was only for a second, an eye-blink, and she was smiling again. 'If you were a gentleman, you would profess your love to me in a long speech.'

I shuffled onto my knees. The mattress sagged under my weight. Lena's naked body bounced as I moved.

I clasped my hands together, looked up to the heavens and said whatever came into my head. In English. 'Once upon a time there was a poor young Englishman who fell in love with a beautiful princess but she would have nothing to do with him. So he went off and became a hero...'

Lena shook her head. 'What? What are you saying? In Russian? English is no good.'

'It's a beautiful language.'

'In Russian.'

'It's difficult enough in my own language.'

'It shouldn't be.'

'Help me then.'

'I know just the thing.' She rolled over onto her front, stretched an arm into her suitcase, her feet sticking up in the air as she did so, and brought back a bottle of vodka and two glasses. 'A toast.'

'Snap.' I showed her my presentation case of lemon vodka. 'Courtesy of Comrade Beria.'

Her eyes lit up. 'Beria!'

'How come you know him? He's local.'

'I've seen him in the papers, he's a rising star.'

'Anyway, a double toast.'

'You must do it the traditional way. "*Litotska*", we say. Fill it halfway.' Her fingers were slender around the glass as I poured the clear liquid. 'Before you drink you must cross the glass, like this.'

'Why do you do that?'

'When you open your mouth to drink, the devil can leap in. The cross drives him away.'

'You don't believe that, surely?'

'You think you know me?' she reprimanded. 'How can you love someone you don't know?'

'I love finding out,' I said.

We clinked glasses. 'There are no devils,' she said. 'Not real ones. But it is custom, I like it. It reminds me of my grandfather and St Petersburg before the revolution. He would sit me on his knee, the bottle in one hand, a glass in the other, and tell me stories and sing the drinking songs. The women there used to call vodka "orphan's tears" because the men would work all week and spend their wages each night in the taverns. They never came home until they were drunk. He told me that while he breathed his fumes over me.' She chuckled, remembering. 'But the tradition is good. It is old. Unspoiled.'

She handed me a glass, put her own between her knees. She dipped her finger in the vodka and swirled it around, then ran her finger over my lips. I sucked the sharp taste off. Then I took a swig, kissed her and let the vodka seep into her mouth. She received it and swallowed.

'So', she said, 'a toast. To all things old and all things pure.' We crossed our glasses and threw it back in one shot.

'To Talbot,' I returned. 'Old but not so pure. Mmm.' The spirit bit at the back of my throat as I breathed in.

Ileana tutted.

'What?'

'You've forgotten something, Mister Grover.'

'What?' I repeated.

'Your speech. In my language.'

'That's not fair.'

'I won't believe you unless you do it.'

'OK, you win.' I took a deep breath. 'When I first saw you, I thought you were pretty. When I saw you again, about two seconds later, I realised you were beautiful. And when you opened your mouth and spoke, a tingle ran down my spine. It's true!

'I spent an idyllic evening with you and a not so idyllic morning without you in the most wonderful city in the world. I spent two weeks dreaming of you, wondering where you'd gone, and one week wishing I'd met you ten years ago. Then I tortured myself wondering how I was going to tell you I had to go and I've just spent three terrible months hoping you would write to me.'

'I did, I said don't write.'

'That wasn't what I had in mind. Why did you do that?'

'Weakness. I suppose I wanted you to know I'd received your letters… But your speech.'

'All right, you ask me what do I love? I love the tiny hairs under your chin that only show up in this light. I love your toes. Your perfect breasts…'

'They are too small! Men like big breasts.'

'No, they are perfect. The French, and for all their faults they do know about love, they say that the perfect woman's breast fits in a champagne goblet.' I cupped her breast to demonstrate. 'I love the ridge of your back, the furrows on your forehead when you frown.'

I stopped for a moment. 'I can't do this in one go, the list is too long. You make me laugh, you make me lose my inhibitions, you ask me questions that make me think. But if I had to pick one thing, it is that when we're together, the world seems better. Everything bad, unfair or cruel disappears and there is only the here and now and that is so perfect, everything else is forgotten.'

Lena closed her eyes, flopped back on the mattress. I waited. It seemed as though she were weighing it all up, taking it in. Then she sat up again and, like a child who cannot stop asking 'Why?' she said:

'More.'

So I leapt on her, two giggling lovers, completely at one.

When I woke up the curtains had stopped fluttering. The air was still and dense. Through the window the sky glowed purple, paling by the minute. Lena's clock clicked away beside my head. I stretched over, squinting at it in the dim light. Five o'clock, but I felt wide awake. Faint leftovers of a dream clung behind my eyes as dots danced around the room.

I sank back into the pillow.

'There was a thunderstorm before.'

I started. Lena was staring at the ceiling, her arms straight by her sides.

'I thought – '

'I didn't mean to make you jump. Sorry... It woke me up and I couldn't get back to sleep. I was just thinking. Things racing round my mind.' She paused. 'Sometimes you can't stop them.'

'What sort of things.'

'Oh, nothing important.' She rolled over to face me.

'Really.'

But there was something behind her expression, something hidden.

'You can tell me,' I said.

She smiled. A smile that only women smile, one that said I could tell you but you would not understand.

'There is nothing to tell.'

'You don't trust me?'

'It's not that. It doesn't affect us.'

'Aaah, so there is something.'

'Brian, please . . .'

'You admitted it!' I tried to sound jocular, cajoling, as though it were just a game. But there was more to it than that. I wanted everything from her. My love was selfish. It required everything.

I had a thirst that demanded to be quenched. It gnawed at my gut that she was holding something back.

'There are secrets that should be left alone,' she said quietly. 'And you must not try to get them out of me! We have now and hopefully we have the future. The past doesn't matter. If you can't accept that...'

I was about to protest then realised I could not. I too had secrets that I wasn't able to share.

I put my arms around her and we lay there, silent, until there were sounds outside - vehicles rumbling down the road, people chatting before they went on shift. Finally, she said to me: 'Some day I will tell you, if you promise one thing now.' I gripped her hand, slipped my fingers through hers.

'I'm sorry Lena. It was wrong of me. You don't have to make a deal with me. I don't deserve it.'

'No, listen! I want you to promise.'

'Anything.'

'Will you take me away from here? Not now. One day. To England. Will you promise to do that?'

I grinned. 'Cross my heart,' I said in English.

'What does that mean?'

'It's an English tradition. It means yes. I promise.'

CHAPTER 14

After the first few days Lena left my room at the complex and went to stay with Lily. It was better that way, fewer questions. Lily, who prided herself on her independence, had been surprisingly amenable to the idea of Lena moving in and the two of them seemed to hit it off immediately. Lily's place was about eight miles from my apartment and the journey soon became very familiar as did the spare room to which Lena quickly added small touches that made it her own. Talbot had arranged for her to be transferred to the local medical unit attached to the wells and she was soon working all hours, tending to patients who had fallen from towers, got their hands caught in lathes with no safety guards, or their skin scalded from boilers which leaked from lack of maintenance. Sometimes she would become frustrated by the pointless inevitability of the injuries, but she knew she could not speak out. To suggest better precautions, to make the most even-handed of observations might be taken the wrong way.

I too was kept busy. The wells demanded most of my time and

it wasn't long before the attitude to our exulted status as local heroes turned to 'If you're so good, you should be able to produce more.' The quotas continued to rise, the equipment to fail. Every time I tackled Sirienko about it, he cut me off: 'Mr Grover, are you presuming to criticise the Soviet system? That is not wise and it is becoming tedious. If you do not like it you can return to England. Of course there is no work there, and you could not take your woman.'

Lena and I lived for the weekends, especially Saturday, the only full day we could be sure we would spend together. During the week we would snatch whatever time we could in the evenings, mainly wrapped up in each other, away from prying eyes. But on Friday nights we'd all get together, Frank, Lily, Lena and I, and we would celebrate the fine things in life in a tavern close to Lily's house. We were a family. Saturday mornings were reserved for the market. It was a ritual we never tired of. Whatever the weather, we'd go into Grozny and lose ourselves in the crowd. This was the time when we felt like an ordinary couple, doing the things that couples had done together for generations. It felt normal and it felt good.

The summer transformed Grozny. With the arrival of the heat, its character shifted and the people emerged as if from hibernation. The river that had become turgid and brown was refreshed by new water from the Caucasus mountains and sparkled blue under a clear sky. Couples walked along the bank hand in hand. Gangs of children with scuffed knees and grubby faces skidded flat stones, forever trying to reach the other side. Old men sat by the bank gnawing at great hunks of bread with toothless gums, remembering when they wore short pants, when they had a young girl on their arm, when their strong muscles obeyed the commands of their brain without protest or pain. The warm sun on their back made them wonder if that strength might just be coming back.

The summer also brought the return from the mountains of the Chechens, the tribe who had travelled these plains for thousands of years. They arrived to sell their wares in the market place and to swamp the town in colour and noise. They were outsiders in their own land but as far as possible refused to acknowledge their rulers from the north and in their turn, the Russian officials largely let them be. Occasionally, police chiefs sent sorties into the hills like eager missionaries hoping to make conversions but the pushes stopped when their comrades failed to return. Then there would be a long period of calm in which the Chechens were left alone until some new career bureaucrat would try to make a name for himself and start the crackdown once again, inevitably failing and bringing to a halt the personal progress he had hoped would shoot ahead.

The local working people looked forward to the arrival of the Chechens with their wonderful food, distinctive because it was fresh, and the beautiful woven cloths of yellow and red, through which golden threads sparkled as they hung over the edge of market stalls. Money that had been squirreled away during the winter was taken from hiding places deep in cupboards and spent with gusto. The scene was often raucous and occasionally over-boisterous but the police let it be, after all they too enjoyed the chance of something new to wear instead of their drab uniforms, and the taste of deliciously fresh food.

For Lena, the market days at Grozny represented everything she had been denied in Moscow - the freedom to wander, to pick and choose at random, and the luxury of not having to queue for hours. Within weeks of her arrival we began to feel as though we had been together forever. Our lives seemed problem free or maybe we just didn't notice them because we were so immersed in each other. We took languid evening strolls in the park, ate candle-lit meals with sweet Georgian wine, shared private jokes that no one else got, and made love passionately in the privacy of our room – quietly, longingly under a sky that found it hard to contain all the stars. We went to work with the secret smiles of lovers on our faces as the summer passed idyllically by, time unnoticed. Until suddenly it was November, one month until my contract ran out.

Lena brought in a tray with coffee and a plate of fried food. I watched her as she placed it carefully in the space she'd cleared. The sheer ordinariness of it thrilled me. I wanted my life to carry on like this. We had only been together five months and now I wanted another five, and five more after that, stretching into infinity. I resolved to renew my permits as soon as possible. I knew there would be endless paperwork but I was reasonably confident it could be sorted out. I was working hard and they needed all the help they could get in the oilfields. There were a few small doubts, no more than a hint of a shadow really, but enough to invade my sleep from time to time and make me grateful when I awoke to find I had been dreaming.

It was little things that concerned me. I remembered one of the ex-pats saying to me in a bar a few days after Frank and I received our medals: 'Watch your back. Success makes some people round here very jealous, especially a foreigner's success.' Then there had been a spate of problems at work. A few things had gone missing. It was only small things like charts, files or tools but it had disrupted shifts for an hour or two. I'd put it down to petty thieving and told myself it was no more than you would expect when people are living on meagre wages. But then an engine broke down halfway through drilling a borehole and set us back several days. A boiler ruptured, bolts were loosened on rigs, more equipment went missing. And most of it seemed to be happening at the wells where I was in charge.

One Friday, Sirienko called a meeting and demanded to know what was going wrong and made it clear he was very unhappy. 'Sometimes it seems that those who criticise the system most are the most accident prone,' he said. All eyes turned towards me.

'It is a coincidence that these things happen on my wells,' I said. 'I have mounted thorough investigations but no one seems to know what has happened.'

Sirienko shrugged and said, 'Well we will all have to work harder to make up the time' and I felt that he had accepted my explanation. But as we left the meeting Nikitich took my arm.

'No longer the golden boy huh?' he said, clearly relishing the situation.

'It happens.' I replied. I wasn't going to let him think I was concerned. 'See you Monday.'

'Perhaps,' he said.

Even I realised my attempted smile was pretty feeble and maybe the chill I felt was the reason I drank far too much that night.

CHAPTER 15

Lena sat on the bed by my feet and shook me. 'Come on, you've got a lot to do.'

'Noooooooo,' I groaned. 'Just leave me here to die. Oh, my head.'

'Sorry, you've got to get up. After all you did promise to help Lily prepare for the party tonight.' Even through my hangover I could sense the delight she was taking from breaking this news to me.

'I said what? How drunk was I? What else did I say?'

'Oh nothing much.'

'I know what that means. Come on, out with it.'

'Oh you just informed the packed bar that Sirienko was a bumbling idiot fit for nothing better than a janitor's assistant.'

'Didn't everyone agree? I seem to remember them nodding their heads.'

'It was your head that was nodding.'

'Ah.' I fell back on the bed and covered my face with a pillow. 'I might as well end it now,' I said. 'Is it possible to deliberately suffocate yourself?'

Lena pulled the pillow away. 'I wouldn't let you, even if it were.'

I smiled and reached out towards her, stopping midway as my memory flashed a warning.

'That man was there again, wasn't he?'

She nodded solemnly, then added quickly. 'It's nothing, He's just another face.'

I'd first seen him about a month ago in the works' canteen. He was in his early thirties with a thin angular frame, blond hair cropped short, and smooth pale skin which was unusual for Grozny at that time of year. But what made me take notice of him was that he was dressed in the regulation works tunic but it was spotless and didn't seem to sit well. He was sitting alone, taking his time over a cup of coffee and reading *Pravda*. He didn't look at home in those surroundings. I wondered why Andrei hadn't introduced him as he did most newcomers. The next day he had gone and when I asked about him, Andrei said: 'I don't know who you mean, there's been no one new arrived that I'm aware of.'

I didn't think any more about it until I spotted the man again a couple of weeks later, this time wearing a suit and sitting on a bench under the poplars in the market square. He was looking straight at me but when I caught his eye, he pretended to read a book. I decided I needed to know more about him but as I started to approach he quickly moved away and melted into the crowds.

I felt uneasy but pushed it to the back of my mind. Now Lena had told me that I had made stupid, vodka-fuelled comments in front of him. I was angry with myself for dropping my guard, for allowing myself to drink too much. It was so easy when I was with Frank - he could drink all night and while he might become a little melancholy, he was never loud. If anything he became introverted and usually mumbled nothing but undying love for Lily. But me, a person who could get tight on what Frank would consider a quick one, I became emboldened, willing to put the world to rights and share my ideas with anyone who cared to listen.

I wished I hadn't done it in front of this stranger. 'He's not just another face. We're being watched,' I said.

'Why would they watch us?'

'My contract is up soon. Perhaps some people don't want me around.'

She gave me a hug. 'They'll renew your contract. They need you.'

'Perhaps.'

I pulled her to me, wanting the reassurance of burying myself in her warmth. If she was there with me, nothing could be that bad. 'Did I really say I would help, Lily with the party?' I asked.

'You did. So let me go and get showered and shaved. You are disgusting.'

Refreshed, I stuffed my pockets full of roubles and a few dollars in case I needed some favours. Lena drew up a list of what we needed which consisted mainly of fiery Chechen spirits and vast quantities of fresh fruit.

Outdoors it was bright and clear, and already very hot. Most people were taking advantage of a Saturday morning lie-in, so as we made our way towards town it was quiet except for the occasional half heard snippets of conversation carried from houses on the breeze and the background steady chug of distant wells. The dusty track wound gently around the slope of a hill. We took our time, Lena pausing to pick wild flowers which she said would look nice on the table that night.

'You'll have no room left to carry the food,' I said.

'You're the one who volunteered so you carry the food. I'm happy holding flowers.'

About a mile down the road a truck trundled towards us, a small speck on the skyline. Lena prodded me. 'If you must pickle your brain with vodka, then you must pay the price.'

The truck was much closer now, its engine spluttering and coughing as it negotiated the incline. It reached the brow of the hill, but instead of speeding up it slowed right down, and stopped about fifty yards in front of us. At first I had assumed it was from the fields but as we approached it became clear it was police issue. There were three men in the front. The driver leaned on the steering wheel staring at us.

As we walked towards the truck two of the men jumped down from the cab, their heavy boots sending up puffs of dirt as they landed. I remembered Talbot telling us to be polite, smile and be dumb, and walked towards them with my arm out as if to shake hands. I hoped I looked more confident than I felt.

Still in the cab, the driver was smiling. He knew what his comrades were up to, had seen it all before, and was ready to enjoy the show. They weren't particularly big. In fact, in workmen's clothes they would have looked like rather nondescript people who held down dull jobs. But when they pulled on the uniform, it gave them a kernel of self-importance and sense of power that they enjoyed being able to wield.

They stood blocking our path until we were within an arm's length. Lena looked down at the ground.

'Good morning,' I said.

'Name?' The first one fired the question at me.

'Brian Grover.'

'You're not Russian. Nationality?'

'British.'

'Papers.'

I produced my passport and permits. The officer plucked them from my hand and painstakingly pawed through every page. I wished I had one of Talbot's letters from a minister that had worked so well on officials in Moscow.

'What are you doing here?' he asked.

'I work on the derricks.'

He nodded and whispered something to his partner. When he turned back to me his face had transformed from vaguely amused to impassive, serious.

'Someone is sabotaging the wells.'

This wasn't the time to argue. 'I know there are problems. We are looking into them,' I said.

'It is funny, don't you think, that all this happened after you came here?'

So it was no accident that it was me they had stopped. I felt blood rushing to my cheeks. 'What do you mean by that?'

He waved a hand in dismissal. 'It is only an observation.' He glanced at Lena, looked her up and down then turned back to me. 'How long do you intend to stay here?'

'Indefinitely.'

'Then you need to extend your visa.'

'I intend to do that.'

'Of course, it might be revoked.'

'I hope not. I'm happy here.'

He gave Lena a leering sidelong glance. 'I can see that.'

There was a pause, as if he was contemplating something more. Then he held out my papers. I reached for them and he let them slip from his hand. The passport landed face down. I stooped to retrieve it. He placed his boot on the cover and pressed it further into the dust.

'You must look after your documents. They are valuable,' he said impassively.

I felt the anger rise in my throat but swallowed it. I nodded, and reached again for the passport. This time he let me take it.

'Well,' he said. 'That's all for now... hero.'

The driver started up the truck, smirking. The two officers turned on their heels and walked away.

As they passed us the truck stopped again. The driver leaned out of the window and called, 'If you're such a hero, why do you bed with the whore of Grozny?' And he started laughing. 'The hero and the whore. We know everything you do. Everything. I've seen it with my own eyes.'

I watched them as they disappeared into the distance. Lena buried her head in my side.

'It's all right,' I said, lifting her tear-stained face up towards me. 'They were just bored, looking for amusement.' Even I wasn't convinced.

'They hate us. Because I am with a foreigner, they call me a whore. Because you were successful they are jealous. Don't you see? And once they get on to you, you're in trouble.'

'Ignore it. Let them watch. We've done nothing wrong.'

'They don't need a reason.' She tossed the flowers aside as if they had been tainted. 'You don't understand. You don't know how difficult this is.'

'It will be OK,' I tried to reassure her. 'Come on, we've a party to prepare.'

CHAPTER 16

We felt safer when we merged into the growing crowd in the market. Canopied stalls ran in lines across the central square then spilled out into the crooked back streets. Men and women called out, proclaiming their low prices or exceptional quality - 'You won't find cheaper in the whole Soviet Union!' or 'Our cloaks are so fine, Comrade Stalin himself would be happy to wear them.' Stallholders bargained and blustered, desperate to outdo their neighbours and persuade the milling throng to spend money on their particular pots and pans or shawls, or hats or fruit or bric-a-brac and knick-knacks. A dozen different herbal potions were highly recommended to fix all your ills. It was a cacophony of capitalism.

I clung on to Lena's hand so we didn't get forced apart in the mêlée. We stopped at one stall and watched an old man, the top of his head as smooth and shiny as a conker, his leathery face a relief map of wrinkles, as he cajoled a group of women into buying ornamental cushions.

'I spent the whole year lovingly making each one by hand along with my dear wife,' he said. 'Surely you will not send me home empty handed to tell her we cannot eat this winter?'

And when this plea to their better nature didn't work, he changed tack: 'Ladies, this cushion will ease your aching back when you sit at night but is also strong enough that your drunken husband will feel its force when you use it to box his ears.'

That brought a laugh, and some sales.

'Let's get our moonshine and go see if Lily's out of bed yet,' I said.

'What's munsheen?'

'The drink. It's English for illegal home-made spirit.'

She tried the word out again, rolling it around her lips. 'Munsheen. I like that.'

We stopped at a stall where an old woman, several inches under five foot, offered us a sample of her home made spirit.

'Just a sip,' she cackled, winking. 'It is very strong. Be careful. If you spill it on the ground, the grass will shrivel.'

Lena tried a drop then fanned her hand in front of her mouth. 'Puh! We will take two bottles. If we don't drink it all I can take it to the hospital and use it to douse the wounds.'

The events of earlier were pushed to the back of our minds for the moment. By the time we ambled out of the market square the contentment of recent months had returned, restored by the sheer pleasure of being in each other's company and sharing everyday things that we both enjoyed.

Lily's place was a small cottage on the south side of Grozny. At first glance it was unremarkable. Square-faced with shuttered windows and walls blackened by grime carried on the air from the factories, it looked much like all the other rather tired houses in the neighbourhood. But one thing marked it out from the rest - it was away from the main road, some distance from the houses on either side, and behind it rolling fields stretched for miles to the hills on the horizon. Unlike so many homes in that area, Lily's cottage offered some privacy, a place where we could talk freely and play the kind of music that we wouldn't admit to liking anywhere else. It was an oasis of freedom in a land where people had learned it was safer to impose their own restrictions, and it was this that made Lily's parties so special.

Only a select few were invited, those among the riggers, refiners and mechanics trusted to be discreet, people who knew a good knees-up when they saw one and weren't likely to say anything afterwards. They were mainly Americans, some French, a lone Canadian named Cahl Tyrone, a couple of Brits who had followed much the same course as me and were happy just to be working, and lastly - and, for the lusty Yanks, by no means least - Lily's numerous girlfriends who flocked there for the attention, the affection and the lavishly bestowed gifts that were heaped on them by the decadent representatives of the bourgeois West.

Lily loved a party but even more than that she relished being surrounded by people enjoying themselves and knowing that she had made it happen. To me, she seemed like a survivor from the more hedonistic days in the Twenties who had been swept up from the nightclubs of London or speakeasies of Manhattan and dropped down improbably in this faraway land that was like another planet. She was long and slim with cropped blonde hair tucked behind her ears. She plucked her eyebrows in high, thin arches and she wore bright red lipstick that glistened when she spoke.

She didn't host her parties, she reigned over them, flitting from room to room to ensure glasses were full and no one was standing alone. People were drawn to her and as they gathered round, she would briefly bask in their adulation then start up a lively debate.

Once everyone was joining in she would slip away to do the whole thing over again in a different room.

She and Frank made perfect partners. Both saw life in simple terms - it's brief and it can be hard so grab every bit of fun wherever and whenever you can. You can't change yesterday and you can't control tomorrow, so you might as well live for today. There were times, when I saw them together and the parties were in full swing, that I was tempted to abandon all my instincts and everything I had been taught and follow them, but I always drew back at the last moment, worried that tackling the mysteries of tomorrow would be better done without the mother and father of all hangovers.

Anyway, I had Lena. She and Lily were by now firm friends and yet you couldn't have wished for two more different people. Lena rarely wore make-up and while Lily loved to parade in flamboyant dresses that highlighted her more obvious charms, Lena would casually throw on something simple and I could tell from the glances she got from men that I wasn't the only one who thought she looked stunning.

When we arrived, Lily was in the living room still in a dressing gown and beginning an hour-long session with her make-up bag and hand mirror. Frank came out to greet us, half-covered in shaving foam and muttering something about Russian razors. We sat down for coffee and made plans for what needed to be done by the evening. I caught Frank glancing wistfully out of the window as the women went through the lists.

'You got roped in too?' I asked in English.

He chuckled and looking at Lily, said: 'Believe me, young Grover, it's a price definitely worth paying.'

'Aha!' I had him, I finally had him. In my most condescending manner possible I said, 'Correct me if I'm wrong but what was that you said to me not so long ago? "Don't get in too deep" wasn't it?'

'Yup, you've got me there. I think that makes the score one hundred to me and one to you.'

I had been to three of Lily's 'gatherings' as she liked to call them - 'We're gathering tonight' she would say in a hushed whisper to those lucky enough to be selected - and each had been a memorable occasion. People sang songs, performed tricks, played cards or generally just lazed on sofas sipping drinks. With the lights down low and snacks passed round on beautiful hand-painted platters you might have thought you were at some high society party in the West. But at Lily's, there was no need for silly rules of etiquette or polite small talk or dressing up in ridiculously stuffy evening wear. People came as they were and left in the small hours.

But as this evening got under way, I found it hard to get into the swing of things and realised that the encounter with the police was still on my mind, no matter how much I tried to shut it out. I'd wanted to ask Frank what he thought but there hadn't been the opportunity before people started to arrive and now he was busy filling glasses and exhorting people to have a good time.

By eight o'clock the house was full of guests relishing the potency of the punch Lily had concocted. She was coming alive, carefully selecting just the right music to get everyone in a party mood between answering the latest knock at the door and greeting newcomers. I was helping Lena carry round trays of caviar and snacks.

Suddenly, the mood changed, conversation halting in a wave through the rooms as people realised there was a commotion at the front door.

I heard Lily's voice shout 'Frank!' and was right behind him as he pushed through the crowd.

Then I heard a second voice that I recognised.

'Let me in. I'm telling you it's for your own good.' It was Andrei

'*Idyi*! You're not invited,' Lily pushed him backwards. 'Frank! I need help here.'

'He's OK Lily. He's a friend,' I called, but she didn't hear me above the confusion.

'I've got to speak to Brian.' Andrei tried to push past but was blocked by a wall of arms and bodies.

Frank reached the door. 'What's going on? What's wrong?'

'This man won't go away. He pushed me against the wall, he grabbed me. I thought – '

'You did what?' Frank made a lunge for Andrei. I got between them.

Scared but determined, Andrei said: 'You must listen. The police are coming.'

Lily looked flustered. 'I don't understand.'

'Please it's not what you think. I wasn't touching you. I have come to warn you. The police are going to make out this is some sort of brothel. I heard it all. Nikitich set the whole thing up.'

'Edvuard?' I said.

'I overheard them,' Andrei said. 'Sirienko and Nikitich. They were in the site office and I heard them mention a raid. They were laughing about it. They tipped off the police about tonight.'

'Why?' I asked.

'They don't like you... ' he started, lost for the right words. Then waving an arm, added: 'They don't like you doing this. Especially you.' He seemed embarrassed. 'You and Ileana, it sets a bad example.'

There was panic in the house. People rushed for their coats and pushed at each other in their haste to get out through the back door. I fought my way back into the living room to find Lena.

'What's happening, Brian?' There was fear in her eyes.

'Get your stuff together. We have to leave. I'll explain later.'

She hesitated.

'Please, just do it!' I snapped.

But Andrei's warnings had come too late. The window in the living room shattered. Outside I could hear screams. Then a clipped voice through a loudhailer commanded, 'Remain where you are. Do not attempt to leave the house.'

I peered round a curtain to see what was happening. Some of the guests who had got out first had been herded into a tight circle. Around them stood a group of officers, batons in hand. A woman tried to break away and was immediately cracked across the head. She fell to the ground, blood streaming from a cut above her eye. No one dared to move to help her. A guard moved over and casually kicked her in the ribs. 'Whore!' he shouted. Standing at the back, beside the parked police vans, I saw the man in the suit from the marketplace, casually smoking a cigarette.

The next thing I knew, they were in the house, a swarm of them, ten, maybe fifteen uniforms, pushing people aside. They were hell-bent on destruction. They pulled pictures from the walls. They smashed plates. Hurled chairs at windows. One just wiped everything off the table on to the floor with one sweep of his arm. We all stood rigid, not wanting to be noticed, fearing to be singled out next. Frank had obviously been in their path as they entered and he was now rubbing a rapidly growing bruise on his cheek.

A senior officer entered and the police stopped their destruction, waiting for fresh orders. He paced around the room staring at each one of us in turn, saying nothing, just looking us up and down slowly, contemptuously. He lingered by me. I felt his sour breath against my face.

'Party's over,' he whispered.

Then he turned and pointed at Andrei, snapping his fingers. Two officers grabbed him, pulling his arms roughly behind his back. He was thrust to the centre of the room. The senior officer looked around at us all again, his face relaxed, as if this were the most normal thing in the world. He took a step forward and punched Andrei in the stomach. As the youngster dropped to his knees, clutching himself and gasping for breath, the officer grabbed his hair and jerked his head back. Then he swung a baton and there was a sickening crack as Andrei's nose splintered and blood poured on to the carpet.

'You only get one warning,' the officer said to us all. Then they left, dragging Andrei, unconscious, into a waiting van.

We stood there in shock. No one knew what to do or say. After the noise of the vehicles driving away there was silence, except a continual taunt from the gramophone: the word 'happiness', over and over again followed by a click. Frank leapt across the room and dragged the stuck arm off the record.

At that everyone started to move. Some gathered their things and left, not saying a word. Others began to pick up the mess from the floor, awkwardly putting the broken pieces on to the table or a cupboard. I looked around for Lena and was relieved to see her and Lily come out of a bedroom. I grabbed her in my arms and clung on to her.

'Brian, what's happening?'

'Ssh. We are all right. That's the main thing. We'll talk about it later.'

Someone asked, 'What about the people outside?'

I looked out. They had gone. I hoped they had not been carted off in the vans but reasoned if they were going to take anyone, it would have been Frank and me.

We tidied up as best we could and gradually the rest of the guests made their way home, promising to return the next day to see if there was anything else they could do. We didn't really expect to see them. Finally just the four of us remained. We all knew this was the end of a special time in our lives but no one wanted to say it out loud.

Frank emptied the remains of a bottle of wine into some glasses and handed them round. 'What will happen to Andrei?' he said to no one in particular.

'We won't see him again,' Lena said.

Lily picked a picture up off the table, its frame broken and the glass cracked from edge to edge. She hung it back on its nail, not bothering to straighten it. Tears smudged her make-up. She took Frank's hand and led him into the bedroom. Lena and I went into the kitchen and started to wash up the dirty glasses and plates. We couldn't think of anything else to do.

When we finally got to bed it was almost dawn. We lay there in the twilight whispering to each other, too tired to sleep.

'You know we have to leave, don't you?' I said. 'First the man in the canteen, then the lorry, now this. They clearly want me out. If we stay we are in danger and so are our friends.'

She nodded. 'Why us, Brian?'

'I don't know. I can only think that I've criticised too much or perhaps it's just that my face doesn't fit.'

'Or because you are with me, a woman from Moscow. Maybe they think we pulled too many strings to get me here.'

'No, it's not you. I should have learned to keep my mouth shut.'

On the Monday I handed in my notice and Sirienko accepted it without comment. Frank said he would stay on to see out his contract. I asked if he was sure and he smiled ruefully. 'I don't want to leave Lily until I have to.'

There was no news of Andrei and when I asked people they just shrugged and moved off, preferring not to be seen talking to me.

Officially Lena couldn't leave without authorisation. I didn't think they would stop her but they might, just to be bloody-minded, so to be sure we told no one when we were going. I got hold of an old truck and set off early in the morning when there weren't many people about. She was curled up in the back under a load of old sacks. We had said no goodbyes. Our summer idyll was over. Ahead of us was the harshness of winter in Moscow. But at least we might be able to lose ourselves in the city, become anonymous once more and try to rebuild a life together.

CHAPTER 17

As soon as we got back to Moscow I contacted Talbot who came up trumps as I'd hoped. 'No problem, old chap. Leave everything to me.'

He employed me as a salesman and managed to pull strings and get Lena back her job at the hospital. After a week, he'd somehow contrived to sort out all our papers and permits so it would be almost impossible to tell that we had recently fled from Grozny. He also gave me a bag stuffed with a few thousand pounds.

'It came for you after you left,' he said. 'An insurance policy you had back in London matured. I have to tell you, dear boy, that it took a lot of persuading before the officials would let the money come into the country. Several days work in fact. So I took a small commission off the top. Hope you don't mind.'

How could I? Without his help, life would have been impossible. Even though I suspected a 'small commission' was at least twenty-five percent, it was money I didn't even know I had, so it was neither here nor there in comparison to being able to live in peace with Lena.

We found a small flat in the suburbs. It was nothing much - a kitchen and two square rooms with a bed, a brown-stained sink and a broom cupboard. The paint was flaking off the doors, the windows didn't shut properly and the corridors we walked along to reach our front door smelled of bleach on a good day and rotting vegetables the rest of the time. But it was *our* front door and we also knew that a block like this was too lowly to include Party officials among our neighbours so we were safe from prying eyes. Our dream was not to move up to a more luxurious apartment but to get away completely and start a new life together in another country where we could just be Brian and Lena and not have to watch what we said or keep an eye out for suspicious men in suits. But Lena could not leave without permission. And I would not leave without her.

We couldn't complain. I was doing well at work and with the cash I'd just come into, we were able to enjoy many of the good things Moscow had to offer. As winter moved into summer, we spent many Saturday and Sunday afternoons at the swimming pool, lying close together with our feet dipped in the water, talking about nothing in particular until it became so hot that we had to slip back into the water. Thanks to Talbot's contacts we were allowed to shop in the stores reserved for privileged officials. As well as better fitting, more comfortable clothes, we could indulge in treats like Swiss chocolate and freshly ground coffee, and I always smile at the memory of Lena refusing to allow me to make coffee until she had buried her nose deep in the packet and inhaled that distinctive aroma. In the evening we would often go to the opera, the ballet or a play or visit one of the elite restaurants where we would eat steak or *Pelmeny* or my own favourite *Vereniky,* and drink French wine.

Just how fortunate we were was brought home when we

visited Lena's friends, young men and women who worked at the hospital. They did important jobs and were committed to the Soviet ideal but their fare was very plain and the wine was local and quite rough. That didn't prevent the evenings being among the most enjoyable I had experienced since arriving in Russia. They were good people, bright and optimistic. They laughed a lot and were convinced that wonderful things were just around the corner, that Stalin's plans would bring every Russian a life that only the elite had enjoyed under the Tsar. All they had to do was work a bit harder and get rid of the dissidents who were holding things back. It was those troublemakers, they told me, who were causing the food queues and the shortages in the shops. I hoped their idealism would indeed be rewarded but I doubted it.

I wondered if I should tell them about the things I had seen in Grozny that convinced me that the bulk of the people were being let down by incompetence, corruption and the greed of their leaders. But I had learned my lesson. One Englishman was not going to be able to change the course of a revolution, but he could easily land himself behind bars, a forgotten man at the far end of an empire. So when Lena's friends asked me what a capitalist like me thought of Russia, I was careful. I told the truth but not the whole truth: 'I admire the Russian character. You make the English look lazy. You have built new roads, new houses, new factories in less time than it would have taken us to start discussing the plans. I love the warmth and friendliness of the Russian people, the way you invite me into your homes and share your food and your vodka.'

'So it is better than the failed capitalist system of your homeland?'

My safety antennae picked up the warning signal immediately. I smiled. 'I am here, aren't I?'

There was less philosophical fervour among those officials I mixed with on behalf of Talbot and who also enjoyed fresh coffee and good restaurants. They were just desperate to meet their quotas and keep their masters reasonably happy so they could hang on to what they realised was a privileged lifestyle. I quickly learned that 'Talbot's Law' - find a gap and fill it - was indeed the way to be successful in Moscow. And there were plenty of gaps. My experience in the oilfields had shown me that while projects were always supplied with massive amounts of gleaming new machinery, there was always a shortage of parts and expertise to get them going again once they broke down.

A few weeks' research convinced me this was especially true in the agricultural system which had been dragged from feudal to the collective in a matter of months, leaving former subsistence farmers bemused by these new tractors that had turned up to replace the horse they had patiently walked behind for years. Over drinks in the Metropol a tipsy official had admitted to me that there were now thousands of tractors rusting in fields because they couldn't get the parts to repair them.

So, today as I went to meet Talbot for lunch, I was feeling quite pleased with myself. I'd managed to source a ready supply of crankshafts, fuel pumps, fan belts and other essentials from England, together with the mechanics to demonstrate how to use them, and now I had a massive order in my pocket.

Talbot beamed. 'Brilliant, my boy. At this rate I will be able to retire before long and let you take over. I will only expect a trivial pension for the education I've given you.'

He called for a bottle of champagne. By the time the second bottle was drained, he had gone beyond celebration and was beginning to get maudlin. He leant across the table, confidentially. 'To be honest, Brian, I'm not feeling my usual self at the moment. My dear wife has left me.'

I hadn't even realised he was married and wasn't sure what to say, but it didn't matter. This was more of a monologue. He just needed an ear to bend.

'You see, Brian, you are a lucky man. You have met Lena - a wonderful woman - fallen in love and that's that. But for poor weak men like me, while love is simple, monogamous lust, I'm afraid, isn't. Somehow my dear wife discovered that I had taken pleasure with my secretary and now she wants nothing to do with me. Nothing at all. We've been married for more than thirty years and it was such a brief episode - it didn't mean a thing. I tried to explain. I told her, "Dearest, it meant nothing. It was just a moment of weakness on a lonely night in town." But she wouldn't listen. She just packed her bags and left. Brian, you just don't know how lucky you are.'

I wondered if it would make him feel any better if I told him about Madeleine and the dilemma that was increasingly keeping me awake at night. Lena would be safer if she were the wife of an Englishman rather than just his lover, but I would be a bigamist, and if we ever managed to get to England and someone found out, she could be deported to a life of shame back in Russia. What made it worse was that I had never found the opportunity to tell Lena about Maddy. I knew I should have told her at the beginning but it had been so long now, I couldn't see a way of raising the subject which wouldn't result in her walking out on me.

'So you see, Brian,' Talbot was still speaking. 'You must make sure you protect the things that are important in life. You don't want to end up a sad, lonely old man like me.' He emptied his glass and slumped dejectedly in his seat.

I saw him home, put him on his bed and covered him with a blanket. Then I set off to find Lena and make things right with her. On the way to the apartment I stopped a woman selling flowers.

I asked her to wrap three bunches together and then gave her a big tip.

'Ah,' she said, 'either a man in love, or a man with bad conscience.'

'Both,' I said in English.

Even before I opened the door I could hear the familiar scrape of spatula against frying pan and sure enough Lena was standing at the stove cooking onions. She was making such a clatter and singing at the same time, so she didn't hear me come in. I put the flowers on the table and watched her for a while, marvelling. Even in her oldest clothes, over which was tied a very un-glamorous apron, and doing such a mundane chore, she still looked stunning. I crept up behind her, circled her waist with one hand while easing her hair to one side with the other and kissed her neck. She gave a little start then relaxed back against my body, slowly turning until she could kiss me on the lips.

'Puh!' she said, feigning anger, 'you have been drinking. My grandfather warned me about men like you.'

'And you,' I said, kissing her again, 'have been eating chocolate. You will ruin your appetite.'

I reached over for the flowers, placed them between us.

'They're beautiful! Are they for me?' she said in mock surprise.

I put a finger to her lips. 'Not a word.'

She wiggled her body, her eyes teasing. 'I love it when you get masterful.'

'I'm serious!'

She rubbed herself up against me, and raised one eyebrow. 'I know you are. It's not that difficult to tell.'

Clearly she had no intention of taking me seriously so I lifted her up and carried her into the bedroom.

'What are you doing?' she laughed.

'You will remain silent until you hear what I have to ask you. Do you promise?'

'Yes, sir, I promise.'

I set her down, thrust the flowers into her open hands and knelt down before her. 'Ileana Golyius Petrovna,' I began.

'Petrovna Golyius,' she corrected.

'You've broken your word already. How can I say what I'm going to say if you break your word so easily? Ileana Petrovna Golyius,' I tried again, 'will you marry me?'

I took her hand and kissed it lightly. Her nails dug into my palms. When I looked up her face was wet with tears, her eyes closed. I couldn't read the expression on her face. She was as beautiful as a Pre-Raphaelite painting and as enigmatic.

It was probably only a few seconds but it seemed ages before she responded. She swallowed, wiped away the tears with the back of her hand and said: 'Brian Grover, you ask the stupidest questions.'

I flinched at the words, at the exasperation in her voice. Then she said, 'Of course I'll marry you.'

I grabbed her and kissed her, making sure she had no time to change her mind, to take it back.

'I love you,' I said. 'I want to spend the rest of my life with you.'

'And me with you,' she replied.

I kissed her again, wrapping my arms around her so she couldn't escape.

'You are crying. You should be happy,' I said.

'I am. I'm very happy, it must be the onions.' Then she pushed me away. 'Oh no,' she cried.

'What?' I said, frightened she'd thought of a reason she couldn't marry me.

'The onions will be burning!'

'She leapt up and ran into the kitchen. As she opened the door she was met by a cloud of black smoke. Dinner that night was a little on the charred side but neither of us noticed.

CHAPTER 18

There was a long line of couples waiting for the big moment, all of us in our finest clothes which had been specially cleaned and pressed for the occasion. The only snag was that in the Soviet Union of 1933 there was no big moment. Marriage was definitely going out of fashion in Moscow, considered too bourgeois and, more important, too time consuming, None of Lena's friends could understand why we were bothering. There were factories to be built, fields to be ploughed. Why all the fuss? It makes good sense for comrades to live together and support each other and produce children for the future of the Union, but why waste time with a silly ritual?

The registry office was as bleak as a railway station on a cold winter's night. At the far end of the plain, narrow waiting room was a door and beside it a pane of glass behind which sat a dour attendant with about as much goodwill as a snake eyeing an unsuspecting frog. Thick lines, running from the edge of her beaky nose, echoed the downturn of her pale lips. Bitterness and resentment were etched in grey, blank eyes. I couldn't help thinking she had been chosen to put off as many people from getting married as possible. She certainly affected the atmosphere. Instead of the bubbling excitement you might have expected, couples sat hardly talking. Grooms smoked absent-mindedly. Brides became irritated because their man was getting ash on his trousers and brushed it away with a warning glare. It was as though most of the people in the room were embarrassed to be caught buying into this ritual yet found themselves unable to shake off the tradition of centuries.

Given the state's desire to cut down on waste, the ceremonies seemed to take an extraordinarily long time. Every three quarters of an hour or so, the attendant would tap on the glass, bark 'Next' and there would be a shuffle of feet as the couple nearest to her made their way through the door and sat in front of her. The rest of us moved up, two places closer to becoming man and wife.

One of the couples must have been warned about the delay because they took out a lunch box and proceeded to munch away on sandwiches. The rest of us could only look on enviously wondering if there was any way we could hold our place in the queue while we popped out for something. We decided against it.

I refused to be sucked into the pervading gloom. This was a special day and I intended to enjoy it. I squeezed Lena's hand. 'You look beautiful,' I said. And she did. She had spent some time that morning pinning her hair up in a bunch on top of her head with little ringlets curled meticulously down each side of her face. She wore a little more make-up than usual, but subtly applied. And to my delight, she was wearing the red dress with black flowers that she had worn the night we met, only now instead of hiding an undernourished body, it hinted at the graceful, curvaceous woman underneath.

The 'ceremony' itself lacked style and had no hint of romance.

We were required to fill in a long form with our personal details and the numbers of our various permits and passes. Then the attendant, without a glimmer of smile, said, 'You are now husband and wife.' She handed us a rather tatty certificate and ushered us out.

I whispered into Lena's ear, 'Look how her nose twitches when she speaks?'

Lena giggled but cut it short when she caught the attendant's icy look.

Wedding rings had been renounced in the Soviet Union as Christian relics so I made a ring with my thumb and forefinger and slipped it over her wedding finger. She put her arm round my neck and we kissed.

'I have something for you too.' From her pocket she produced a square silver case. She placed it in my palm.

'Open it.'

Inside was a miniature portrait of her in watercolour. 'I had it done by a street artist in the market at Grozny. I was going to give it to you on your birthday but I thought this was more appropriate. The case is very old. It's an heirloom that has been handed down through my family for many generations.'

'It's beautiful. Are you sure you want me to have it?'

'You must keep it on you all the time. It's instead of a ring. Do you promise?'

'I promise.'

As we strolled across Red Square that day, Lena's feet tapped the cobbles in time with mine. I remember the sun stroking our backs as it sank behind the Kremlin wall. At the edges of sharp shadows cast by *Spasskaya* Tower, the tower of the saviour, we danced as Lena hummed Tchaikovsky's *December Waltz* to keep me in time. Small groups stopped to watch. Some smiled, some clucked their tongues in disapproval, a few clapped, sharing our happiness. She was finally teaching me how to dance properly. Slowly I became sure of the movements, the simplest steps in the book but for me a feeling of freedom. At last I didn't have to look at my feet. Soon we were spinning round and round, the Kremlin's barricades looming over us dark but irrelevant. I knew we were just a fleeting moment in the lives of those around us but I hoped they would tell their family about us when they got home. Perhaps they would remember us in years to come. I knew I would remember this day for the rest of my life.

We finally stopped. Lenin's mausoleum stood before us and I remarked how it looked like a pile of matchboxes stacked up. Lena frowned at me and said, 'Don't be so disrespectful,' and I laughed at the smirk behind her scowl. But I also knew she was being careful for just across the cobbled stones a queue snaked up to pay homage at the place where the man had been laid to rest.

She grabbed my hand and yanked me through the crowds. 'I want to show you something,' she cried as we ran through the gateway to *Sobornaya Ploschad*. 'There,' she said, and pointed to the soaring white bell tower of Ivan the Great. I let out a deep whistle of admiration, even though I had seen it before.

'Don't pretend,' she said to me. 'It's obvious you know it. That's not my surprise.'

We went right up to the base of the tower where the enormous Tsar Bell lay. It had been left where it was made after it was damaged while cooling. Lena walked around it, tapping her nails against the metal. 'Listen!'

The tiny chimes came in quick succession as she tapped, tight and metallic at first then folding over themselves and building up to a deep rumble like a far off thunderstorm as she rapped harder. She ran around the bell, now banging it with her fist. I chased after her and as she speeded up, the rumble turned into a roar. When I caught her, she flopped back against the bell. The vibration thrummed through our bodies.

'It was cast two hundred years ago, almost to the day,' she told me. 'This sound is centuries old,' she whispered. 'It's for us. It's our celebration.'

'But the bell was never tolled,' I said.

'I know. That's why I'm doing it now.'

I looked up to a see a uniformed guard striding purposefully towards us. 'I think we'd better go,' I said. We sent him a friendly wave and ran off. He was too fat to chase us and too lazy to get someone else to make the effort.

Later we met up with Talbot at his flat. We knocked on the door and it swept open immediately. I wondered how long he'd been standing there waiting for us. He looked immaculate in evening dress, glistening starched shirt with a bright red bow tie. He bowed to us like a butler in an English country house.

'Greetings good lord and wife,' he said humbly. As we walked in he nudged the door a little further and a bucket flipped over on a string above him but instead of catching us, confetti showered over his head. He stood there rigid as his pristine black jacket, becoming covered in multicoloured flecks of paper. When the last piece had dropped lightly on to his shoulder, he calmly brushed himself down. 'That,' he said, 'was not meant to happen.'

I whispered to Lena, 'They say in England, "It's the thought that counts".'

Talbot turned on his heels, 'This way lady and gentleman.'

He must have spent the whole day cleaning the place up. Normally, it was a nightmare of old newspapers heaped on chairs and scattered correspondence 'filed' on the floor, but today his flat glistened. Along the hall ornamental lamps glowed dimly, their brass fittings glinting from a recent polish. We turned into the dining room and there above the fireplace hung a banner printed in blue. It said simply 'Good Luck'.

Lena smothered him with a hug. 'Stephen, thank you. It's a lovely surprise.'

'The surprises,' Talbot declared grandly, 'haven't even started.'

For once, he wasn't exaggerating. He left the room, returning with tray after tray of luxuries: chicken, steak, caviar, of course, champagne and a gargantuan cake encrusted with thick layers of chocolate. Talbot was our humble servant and he made us feel like royalty. After he'd finished his last mouthful he made a speech, giving us advice on making the most of married life as if we were a naïve young boy and girl with no idea of what should happen next. We held hands and let him talk.

Finally, when the air was woozy with alcohol and the candles had burned down to the wick, Talbot heaved himself up from the table and informed us with a slur, 'Almost forgot.' We groaned, our insides tight and hard from overindulgence.

'I can't eat any more, I can't drink any more and I don't think I can even speak any more,' I said.

'I should have given you this at the beginning of the evening but with everything else it slipped my mind,' he said.

He walked up to Lena, stood behind her, reached up and placed an exquisite garland around her head. 'I wanted to show these flowers what true beauty looks like, Lena. They should wither in shame at being next to you. My dear, you look radiant. Absolutely wonderful.'

'Thank you.' She looked at me. 'You see, some men know how to talk to a woman.'

'My dear, you should be flattered that I married you at all,' I replied in my most pompous voice. Lena threw a napkin at my face. I ducked and it missed. I grabbed her and drew her into my arms.

Talbot laughed. 'She's quick off the draw, old man. You'll have to watch your step.'

Midnight came and went, the last bottle was drained and finally we bade Talbot goodbye, thanking him a thousand times. A horse-drawn cab was waiting for us outside, just like the night we first met. He'd thought of everything.

I carried Ileana Grover, my Lena, giggling and tipsy over the threshold and into the bedroom. Then, falling on to the bed, we passionately made first-night love by candlelight, for once, without a thought for the thin walls and the neighbours.

The next morning I shook Lena at six o'clock. 'Come on, wife, it's time to get up. Stop being so lazy, you have chores to do.'

She ignored me and just curled up into a smaller ball under the blankets. However, she had left her feet peeping out, inviting someone to tickle them. I obliged. She groaned, then yelled and finally jumped out of bed looking far from pleased.

'What do you think you are doing? What time is it? It's still dark outside. Are you mad?'

'All right, all right. But you have to get up. We're catching a train at eight.'

'Where to?' she demanded.

'Mmm, I don't know, the name seems to have slipped my mind.'

'Where to?'

'Not telling.'

'Tell me!' And she dived on me, her fingers seeking revenge in my ribs.

After a while, she gave up. I wasn't going to tell her, no matter what she did. We packed in a frenzy, throwing things haphazardly into a couple of bulging suitcases. As we stood looking around to see if there was anything we'd forgotten, there was a click from the letter box out in the hall. Lena raced to it saying, 'It's probably a good-luck card.'

She came back looking puzzled. 'It's in English. I thought you didn't tell anyone?'

My stomach churning, I reached over for the letter. 'I didn't...' I said, and then stopped cold. On the back, in a scrawled hand were the letters 'MG'.

Madeleine.

'Who's it from? Who's it from?' Lena asked, excited at the prospect of a letter from overseas.

I ripped it open, saying the first thing that came into my head. 'It's probably just an old mate from the oilfields in the States.'

'Who?'

'Mark. Mark Green.' We'd been married less than twenty-four hours and already I was lying to her.

'You haven't mentioned him before.'

My brain was racing, trying to invent something near enough to the truth that I would be able to remember it. I'd already conjured a name out of thin air. If I wasn't careful I would make up another small lie to cover the first and then another to explain that and then another and another until I'd weaved a web that would trap only me. But I had to buy just a little more time. I told myself I would sort it all out after the honeymoon. Everything felt so right between Lena and me, surely one wrong decision, a terrible mistake from the past, couldn't be allowed to destroy that?

I said, 'I'd forgotten about him. It's been so long. I'll write after we get back.'

'We'll send him a postcard together,' she said. 'He'll want to know about me.'

'Yes,' I said distractedly, trying not to worry about why Madeleine had written, 'I should imagine he would.' I made an excuse, went quickly into the bathroom, shut the door and sat down to read.

So, I tracked you down at last. You're like a ferret, Brian. You think you can slip in and out of anything. Well, I wanted to let you know that you can't. I'm not someone you can leave behind like a bad memory. I am not someone you can ignore.

I waited and waited but heard nothing so I got in touch with a private investigator. He's expensive but very effective. You wouldn't believe what he can do - he has contacts everywhere, even in the Soviet Union.

I know all about you, and the slut. I don't suppose she knows about me.

Think about this. People aren't stupid. And nor am I. It just needs a word in the right ear to confirm their suspicions . . .

I returned to the room, my toothbrush in my hand.

'Brian,' she said, 'how does - what's his name? Mark? - how does he know our address?'

There was no answer to that. I couldn't exactly say to her, well darling he's so keen to get in touch he's put an investigator on our tails. All I could manage was: 'I don't know. It's funny, I really don't know.'

It was enough. She just shrugged her shoulders and slipped on her coat. I was grateful for her trusting nature and swore to myself that I would make amends. I glanced at the piece of paper that I wished would disappear. But I knew it wouldn't, I knew it was just the start of my problems. The final few words echoed in my head.

I could make life very difficult for you Brian. And I will. Come back to the States. If you stay in Russia you're finished.

Madeleine.

CHAPTER 19

There was a gentle breeze at our backs, just enough to make the palm trees bob gently at the edge of the white sand beach and to make the bright afternoon September sun less oppressive. We stood at the waterline, the Black Sea nibbling at our toes and tidying up the footprints we had left behind us in the wet sand. Gentle, tree-covered hills swept down to the bay which we had to ourselves, and beyond them the Caucasus Mountains were blue and solid in the distance. If Sochi wasn't paradise, it was not a bad imitation.

'Imagine we are the last people on earth,' Lena said. 'What would it be like?'

'It would be fine by me,' I replied.

'Wouldn't it be lonely? Can two people really be enough for each other?,' she said.

'I don't know. Right now I would be quite happy for someone to tell me that you were the only person I would ever see again in my life. In fact it would be rather nice.'

We slowly made our way along the shore to where Ivan had his shed. He had promised a boat would be ready for us to take out but as we had discovered, in Sochi you didn't bother to fix a time. 'Whenever you get here, she will be ready,' he said.

'It would be good if you knew there were other people but you only saw them when you wanted to,' Lena said quietly.

I nodded, watching the water splashing over my toes. Lena stopped and sat down on the sand. She wrapped her arms around her knees and stared out towards the horizon. I sat down beside her.

'What's wrong?'

'I don't want to go back. Here we can do what we want. The people like us and we like them. Why can't we stay?'

I hugged her. 'I know. I feel the same. But we have to go back.'

'Puh! And you said you would give me anything I wanted. The stars and the moon if I asked. Now we have only been married two weeks and already you refuse me something as simple as to remain on honeymoon for the rest of my life. Men!'

She went into the sea, scooped up some water and threw it over me.

We'd arrived in Sochi weary from the journey but elated at the prospect of two weeks' holiday. When we boarded the train in Moscow it had been all hustle and tension. The contrast when we got off couldn't have been more marked. The early autumn chill had been replaced by a warm sun that beat down on the brown-brick platform. Laziness hung in the air and I would not have been surprised to see porters dozing in hammocks slung between the wooden uprights of the old fashioned station. They were certainly in no hurry to come and take our cases and the other bags Lena had insisted on bringing.

A faded blue sign hung from the canopy of a wood-slatted shack at the end of the platform. It looked like a holiday chalet that had been built in the wrong place and left untended for years. On the sign in a yellow hand-painted scrawl was the word *Informatsiya* but when I went to it, the front window had been closed with a rusty bolt.

Somehow it didn't matter. It was as though you breathed in something with the air that told your brain 'relax, there's no rush'. Lena surveyed the scene, stretched and looked up at an almost cloudless sky.

'I don't care where she is,' she said. 'I'm just happy to be here.'

'She said she would meet us,' I replied, the Englishman still able to push his way through the veneer.

'Who cares? We can leave our baggage in the waiting room and wander round for a while. It'll be safe.'

Somebody waved from across the road. A stout woman with a dark oval face puffed towards us. It was Mrs Sakharin, who had promised to be at the station and take us to our apartment.

'Greetings, greetings!' Her head bobbed as she talked, causing her hair, pulled back in a floppy bun, to lurch from side to side.

'Are we that obviously tourists?' asked Lena, warming to the woman immediately.

'Anybody who has spent time in Moscow is obvious,' Mrs Sakharin whispered. 'Too much tension. They move like this . . .' She stuck her chest out, angled her arms like wings and strutted in a circle around us. In Moscow that would have been heresy but here nobody seemed to think anything of it. The ticket inspector in his booth glanced up, shook his head and smiled.

She stopped abruptly, as if suddenly remembering she had an audience. 'I mean no disrespect of course - and you,' she pointed at me, 'are clearly not from Russia at all.'

'I'm English,' I held out my hand. 'Brian Grover.'

'We don't shake hands here,' she cried. 'We either embrace or we fight. No in-betweens!' She grabbed me in a bear hug and nodded to Lena. 'I know you are just married, dear, but I don't often get a chance to wrap myself around a handsome stranger. And exotic foreigners are unheard of.'

Lena laughed: 'Ah, feel free. But let me warn you, when you get to know him he's neither that handsome nor that exotic.'

'Like all husbands,' Mrs Sakharin chuckled. 'Now, let's get you to your flat.' She snapped her fingers at a young porter, half asleep in the shade. He came to with a start and rushed over.

'The trolley, idiot!' she barked at him and he ran back to get one.

'My son,' she explained with a dismissive wave of her hands. 'Heart as good as Christ himself, but so lazy. Just like his father.'

'It must be the heat,' Lena responded helpfully.

'It is. Everybody is like that here.' She sighed. 'Better that I suppose, than the dreadful busy bees up north.'

The trolley was loaded and we trundled out of the station. Within a minute she was showing us to our home for next two weeks. With obvious pride Mrs Sakharin proclaimed: 'Close to the station and close to the sea, I deal in nothing less than perfection.' She wasn't exaggerating. The house was bright, clean and friendly. She had put fresh flowers on the table and there was fruit in a bowl on the sideboard. She flung open the French windows and invited us to step out on to the veranda. The view was stunning. There was a small garden and beyond it the sea, almost flat at low tide, rippled away towards the horizon. To left and right, at the far ends of the long beach, the bay curved out like fingers beckoning home distant boats.

'This is a part of the Soviet Union that most people never see,' Mrs Sakharin said. 'The grey men come here on vacation to restore their bodies and souls. They've wrecked everything else but they will never spoil this. They know they need it to survive. So you must make the most of it. It is a perfect place for newlyweds to be in love, to be happy and to spend time with each other they will never forget.'

She had been right. Sochi was sublime. We walked, we swam, we ate great food, and lost ourselves in love to the soothing soundtrack of the ocean as a warm breeze floated in through the open window. One night we ate on the veranda, looking out over the strings of lights that lit up the piers. It was wonderfully clear and Lena leant back in her chair and gazed at the swirl of stars overhead.

'My mother once told me that each star is a child that might have been born. But that some children will never be born because the right people don't meet each other. They are the ones that chance never made. I want to make a child with you, Brian.'

I was silent, moved by her words but also troubled because of all the complications about which she knew nothing.

'One day, when we can, when things are sorted. What is it, Brian? What's wrong?'

'Nothing,' I lied. 'Who knows, maybe we already have?' Then I steered the conversation back to our holiday and the plans we had. They had all turned out perfectly, but today was our last day and I was aware that we must not waste a second of it. There would be time to regret its passing in Moscow, not now.

I grabbed her hand and pulled her to her feet. 'C'mon, Ivan will be waiting for us.'

An hour later we were in the sea up to our waists feeling slightly ludicrous in inflated lifejackets and holding a yacht as it rocked against the waves. Ivan stood on the stone ramp that led from the boathouse to the water. He was an old man, seventy maybe, with a weather-beaten but contented face. It was hard to picture him anywhere else but in his shed surrounded by lobster pots and fishing nets and shelves of waxes and polishes and old dusty clamps. The place was so much a part of him that it seemed to me it would have to be closed up when he died. I doubted it would accept a new owner.

We had met him a week ago, as we took our morning walk along the beach. He was patiently sanding down a small patch of wood on the hull of a dinghy. His hands moved to and fro in a firm, steady rhythm, over and over until the surface was like glass. He was so engrossed in his job that we stood back, watching from a few yards away so as not to disturb him.

His fingers were like thick gnarled twigs but they moved quickly, flicking off the dust then sliding over the same area again and again. It was deceptively hard work and his thin grey hair stuck to his forehead in damp curls. Eventually he stretched and surveyed his work, satisfied. He turned to us and said: 'It is not ready until it is as smooth as the skin of your first lover.'

His face collapsed into a sea of wrinkles from which appeared a huge grin. And he spoke completely unselfconsciously in the way that only old people feel they can. 'You two are lovers,' he said. 'You hold hands like tomorrow may not come. So you know what I mean.' We got to talking and he wanted to know everything about us.

After that, we dropped in to see him most days and on one fine afternoon we took down a picnic to share with him. Later, when the wind got up, blowing sand on to our tablecloth and food, we salvaged a bottle of vodka and retreated into his shed. The next few hours slipped by as we contentedly drank, told stories and listened to the wind rattling outside. I asked him if we could go out on the water sometime and he said, 'Maybe - if your vodka is always as good as this.'

Ivan had given in to our pleas and generous alcoholic bribes and told us: 'You can take *Alba*,' he said, 'she's my finest and oldest.'

'What does Alba mean?' I asked.

He grinned. 'Short for Albatross.'

'You can't call it that!' I cried out and Lena laughed.

'I can and I did,' he replied. 'Fifty years ago. And it's still one of the most reliable boats I ever built. It's all superstition, I have no time for that. Sea, wood and air - they are the reality, they are what determine what makes a boat stay up, not a name. My friends thought I was mad too... Take it or leave it.'

We looked at the Alba, carefully assembled all those years ago but still handsome despite the odd repair, and with a sheen that showed the wood had been lovingly cared for ever since. We took her.

As we moved out of the harbour, it seemed that Ivan was having second thoughts. He was waving his arms and shouting to us. I knew he wasn't convinced I knew how to sail and, admittedly, it had been years since I had taken a boat out by myself, but I thought I was doing OK and didn't know why he was making a fuss.

He was pointing at us then at the sea, yelling instructions that made no sense at all against the noise of the waves.

'What's he saying?' I asked Lena.

'He said the wind's changed. I couldn't catch the rest, but I think he wants his boat back.'

'Feign ignorance. I bought half the vodka in Sochi so we could do this.'

So we pretended to take his gyrations as some sort of farewell and with broad smiles waved back at him. Soon he was just a dot in the distance, still scurrying up and down the ramp. We moved beyond the headland and out of the sheltered bay. The sails cracked as they bellied out. I was a bit surprised at the power of the cold wind that tumbled down from the mountains and gusted urgently over the open sea. It was unexpectedly choppy, waves smacking noisily against the hull. But as I felt the boat respond to the freshening wind, my momentary doubts disappeared. This was exhilarating. I showed Lena how to adjust the gib rope so that the sail curved true without flapping. She soon got the hang of it and appeared fearless of the water.

'Lean back over the side when you feel the yacht tipping forward,' I called to her. She did and almost fell in. I grabbed her and she gave me a petulant look.

'What? I did what you said!'

'Sorry, I forgot to tell you to put your feet in the loops.'

'So you want to drown me? Already?'

We were about half a mile out and still travelling in a straight line.

'When we turn, I'll give you a shout. Duck and go over to the other side. OK?'

She nodded. I turned the nose of the yacht into the eye of the wind and we tacked. Lena moved round the boat like a natural.

The sun was at our backs now, warming us up in between the bouts of spray that burst over us with every big wave. The bow cut through the water like an animal trying to free itself from a constraint. Our legs were taut as we hung over the edge and I felt elated at the ease with which it had all come back. It had been over ten years since I had first sailed. I'd been travelling round Europe after leaving Cambridge, and stayed by a lake in central France for a while where I met up with a friendly group of rich young 'down-and-outs', idling away their lives. A couple of them had been keen sailors and had taken me out on the lake a few times and shown me the basics. I had promised myself that one day I would take it up seriously but like so many other youthful dreams, it had been put on hold while I tried to forge some kind of living. But now it felt as though I'd been sailing every day.

We tacked around the headland of our quiet bay and looked back at Sochi, nestling close to the waterline. From a mile out it looked tiny, like an artist's idealised view of a town.

'Can we stop?' Lena asked.

'Sure. Why?'

'It would be nice to just sit and watch for a while.'

I let the sails flap, stuck the rudder full down and we drifted. Lena snuggled up beside me.

'It looks so different,' she said. 'From out here, everything looks quiet, no people, no trucks. The only sound is the water... I like it out here.'

I squeezed her hand. 'It gets cold after a while.'

'Not yet though. Where shall we go now?'

'Find a landmark. Pick one.'

She looked along the coastline. 'The church on the hill over there, with the tower.'

It was about three miles away on the next headland, standing exposed to the ravages of the seasons. It seemed a bleak place to worship, stuck at the end of a long, steep walk unsheltered by trees. I imagined it would take a fiery preacher to stop a weary congregation from nodding off during the sermon after that climb.

Lena adjusted the sails as I pushed the tiller left and we headed for the church. On the horizon dark clouds were thickening in curls but I reckoned we had a while before we should turn back. I was thrilled that Lena was so obviously happy to be sailing. Many of my friends had told of wives who did nothing but complain about getting wet, cold and miserable but she seemed to shrug off the discomfort. I watched her adjusting her position to balance the yacht. Her knuckles were white with cold and her hair was salty and tangled by the breeze but she was laughing, lost in the rush of something new, something exciting. I thought how nice it would be to take her back to England, up to Windemere, perhaps, where we could rent a country cottage and stay there as long as we wanted. We could go for long walks, sail in the evening, drink in a real pub.

The memory of Madeleine's letter cut across my fantasy. I was a fool. I had allowed my life to become so complicated that now I had found the perfect partner, the perfect life, I was in danger of losing it all. How could I even think about a family or life in England? I was a bigamist, a liar, a cheat.

I yanked at the tiller and the yacht lurched in the waves. Lena scrambled to the safety of the deck, suddenly unsure.

'Brian, perhaps we should turn back.'

'It's just the swell, Lena. Nothing to worry about.'

We had lost our momentum and we were bobbing around like flotsam. I looked at the marker. The yacht was upwind of the church now. About two miles to go. It became a battle, a test of will. With the wind almost behind us I was sure we could get all the way there ahead of the storm. I let the rope out a few degrees, until the sails flapped. I smiled reassuringly to Lena. 'Now we're going to go really fast. But you have to lean right back.'

She looked apprehensive.

'Come on, you did it without thinking before.'

'I don't know.'

'It'll be all right. Don't you trust me?'

'I trust you, but I don't trust that.'

I followed her gaze to the black clouds that were gaining on us rapidly. Between us and the clouds, the sea was a misty wash of grey. I knew that meant a squall but I didn't want it to beat me. I turned back towards the church which was still in sunshine. I gripped the rope and pulled it in hard.

'Ready?'

Lena gave me a quick half smile.

'Lean out!'

I turned the boat so the wind was full at our backs and soon we were racing along. The hull lifted higher in the water and surged forward, clipping off the top of waves. I felt blood rushing through my limbs as I pumped the mainsail. My hands were numb with cold, but I didn't care. It was like riding a runaway stallion and I wasn't sure any more who was in control.

We veered slightly. The yacht cut the waves at forty-five degrees, yawing wildly sideways with each impact. My focus had narrowed. I was hurtling down a tunnel. Only the church, now grey under the sweep of clouds, mattered.

'It will be all right,' I thought to myself, not sure if I meant our present adventure or my desire to divorce Madeleine, to take Lena to England and to have my parents love her and welcome us as a family.

'Brian, it's raining.' Lena's voice cut into my thoughts.

The swell was now ten feet. When we were at the low point, there was no land or sky, just a wall of water.

'We're wet through already, what does a bit of rain matter?'

'Brian, it's a storm! Turn us round. Please!' she sounded scared, but I didn't want to stop.

'A few more minutes, then we can ride the swell back. It'll be fun.' The fact that I had to shout out the words did nothing to reassure her. We carried on.

Then the real rain swept over us. Huge drops, driving almost horizontally, stung as they hit my face.

Lena dragged my head round to face her.

'What the hell's got into you? Turn around now!'

There was hardness in her eyes, a speck of flint that I had not seen before and it snapped me out of my madness.

'Yes, you're right,' I said quietly.

The words were lost in an explosion of sound.

A gust hit the boat, making it shudder. For a second the air seemed solid. I struggled for breath. I tried to turn into the wind, into the waves, to give us some respite. But I was too late. A wave crashed against our port side and both rope and tiller slipped from my hands. Unguided, the boat lurched round. I caught a glimpse of Sochi but it was obliterated by the boom flapping past me.

'Lena! Heads!' I screamed.

There was a crack as we jibbed, and another crack as the boom hit Lena just above the ear. The force knocked her overboard. She slumped face down in the water, the lifejacket keeping her buoyant. I was about to jump in after her when the next gust hit. The yacht went over. As I hung in the air, it seemed to be plunging nose first into the ocean.

Then I was under. Nothing but a blur of bubbles. The roar of the outside world was only a rumble, getting quieter. Something was dragging me down. I could feel the upward pull of the lifejacket under my arms but it was losing the fight. The sounds kept receding. Something was around my foot. I opened my eyes. There was nothing but green. I was desperate to breathe. To cough. I knew I mustn't. I had to go up. I fought the panic that was building up inside me. Use your hands. Free your foot. Get rid of your shoe. Quickly. That's it. Now kick up.

I broke the surface, gasping and retching.

'Lena! Lena!' I screamed as hard as I could but it was lost in the roar of the storm.

As I rose to the high point of the swell I caught a glimpse of her. The upturned yacht with the rudder sticking hopelessly in the air looked like a shark. Lena was on the other side. I struck out for her, losing sight each time surf crashed over the boat. I swam as hard as I'd ever swum but seemed to be making no progress against the torrent. Seconds were hours. My mind was suddenly filled with an image of us drinking coffee in front of a warm fire. Fool! Concentrate! Swim!

When I reached her she was limp. I grabbed her under the arms and pulled her back to the upturned boat. There was a gash on the side of her head. Blood ran on to her face, only to be washed off a moment later. I pressed her, limp, up against the side of the boat, holding the rudder for leverage. Wrapping my legs around her waist I thumped her in the chest with my free hand. Water dribbled from her lips and she let out a gurgling moan. I did it again and this time she shook her head and choked.

'Lena, can you hear me?'

Her head flopped to the side. I slapped her cheek. 'C'mon! Wake up, please, wake up.'

'*Nyet.*'

'Lena. We have to pull the boat upright. Can you help me?'

Her eyes opened momentarily and I grabbed the opportunity.

'Think of a hot fire and a nice bed. If you help me now, we can get back. You can be warm and snug and you can sleep for as long as you want. Just a few minutes, please.'

I could see her summoning some strength through sheer willpower. First her arms, then her legs began moving of their own accord.

'That's it. Hold the rudder. Hold it tight.'

She wrapped her arms around it, clinging on with every ounce of strength she had left. I knew if we stayed in the water much longer we wouldn't be able to move at all. I clambered up onto the hull, slipping on the shiny surface. Damn Ivan and his polishing. A toggle was floating on the other side. I leant over, wanting to lunge for it but knowing I would only slip over headfirst if I did. It bobbed in the waves a few inches out of reach, mocking me. I willed it forward, splashed my hand in the sea trying to create some pathetic current that could compete with the ravages of the storm.

'Think,' I said to myself. 'Keep thinking. Attached to the toggle is the rope. Attached to the rope is the yacht. If 1 can catch hold of it, 1 can pull it upright and we can get in the boat and everything is all right.'

I felt the boat dip suddenly, much deeper than before. I looked up and cursed. In the seconds before the wave hit us, I locked Lena's hands in mine around the rudder.

It passed over in a roar, jerking and pulling ravenously at every part of my body. I clung to Lena and the boat with all my strength. We tipped sideways and something slapped me around the shoulders.

It was the rope.

Lena was flailing in the water. She had no idea where she was. I grabbed the rope in both hands, stuck my feet against the hull and pulled. Slowly, the submerged mast came into sight, the sail dragging behind it. I tugged Lena over beside me.

'Grab hold of the side - use your weight.'

She nodded slightly. Somewhere inside her confusion of pain and cold she heard me. Agonizingly, the mast started to move in the right direction. As the sails emptied of water, they became lighter. The yacht tipped upright. I clambered in, rolling on to the tiny deck. Lena clung to the side, her hands like a corpse's.

I dragged her inch by inch over the side, careful to balance her weight. She flopped in beside me, a dead weight. What now? The gale was directly astern, the boom was swinging dangerously. Rain like blades sliced at the back of my neck as I pulled the boom sail flat against the wind. The gib would have to flap, I didn't have three hands and the two I had were so numb they were near to useless.

The yacht surged forward as the sail snapped taut. Lena jerked on the deck with the force of the movement. I positioned her head between my feet to stop it from rocking.

'We're going to be OK,' I yelled to her in a daze. 'We're going to be OK. I'm sorry. I'm so sorry. I should have told you about her, I should never have lied. I was scared you would leave. I should have told you about Madeleine...'

It streamed out like a crazy mantra, the same guilty words over and over again.

Lena's eyes were wide open. She stared up quizzically.

'That's not rain,' she said. 'That's tears. You're crying!'

And then she smiled as if the storm had moved away from her. She was basking in some sunny place in her imagination.

'Tell me about her when we get home,' she murmured and her eyes closed.

CHAPTER 20

B y the time we got back to the beach, it was crowded with
people waiting to see if we were still alive. As soon as we
were close enough, a group of fishermen waded into the water,
defying the waves that heaved past their chests. Ivan headed the
pack, waving his fist. The yacht finally came to rest as ten pairs of
hands grasped stern and bow. Inside my head, my body was still
in motion. It became harder to stand.

Everyone was talking at the same time, firing questions, yelling
accusations. I tried not to meet any of their eyes, especially Ivan's,
and just waved away their words with my hands. 'Please, see to
Lena,' I said.

They lifted her gently from the deck. I couldn't help. All my
strength had drained from me and I just slumped down, too
exhausted to move. A pair of strong arms heaved me from the
boat. I closed my eyes. All I wanted to do was sleep, or perhaps
wake and discover it had been a bad dream. Right then either
would have been good. I was aware of the sea surging against my
freezing body, then felt my legs falling. They landed against
something solid.

'Try and stand,' a distant voice said.

I couldn't. I collapsed on the beach and the man who had brought me ashore knelt down beside me. Fingers prised my eyelids apart. I blinked. It was Ivan. He looked like a wizened gnome crouching there on the beach with the storm hammering at his back. His eyes showed only concern.

'You're a strong man,' I managed to get out.

He smiled. 'Not bad for seventy.'

My mouth felt thick and rubbery. I forced it to work. 'Lena?' I asked, not sure I wanted the answer.

'She will be fine,' he soothed. 'Just cold, and a hefty bump on the side of her head. She's with a doctor now.' There was silence and then he said. 'You forgot to pull the rudder up when you came in.'

'I'm sorry. I've been a fool. Really, I – '

'It happens.'

'What, fools or storms?'

He sighed. 'Sometimes both at the same time.'

'I was angry.'

He raised his eyebrows. 'What about?' he asked.

I shook my head in response.

'You were angry at Lena? Why? What has she done?'

'No, no. It wasn't her. I was angry at myself.'

'Ah,' was all he said.

Back at the apartment the doctor looked me over. She checked my pulse, temperature, blood pressure, each time writing the details carefully on to a form on her clipboard. I noticed there were two leaves of carbon paper underneath her main sheet. Information was important even in this paradise.

She tapped my chest. It sounded empty.

'You can put your shirt back on now. Nothing wrong with you

174

that a hot shower and a long sleep won't cure. Your wife will be up and about by tomorrow. Mild concussion, that's all.'

We both looked through the open door into the bedroom. Lena was lying on her back, blankets up to her nose. She was snoring.

'I've never known her make a noise like it,' I said.

The doctor gave me a reproving look. 'Be thankful she's making any sound at all. You were both very lucky.'

'I know. Look, I'm really grateful for all you've done.' I offered her a handful of pound notes.

'That won't be necessary,' she said, her voice crisp and businesslike. 'I don't accept illegal currencies. One of the advantages of the Soviet system, you might say 'a perk', is that healthcare is available and free. For everyone.'

'I meant no offence.'

'If you need any further aid, do not hesitate to contact me. I will see myself out.'

I sat down beside Lena. The movement woke her up. I leant down to kiss her on the cheek, but she moved her lips to mine. She ran her hands around my head. 'It's not fair. You have no bumps. My hero has no battle scars.'

'I'm not exactly a hero.'

'You saved my life.'

'Lena, I nearly killed you!'

'Why would you do something like that?'

'Sometimes, you're impossible. Is there room for two under that blanket?'

She shrugged. 'That depends.'

'On what?'

'You know.'

'I don't.'

She looked through the French windows, her eyes focussing on nothing in particular. 'Brian, let's not pretend any more. We can't do that any longer.

Sometimes, you think you know someone and then he does something that surprises you, really shocks you. And you wonder if you really know him at all.'

'Lena – '

'Please, let me finish. But you realise that you understand him perfectly because you have felt the same things yourself. You too have chewed at something endlessly but found it always too tough. You have pulled a problem apart heaven knows how many times, trying to reassemble it a different way, but it comes back the same each time, still insurmountable. And you fear there is no escape because to do the one thing that would lead you to where you want to be would surely destroy the thing you want most.

'When we meet people, we sometimes create an image of ourselves, our best selves, the self that has no skeletons hidden away in closets. And in time we become afraid that the person we care about is in love with this image and if he were to know it is false, everything we treasure will disappear. We are trapped in a lie and no matter how much we try to forget it, it still haunts us.'

She paused, wiping away a tear. I was aware of the switch to 'we'.

'The longer it goes on, the more it festers inside. Much of the time we are happy, sometimes blissfully happy, but even that happiness is not complete because it is tarnished by the deceit.'

'Lena, you're tired, you got a nasty slap on the head courtesy of your hero...'

'Don't patronise me!' She snapped, that flinty hardness flashing in her eyes once more. 'That is something I wouldn't expect from you.'

'I'm sorry.'

'Look,' her voice softened. 'I'm going to tell you a story and it's the only time I'm going to tell it, so please don't interrupt me. Let's find some coffee and go out on the veranda.'

'Are you sure you're up to it?'

'Quite sure,' she said, swinging her legs out of bed. The aftermath of the storm had left the air fresh and clean. The cloud had broken up into little balls. Below us puddles were drying on pavements and the Black Sea was mirror smooth in the evening sun. It was as though the afternoon storm had never happened. But I knew only too well that it had and that the consequences for me were far more than just a bad scare and a soaking.

CHAPTER 21

Lena stirred cream into her coffee, then rapped the spoon on the side of her cup. 'You know the first part of the story,' she said, 'about the little girl who grew up in St Petersburg before the revolution, who loved her mother and father, who trained to become a nurse because there was too much blood and too much hate. After that the story changes.

'This little girl grew up to be a woman who thought she could make a life for herself in a quiet little backwater, away from the turmoil. Somewhere warm and easy. Leningrad was too cold, too harsh and besides, how could she live in a place that couldn't even decide on a name for itself?

'Most people went to Moscow, if they could get a permit. It was the centre of the world, everything happened there. But not this young lady. It was too close to the carnage, too frantic. No, she applied for a position in a nice little hospital in the South, where people smiled at you as you went to work, where the days passed slowly and you didn't have to wear ten pairs of socks at night. A place to the west of here - quite near actually. Her application was accepted, so she packed her bags, got on the train and went to Grozny. She was only twenty-two, much of the world was new to her...'

'But — ' was all I got in.

'Please Brian, don't make it hard for me.' She stretched over the table and took my hands in hers. Her hair fell over her face. I wanted to move it away, to kiss her and hold her so there would be no more story. But Lena was stronger than me. She pulled away and forced me to listen.

'For six months, life carried on quietly. She felt happy there. For the first time in years she could see the results of her work. She was helping people, not patching them up so they could be sent out and butchered again. She decided she would like to stay there a long time.

'Then she met a young woman, about the same age as her, called Natalia Oblonsky. She was outgoing, very popular. Everybody knew her. You could say Natalia adopted this naïve young woman. She took her everywhere, introduced her to a whole new set of friends. Before that, the young woman had buried herself in her work and her social life had consisted of earnest conversations about debilitating diseases over a cup of coffee in the hospital canteen. So these diversions were welcome and exciting.

'One evening, Natalia invited her round for dinner. She loved playing host. She had said she was having a "gathering" but when the woman arrived, there was only Natalia and an older gentleman. The woman wasn't early so she knew something was up when Natalia said: "Now we're all here, we can eat." Natalia introduced her to the man, and the woman thought he might be a boyfriend or a brother. But there seemed to be no affection between them. He introduced himself as a doctor. The woman was curious. She hadn't seen him around before which was strange. They got talking and she noticed Natalia became quieter, but when she looked at her Natalia was smiling, not in the least put out. Then it clicked - sometimes this woman was very slow - her friend was matchmaking. She felt embarrassed about the situation but had to admit to being attracted to him. He was fatherly, sure of himself, and for an older man quite handsome with deep brown eyes and thick dark hair. He knew what he wanted, he was a good talker and an even better listener.

'They... they started meeting up together, going for walks along the river. He took her to the theatre. He was quite wealthy but he never flaunted it, never took it for granted. He told her about himself. Before the revolution he had been a private doctor and was well respected locally so he escaped the changes forced on most in his profession. He had a sort of special status with the authorities because of his standing and they left him alone. And he had a private house which was most unusual. It was nice when they went back there alone, in their own space with no one to tell them what to do. He was kind to her, he made her feel special . .

'She fell in love and it seemed that he loved her. They got married within months of that first meeting and naturally she moved in.'

Lena paused for a while. She was breathing raggedly, trying to calm herself. I said nothing.

'Then, about a year later, she woke up one morning and there was an empty space next to her in bed. The sheets were still warm and crumpled. Maybe, she thought, he was up early studying. She went downstairs. There no sign of him. She went into the surgery. His briefcase was gone. She went into the kitchen. The kettle was still steaming on the stove and there was a full cup of tea beside it untouched. Underneath it there was a note with a scrawled, "No time to explain". That was it. No love, no apology, no goodbye.

'That day she sat at home by the kitchen table going over the same questions time and time again. Why did he leave? What had she done wrong? Where had he gone? Why? She felt scared, lonely, guilty. That evening there was a rap on the door. She rushed to it, hoping he had come back but when she pulled it open the police burst in. One of them grabbed her, shook her, shouted in her face, "Where's your murdering husband?" She could hardly speak. She shook her head. "He wouldn't murder..." The others were ransacking the house, ripping it apart. "He murders babies," he said. "You know where he is." She said, "No!" and the man slapped her, "Tell me and you will be all right." And she screamed: "I don't know. He ran away! He ran away! The bastard ran away and left me." And she crumpled in front of the men and she was ashamed of it. But they left her alone after that.

'One of them knelt down beside her and told her all he knew. It seemed her husband had been carrying out illegal abortions. That's where all his money was coming from. He must have found out that Intelligence was on to him.'

Lena stirred her cup of coffee, now cold. 'He didn't trust me, Brian, he kept his secret and left me to face the consequences. I was obviously nothing to him and now I was garbage in the neighbourhood. Nobody spoke to me, except Natalia. You know her as Lily. I had to leave, start again in Moscow. I gave the house to Lily. I vowed that I would never deceive another person the way he did me... But I broke that vow when I met you. I never saw him again.'

She rose and leant against the balcony, her back to me. A dog barked in the street below. It all made sense. It explained how she'd heard of Beria - she'd covered that slip well - and it explained her rapid friendship with Lily. They must have had a lot to talk about in private. So many secrets. But who was I to judge?

She hadn't finished. 'This is very hard to say. A few weeks before I met you, I received a letter from him. I thought he was dead, or had left the country. He said he'd made a new life for himself, got a new identity, a new woman, children, somewhere far away where no one could touch him. He didn't say where, that would be too dangerous. He was coming to Moscow. He said he wanted to explain, to make it up. With the letter were two tickets to the Bolshoi. He was coming to ease his conscience. I didn't want his money, though God knows he owed me. I just wanted him to know how much he'd hurt me, so I went. As you know, he didn't turn up. I just sat there with you staring at me, thinking "Where is he? Where is he? After all he's done, he couldn't do this to me." But he did.

'So now you know who the empty seat was for. I was scared he'd been caught. I thought you might be the police waiting for him.

'Then when you said you were going to Grozny, I couldn't believe it. It was ten years ago, maybe all had been forgotten, but could I go back? And that first night with you, home again in Grozny - I nearly told you then when you pressed me, but I thought you would leave me.

'You see, I know what it's like to deceive someone you love. I've lied to you and I understand the turmoil it creates.' She turned to face me. 'Brian, I've known for a long time that you were hiding something. The letter that arrived before we came here, I saw the effect it had on you. When I woke up just now I thought I'd dreamed what you said on the yacht but I didn't did I?'

'No, you didn't.'

'Tell me about her. Tell me about Madeleine.'

There was no other way to say it. 'She's my wife.'

'Is?' The pitch of her voice rose a little.

I nodded.

She looked startled. She had worked out a lot but not that.

'I want to know everything,' she said.

'I was twenty-six,' I began. 'And I was stupid.'

I poured out the whole story, like a converted sinner in a confessional box, the details tumbling over each other in their haste to be in the open. Eventually I ran out of words. Lena had kept her promise and not interrupted and for a while she said nothing. The only sound was the gentle swish as the sea curled up the beach and the sigh as it retreated again. It had been doing that for millions of years and would probably continue to do so for another million years, not caring about the troubles of two people whose lives were less than a blink in that vast time frame.

Eventually Lena said: 'When you first met me, did you still love Madeleine?'

'No. The whole thing was a mistake. I came to Russia to forget it. I was a coward, I should have finished the matter properly. But as far as I was concerned when I met you, I was divorced in everything but name.'

She nodded her head, thinking it through.

'Lena, she means nothing to me. I mean nothing to her – '

'Then why does she write you this letter? Why does she track you down? Perhaps she loves you, Brian, and you are hurting her.' She shook her head as if doing so would also shake away the thought.

'No. She left me.' The words came out in a growl. 'I wasn't gentlemanly enough, I didn't live up to the promise of my accent. It got so that she couldn't even bear to touch me!'

Lena ran a finger down my cheek. The few harsh words in her were spent. 'Then she was a very foolish woman,' she said.

'And I am a very foolish man.'

'It changes nothing,' Lena said. 'We are both guilty.' Then, ' Do you remember the promise you made on our first night in Grozny?'

'Cross my heart?'

'Yes. Now, you must take me back to England.'

'I'll have to go alone first Lena. Madeleine won't agree to a divorce without a fight. I couldn't bring you to London, the bride of a bigamist.'

Lena took my hand. 'How long?'

'I don't know, really. Not long, I hope.'

She gripped harder. 'Don't avoid my eyes. Tell me!'

'It could be some time. Up to a year.'

She let go. My palm felt cold and damp without her touch. She let out a long sigh then left the table, walked to the balcony railing and leaned into the breeze. I was going to follow her but something in her movements told me she wanted time alone, time to mull over the implications of this twist in our lives.

'A year,' she said, turning to me finally. 'Then that is how it must be.'

Ivan came to the station to wave us off. We were leaning out of the carriage window when he passed me a small package wrapped in newspaper.

'It isn't much,' he said. 'Go on, open it.'

Inside was a perfect wooden model of the *Alba*. Only, it was no longer the *Alba*. Painted on the hull in Russian was the name *Angry Storm*.

'The big one's changed its name too,' said Ivan.

'It's beautiful,' I said. 'How did you do it so quickly?'

'With fast hands,' he replied.

The guardsman whistled and a plume of steam filled the platform. The train wearily ground into motion. Ivan waved and as he disappeared from view he called out, 'Come back another time. I'll show you how to sail properly.'

'We will,' I called back.

We all knew we would not return. It was another lie. But a warm lie told by strangers who for just a moment have become as close as brothers.

CHAPTER 22

I felt again for the letter in my pocket. Just to be sure it was still there. I had been tempted to tear it open when the rain-soaked postman handed it to me as I left the house but I didn't want to read it in the street. Just in case. I needed to be somewhere private. I was frightened what it might say. It had been two years since I'd last received a letter with a Russian stamp. Two desperate years. And I didn't know if I could bear it if it contained bad news.

Now I peered through the smudged window at the raindrops that had no chance of cleaning away the grime that had accumulated over several years. As the bus changed gear, I lurched against the fat man beside me in the brown suit that had been bought when he was a stone or two lighter. We glanced at each other briefly but didn't say anything. I turned back to the window watching the grey London streets pass by and listening to the nonstop banter from the conductor as he hung from the pole on the platform of the bus.

'Hold on a minute! Lerremofffirstifyoupleeeeeeeeese!' he cried at every stop, holding out an imperious arm. It was a routine I'd got to know well. When I first started taking the bus from Earl's Court each morning he had seemed quite amusing. He was reassuringly constant and soon got to know his commuters, treating them with the same courtesy as a pub landlord would his regulars. 'Morning, my darling, you are looking very glam today. Got a hot date, have we?' or 'Hello, guv. Nice tie. Must be a big meeting.' But as the news from Germany got worse - Hitler's armies had just gone into Austria claiming it as 'a province of the Third Reich' - his constant cheeriness seemed somehow out of step with the times. Everyone feared war was imminent despite Neville Chamberlain's recent hopeful message on his return from Munich. The old, who had seen it all before, were resentful that the 'war to end all wars' had turned out to be little more than a preliminary bout. The young were in turn fearful and excited, wondering what fate had round the corner for them but also thinking that their ordinary lives might soon open up into something extraordinary, even heroic. Meanwhile our conductor seemed not to have noticed that anything was happening outside his daily routine.

Maybe I was being unfair. Perhaps he was whistling in the dark for everyone, trying to keep all our spirits up. I was just too wrapped up in my own gloom to appreciate it. War seemed just another obstacle among all the others I was facing and as I'd singularly failed to overcome most of those, what chance did I have against a tidal wave of history? I'd come home for a year to sort out everything then return and collect Lena, but here I was, five years later, in a mundane job in the sales department of an engineering firm in Chancery Lane with no sign that she would ever be able to join me. And for two years, no reply to my letters.

At least I'd got rid of Madeleine. It had taken a long time and cost me dearly. I still found our final meeting very bizarre when I thought back on it.

We arranged to meet for tea at Brown's Hotel on Albermarle Street. I got there early, anxious to get it over, and I heard her clipped voice giving some poor bellboy orders before I saw her.

Then she swept into the dining room.

'Brian, my dear, how wonderful to see you,' she said, as though we were old friends who had been away from each other for just a few months. She kissed me on both cheeks and I had to admit that she looked good but I noticed that her broad smile was still not reflected in her eyes.

'Now, come, my dear, let's have some tea and you must tell me all about what's been happening to you. We have a lot of catching up to do. If you don't mind me saying so you look a little thin and tired.'

My hackles started to rise. If I was thin and tired it was to a great extent because of her. She had shilly-shallied around, refusing to answer most of my letters, and never giving me a straight answer when she did deign to reply. Then she would get her solicitor to send me a thinly veiled threat, implying she could still make life very uncomfortable for me 'unless you come to your senses and resolve this in a proper way that is acceptable to my client'. But there was never any indication what the 'proper way' should be.

'Isn't London interesting?' she gushed. 'A little tatty at the edges perhaps, but so much history. And I am so enjoying the theatre and the shops. I just love Fortnum and Mason - I went to their store on Madison Avenue, you know. So sad it closed.'

I couldn't put up with any more of this senseless chat. 'Madeleine, can we please talk about what we came to discuss. We both know why we are here.'

'Oh, Brian, I'd forgotten how handsome you look when you are angry.' She was enjoying this.

'Madeleine, I want a divorce. What is it going to take to get you to agree?'

She ignored the question, leaned down to her handbag and took out a package.

'I've brought you a present to remind you of home.'

I was stunned. 'What do you mean home? We hardly lived together for more than a few months and that was in Trinidad and you hated it.'

'Now, now. Open it.'

I unwrapped the parcel. Inside there was a maroon tie with thin, yellow, diagonal stripes and the insignia 'ABF'.

'Who or what is ABF?' I couldn't help thinking I was in an *Alice in Wonderland* world.

'Alabama Banking Federation. Daddy says there's a great job going just now, perfect for someone with your experience, and with the right help and the right contacts, it could lead to much bigger things.'

I thumped the table and a dozen heads turned our way. 'Madeleine!' I tried to stop myself shouting. 'I don't want to live in Alabama. I don't want to work in a bank. All I want is a divorce.'

'You seem to have got things a little the wrong way round, don't you, dear.'

I tried to calm myself. 'Madeleine, what is this all about? You don't love me, so why do you pretend?'

She didn't answer.

'Divorce will be better for both of us. We can both get on with our lives. You are an attractive woman, I'm sure you will meet someone.' She wasn't listening. I raised my voice. 'Madeleine! You will give me a divorce eventually. If you don't, I'll – '

'You'll what?' Her face was harsh. 'What will you and your slut do, Mr Bigamist?'

So she knew.

'Why are you doing this?' I pleaded.

'Because I can. And because you hurt me and humiliated me in front of my family and friends. I don't want you any more, Brian. But I do want to hurt you.'

She left, her words ringing in my ears like a death knell.

It took another year before her solicitor finally drew up the papers that freed me. It cost me the £2,500 annuity I'd received from the company in Trinidad but it was a small price to pay as far as I was concerned. The relief was incredible, only spoiled by the fact that Lena was not there to share it with me and because I knew my problems were only half resolved. I still had to get permission to return to Russia and every effort had been met with a firm *Nyet!*

I'd tried to contact Talbot to see if he could help, but he'd disappeared along with several of his best Russian contacts. The entrance to his office in the Strand was boarded up and the sign gone. In my desperation, I'd even taken a job in Persia, spending six months there, hoping to cross the border but there was no way. I was turned back every time I tried.

That had been three years ago. Since then I'd returned to London, found a job and hoped that if I became just an ordinary, respectable, hard-working citizen for a while, the Russian authorities might relent and let me rejoin my wife. It had been her letters that kept me going. She never failed to say that she still loved me and that she would wait for me. But suddenly they had stopped coming. I'd enquired at the embassy, asked for special permission to go to Moscow to see if she was all right but each time, I'd been rebuffed: 'If you wanted to live in Moscow, you should have stayed there when you had the chance. Why would you leave your wife behind and come to London to live?' There was no explanation I could give that would sound half true and even then they would probably not be satisfied. One less westerner in Moscow was always a bonus as far as they were concerned. 'Please don't keep coming back, Mr Grover. We are unlikely to change our mind.'

'Chanceureeeeeeee Lane! Your stop, Mr G.' The familiar voice cut through my gloomy daydream and I clambered over my portly companion, opened my umbrella, pointed it into the rain and headed off to the office. I hated the thought of reading my letter with my colleagues: small-minded, minor aristocrats – Nigel and Alexander ('Never Alex, if you don't mind, old boy') – whose idea of adventure was a weekend in a hunting lodge in Scotland, with 'a filly or two'. They had quickly written me off as a lost cause, a rather dour chap who was growing old before his time and wouldn't join them for the important things of the day like lunch, and a 'pre-prandial pick-me-up' after work.

I decided that for once in my life, I would be late for work. I passed the Old Square by Lincoln's Inn and splashed down Serle Street towards Maisie's, a little café nestled between a shoe shop and a tailor's that had fallen on hard times. I'd used the café a number of times for lunch and reckoned it would be quiet at this time of the morning. I ordered a pot of tea and slice of toast and turned the letter over in my hand while I waited for the waitress to bring it over. I scanned the handwriting for a clue to the contents and couldn't help thinking that Stalin looked rather smug on the stamp. I hoped that wasn't an omen.

My hands were trembling. I thought about waiting until the evening, reading the letter in the privacy of my own room.

This was silly. I ripped it open and the cheap paper crumbled at my touch.

My dearest Brian,

I am in Uren now. It's a small town on the banks of the Usta River about a hundred miles from Nizhny, I was transferred here two months ago. I give you the address in the hope that one of your letters gets through to me. I know you send them.

This is a terrible place, an industrial town surrounded by mile upon mile of flat farmland. There is no colour here. It is a place to work and produce, not to live. But that is not why it is terrible.

You and I were sheltered, Brian. We thought life was as we had seen it in Moscow, Grozny and Sochi, at times harsh and difficult but on the whole improving. I only realised how wrong we had been when I came out here. It's almost laughable to think that I volunteered. They needed extra nurses at the hospital and I wanted a change, and I also had the impression my old employers wanted rid of me for a while. I am not their idea of a model citizen.

I thought a country town would be nice, somewhere I could live quietly and do something useful for people. I couldn't have been more wrong. There are no farms and there is no countryside as you would recognise it. All the food goes from the collective to the army and into the cities. They leave a little when times are good but this year the harvest failed almost completely - the soil is overworked and so are the men who plough it - and what little is around is snatched away.

I am here to help patch up the mess but I am of little help to starving patients. They don't need nurses and medicine, they need cooks and food.

There is nothing in the shops. There is no grain left to make bread. I have seen old women chew on cardboard as if it were a feast. They eat their food vouchers for dessert. Children dip their hands into glue pots for nourishment. They come into the hospital because they can't get their hands out.

Fuel is running out. The coal goes to the furnaces to make more steel, to make more machines and more tanks. Pravda tells us to be vigilant and strong. These are trying times, it says, the mother nation must stand firm against foreign intervention. It does not say: 'Warning, this paper is not edible.'

There are organised groups now, going round the apartments to take your furniture while you are out. If you see them and challenge them, they say they are with the police and you cannot argue just in case they are telling the truth. Some are just desperate and use the wood to burn, to keep their families warm. Human nature being what it is, others sell it on the black market and grow rich from their neighbours' suffering.

Yesterday was the worst. Up to then I had been able to persuade myself that I might be of some use but yesterday I realised that in Uren I am just another hungry mouth to feed and I want to get out. I saw a young woman, a mother with her baby wrapped under her arm. She was scrabbling around in the frozen earth for something, anything, to eat. Her fingers were bleeding, but she kept going. She didn't know how to stop and no one else had the strength or the inclination to stop her. I took her to the hospital. All the way there she was thanking me, telling me she hadn't eaten for days and had run out of milk for her baby. I tried to reassure her but when we reached the hospital the admittance officer shook his head. I shouted at him, told him it was an emergency.

'They are all emergencies,' he replied. He had taught himself to be hard.

There was nothing he could do. I had to lead her back out into the snow. I was in my uniform, the uniform that declares the wearer is a person who helps people, and I had to push her out into the freezing cold. She was screaming. It woke the baby up and he was crying too. I just ran away. I have never done that before.

It is only October, Brian, and it is already so very cold, but people know there are much harsher times to come and that they will soon yearn for days like this, long for days when there is no wind and the sun brings a little relief.

It is ten o'clock and I am starting night duty. I will be here till morning, alone with my friends. I wonder what you are doing now. I want you. Even after all this time, I want you.

2am.

Most of them are asleep now which is a blessing. It is snowing outside. It is very solitary doing night duty. You have eight hours alone with your thoughts. My only company is a desk lamp and a line of men too weak to groan. Thinking about you helps me through the long dark hours. I long to see your smiling face. I would love to look up from this piece of paper and see you striding down the ward. What would you bring me? I would ask only for your arms around me. Or perhaps I would ask for a pair of thick socks too!

I know in my heart that this letter will not get through but I write all the same, for myself. Do something for yourself, Lena, I say. And I do try. I curl up in the memories of the times we had together. They keep me warm while outside everything is dead and hard as the concrete they keep churning out. Who can eat concrete?

Have you seen Talbot? He had to leave a couple of years back. He was very kind to me after you went but he could not help in the end. I still have the flowers he presented to me on our wedding night. They are pressed in the copy of Anna Karenina that you gave me for our first Christmas. I have read it countless times and when I get to the last page, the flowers fall out and it reminds me of that night. And can you believe it, they still smell? They are fading, but they will be good for a few more years yet.

It is a long time since I heard from you but I cling to the belief that you still write. I imagine your letters read by some bitter, drunken clerk and ogled over. I imagine a dustbin full of them waiting to be burnt in the back offices of some government building and I curse them.

The other alternative I do not wish to think about. Perhaps you have given up? Perhaps it is better that way. Five years is a long time. If we saw each other maybe there would be nothing left. I know of friends, best friends who meet again after so long and they have nothing to link them. They sit in cafés and talk about old times, other people who they will never see again. They cannot look forward.

I'm in a black mood. I cannot cope with the patients. It's strange, I thought I would become hardened as I grew older but it is quite the reverse. I remember my head nurse in training telling me to prepare myself for my first day on the ward. There were soldiers with their legs blown off, little babies whose faces had been cut by shrapnel but I was all right. I sailed through and everybody was impressed with my calmness. Back then, it was possible to believe the suffering was worth it, that there was something to fight for and perhaps die for. Not now. It is an endless, weary line of shrunken bodies with no meat on them, bulging ribs and cracked skin. And their eyes, Brian. Every time I walk down the ward between the two rows of beds, I pray for them to be sleeping, or unconscious. I know it is selfish but I can't help it because the eyes are unbearable. Those that are awake stare at me as they would a saviour. And I suppose I am, for I represent heat and some food. But those eyes also say: 'I am the thousand people who are not here.' They feel lucky and they feel guilty. Why should people about to die be grateful? I know the answer - they at least have some dignity. They won't die in the dirt and the gutter; they won't die in a frozen shack; they will die in hospital where the sick are meant to die. But I tell you there is no dignity in a five-month old baby, looking like an old man. There is no dignity in that.

I wanted to write something that would make you smile but I am not the person you knew, Brian. I am older, I am bleaker. Perhaps if you saw me, you wouldn't love me any more. I was never a coward, but now I want to run away completely. The incident with the young woman yesterday was the last straw. Working in this hospital saps my soul. I will go back to Moscow soon, but I have seen too much here.

It is much worse than when you were last in Russia. The trials have shaken people to the core. I am not political, you know that, but I believe that people should have friends. But now having friends is dangerous. They might snoop, they might say something about you in the wrong place. You might laugh at the wrong joke. I can only talk to a letter that I should not send.

Brian, please don't forget me. I can live without you, but I couldn't live with the idea that you never think about me. You are in my thoughts all the time. Sometimes I am walking down the street and there is a face in the crowd, slipping out of sight. It is foolish but there have been several times when I have run to try to catch up, but it is never you. I should know that by now.

It is no good. We must release each other. There, it is out, finally. It cannot be retracted. I want to be with you at this moment and forever, but it cannot be. Thinking about the possibility only makes it worse. It is like a slow death, not to accept the inevitable. It is futile to keep hoping, when there is none left.

You have done your best to return and the answer was no, I know that. I have done my best, God knows a thousand times, and the answer is always no. It seems now that we were never meant to be together. We should find peace in accepting this and be thankful that we at least had a short time to share our lives.

I am your wife and you are my husband but you must live your life and I must live mine.

You may uncross your heart, Brian. I know you did what you could. I release you from your promise.

I love you,

Lena

CHAPTER 23

*W*e must release each other.

The words were like a slap in the face.

I became aware of a voice beside me. 'More tea, dearie? Aw, you haven't drunk that one. It'll be cold now. I'll make you another.'

'What? Er, no, I'm fine. Thanks.'

I re-read the whole letter. When I reached the final few paragraphs, I read them over and over again, trying to see if I had made a mistake, misread what she had said.

It seems now that we were never meant to be together. We should find peace in accepting this and be thankful that we at least had a short time to share our lives.

I am your wife and you are my husband but you must live your life and I must live mine.

In my head, I could hear Lena's voice saying the words, see her lips moving and sense her strength as she forced herself to write down what she had been thinking about for some time. I remembered how strong she had been that night in Sochi when she finally unburdened the secret she had hidden fearfully away. She truly was a very special woman. At that moment, sitting in that tiny, slightly dowdy café thousands of miles away from her, I felt I had never had more respect for her. I had never loved her more.

'No!' I shouted. 'I'm damned if I will.' I jumped up, pushing back the table so that the cup and saucer rattled and the tea slopped onto the tablecloth. The waitress looked startled, especially when I kissed her on both cheeks and said, 'I'm going to Russia if it kills me.'

'Good for you, dearie,' she said. 'That'll be thruppence ha'penny for the tea and a penny ha'penny for the toast. Call it a tanner to cover my trouble wiping up after you.'

I threw half-a-crown on to the table and rushed outside. My first instinct was to take Lena's letter to the Russian Embassy and beg. But I realised it would be a waste of time. I had to think of a way. I walked blindly into the street, halted by the honking of a car horn and the curses of a cabbie.

'Bloody idiot! Are you trying to get yourself killed!'

I pushed on up towards High Holborn, bumping into people all the way. My head was spinning, desperation supplanted by optimism then lurching back to despair. Ideas flooded in on each other but then disappeared like bubbles before they had really formed. I wasn't even sure where I was going but I had to get there quickly. I suddenly realised I was sweating and panting.

'For God's sake stop!' Embarrassed, I realised I'd said the words out loud and people around me were staring.

I crossed the road and sat on the ledge along a wall. The rough coarse brickwork felt good, it felt real. I started to calm down a bit.

On the other side of an alleyway, I noticed a shop selling model kits. I must have passed it a thousand times without noticing.

While the inside of the shop seemed dimly lit, the window was bright, as if the owner cared more that you should see his display than buy from his stock. When I went over and peered through the glass, it was a little masterpiece, put together lovingly, I guessed, by a man who still had a boy's heart. Rows of tin soldiers marched over fake felt hills, tanks negotiated a sandpit desert, Jeeps chugged in Indian file along a painted black-top road. And above it all, suspended by a wire from the ceiling, a beautiful model of a Fairy Swordfish banked in the air, its single torpedo slung beneath it. It had been painted in minute, accurate detail, the product of many hours on a dining room table late into the night. A small sign behind it read: 'Not for Sale'.

I was completely charmed by it all. I noticed the plane even had two little figures in the cockpit, complete with goggles and leathers. One of them was looking down, waving to the troops below, or maybe to a girlfriend standing in the doorway of her home just beyond the edge of the window.

I knew what I had to do.

Heston aerodrome was about twenty miles north-west of London so it was late afternoon by the time I arrived. It was an impressive site, a great flat stretch of fields crisscrossed with runways and a number of smart buildings including the newly erected British Airways hangar.

I signed up for a 'compressed' course of flying lessons. After filling in my form, I took it to the bored-looking desk clerk and was about to ask him a question. He stopped me in my tracks. He obviously thought I was about to make small talk because he pointed his pen over his shoulder and turned away. I looked past him to a hand written sign pinned on the wall: 'NO CRASH COURSE JOKES PLEASE. CONTRARY TO WHAT YOU

MIGHT BELIEVE, YOU ARE NOT THE FIRST PERSON TO HAVE MADE THAT JOKE. Signed, by order, Irritated Admissions Officer.'

I smiled and said, 'Fair enough.'

'You wouldn't believe how many ignore it. Do you have leathers?'

I looked at him, bemused.

'Flying leathers, gloves, jacket, goggles. We can provide them, but they cost extra. You'll need them. It's cold up there.'

'How long will it take?' I asked.

'Until you are proficient and the instructor passes you? Well, things being what they are in the world, they are asking us to push people through as quickly as we can but it really depends on you. Some people take a couple of weeks, others a couple of years.'

I had no choice. It would have to be a couple of weeks. The longer I left it, the worse the flying conditions would be.

He took my form and consulted the big diary on his desk. 'You're in luck. We've had a cancellation so if you can be here at eight tomorrow morning, you can start then.'

'That's great.'

'Just ask for Ray Sedgely - he'll be expecting you.'

I liked the idea that for the first time in what seemed like an age I was 'in luck' but it didn't last long because when I found Ray Sedgely the next morning there was a bitterly cold gale sweeping down from the north.

'We won't be able to go up today, I'm afraid,' Ray said. 'Too dangerous. But perhaps it's better that way. You can get to know the old girl before you give her a work-out.'

On the runway he said, 'I'm afraid she wasn't taken inside overnight. We were caught a bit off-guard by the weather. But you don't mind a wet backside, do you?'

He had the quiet authority of a man who had been through this routine a thousand times before but didn't mind doing it all over again. He introduced me to the dilapidated First World War Gypsy Moth, a bi-plane which had seen better days. He must have seen the doubt cross my face because he laughed and said, 'Don't worry, she's a beauty. The most solid plane of them all.'

I climbed into the cockpit, feeling a mixture of excitement and apprehension. What if I couldn't master it? I'd taken a while to come to terms with double de-clutching on my father's car and surely this must be a lot more complicated than that? And the conditions weren't really helping. Rain was lashing into my face and within minutes my fingers were numb. Just concentrate and listen. This is for real. I sat there, the buckles digging into my legs, the wind howling under the wings. Concentrate, take notes, you can do this.

Ray methodically explained each dial, how to read the altimeter, the fundamentals of manoeuvring up and down, banking left and right; all the basics that would get me off the ground and with a little fortune keep me there. The hour was up quickly. As we went back to the cafeteria for a drink Ray said to me: 'The most important thing, more than any technical detail, is to remember that a plane is like an untrained animal. It's wilful. You must always remember that you are the boss. You must anticipate rather than react.'

I handed in my notice at work so I could spend all my time on what I had to do. I took lodgings off the Holloway Road and, as always, dropped my parents a note with my new address. They never replied but I assumed that if anything had been wrong, they would have got in touch. From a secluded room at the back of the house I put flesh to my plan, scribbling down notes and making lists of things I had to buy and do. In between, I read every book

I could lay my hands on about navigation and flying. For the next three weeks, I travelled up to Heston daily. I would sit in the front of the plane while Ray barked instructions from behind. I was surprised how sensitive the plane was and it took me a while before I could keep it on an even keel. And Ray had been right about it having a mind of its own - I quickly learned that unless you kept alert, it would start to drift away on the wind, taking you off the route you wanted to follow. But by the end of the first week, I could do a figure of eight over the aerodrome, and by the end of the second week Ray let me up for my first nerve-wracking solo flight. The exhilaration of being up there on my own was tempered by the knowledge that if anything went wrong, there was only me to handle it. I swept around the Heston area as Ray had told me, desperately trying to maintain a steady altitude. He was assessing me from the ground and I'm sure he must have winced as I bounced his poor old plane along the runway as I came down. Two days later, I was taking written tests on navigation, air law and mechanics. And on the 23rd October 1938, I was awarded my pilot's licence.

'No distinctions, no merits,' Ray said as we shook hands, 'just enough to keep you alive and stop you from killing anyone else.'

I thanked him for everything, privately vowing to send him a postcard when it was all over. His final words to me were, 'Go easy old man.' He looked a little worried.

From then on every night, and far into the small hours of the morning, I pored over the route I planned to follow. The obvious way was through Poland and Latvia, but I realised both countries would insist on knowing all about my business before letting me into their territory. I looked for an alternative and the best bet seemed to be via Stockholm.

There was a knock at the door. Probably my landlord again. He didn't like the hours I kept, thought I was using up too much electricity. I opened the door ready to tell him once again that I would appreciate a bit of peace.

But it wasn't my landlord.

Frank stepped straight into the room. 'So this is what you've come to? He glanced around at the papers and maps strewn across the floor, at my unmade bed. 'You've gone up in the world.'

I stared at him. He looked just the same. The hair a little faded perhaps, a few more wrinkles around the eyes. A million questions and greetings came to mind but in the end I settled for a rather pathetic 'Frank!'

He grabbed my shoulders with his great paws. 'Well you could try a hello, at least. Surely I deserve that?'

'If you refrain from crunching my bones, I might even find you a seat.' I cleared a space on the desk. 'Sorry about the mess. Been a bit busy lately.'

'I can see.' He put on a hurt face. 'Too busy to keep in touch?'

'I could say the same about you.'

'Took a while to track you down, nearly a full day getting your address out of your mother. But I did it.' Accusation lay at the back of his voice, but it was playful, a throwback to the verbal duels we'd had so many times in the past. There was a pause. It had been six years and the silence was a little awkward.

'I think a drink is in order,' I said, guessing that whatever else had happened to Frank since we'd last met, he wouldn't have become teetotal.

At the pub on Seven Sisters Road we bought each other rounds of bitter and relived old lives and caught up with new ones. After the third pint, all the strangeness had evaporated and it was as though we'd not been apart. Frank told me the situation had worsened in Grozny after Lena and I had left. Open hostility became the norm, so he simply packed his bags one night, snuck away and gradually made his way back to the States.

'Lily didn't really mind,' he said. 'There'd be many more like me. It was just a bit of fun for both of us.' He looked at me over his pint. His eyes didn't look as philosophical as he sounded. 'Seems like it didn't work with you and Lena in the end either?'

I explained everything to him, right up to me leaving my job but no further. I wasn't sure I should tell anyone my plans, and I decided I wasn't going to until Frank said, 'Sometimes, you just have to give up. Sometimes it's best to let it go.'

I avoided his gaze. At the other end of the room an old man with a hand-rolled cigarette hanging from his mouth methodically potted a black on a rickety snooker table.

'Is that what you really think?' I asked.

'Yep,' he said, gulping down to the bottom of his glass.

I leaned forward. 'And has it made you happy?'

'Nope.'

All his relationships had been 'just a bit of fun', and that was fine if it was all you wanted. I imagined us both in thirty years' time, saying the same thing, quietly wishing we'd taken a different course in our lives but never quite admitting it to each other. I saw us both sitting there, in the same position, thirty years older, fingering our pints, and knew absolutely that I was making the right decision.

I thought it would be good to share my secret with him. So I said, 'Sometimes you've got to think "what the hell".'

'That's what I mean,' he replied.

'No, you don't understand. Sometimes, you've got to risk everything.'

He perked up a little at this. 'What do you mean?'

'I've been taking flying lessons.'

'With you at the controls that probably is risking everything.'

I shook my head and smiled. 'I'm not doing it for the thrill,' I whispered. He looked puzzled.

'Work it out.'

I watched his contorted face relax, smooth out, then tense again into a look of horror as realisation dawned.

'Uhh - Uh,' he mumbled. Then, 'Ah, Christ man, you're not!'

I nodded.

'Tell me this is a wind-up Grover.'

'Not this time.'

'They'll shoot you down. And if they don't, they'll shoot you after you come down.'

'No, I've worked it all out, Frank. If I fly above the cloud they won't see me. And once I'm in, I'll just ask to be arrested.'

'And believe me they will be happy to oblige.'

'I'll explain my case. They might listen.'

'Oh, they'll do that all right. Then they'll take you outside and line you up against the wall with all the other losers.'

I shrugged. 'If it happens, it happens.'

Frank's face reddened. 'How can you say that?'

'Very easily,' I said. 'Frank, for the last five years I've been dead anyway. I've been in a boring job, living on my own and all I've wanted is to be with Lena. At least this way, if the worst happens, I'll die knowing I did everything I could.'

'You're crazy. You're insane.'

'They mean the same thing, Frank.'

'Someone's minced your brain,' he spluttered.

'Feels good that way,' I replied. 'Fancy another beer?'

'Think I need one.'

When I returned from the bar, he was a little calmer. He eyed me slyly. 'There's just one thing I want to know.'

'Name it.'

'Does this mean I can have your room while you're away?'

I said goodbye to him that same night. I insisted that I didn't want him around because he'd only try to dissuade me, and I made him promise not to tell anyone else. He reluctantly agreed to both demands. We shook hands and I realised how pleased I was that I had seen him again. He must have felt the same. He said: 'Six years I don't see you, and when I do it's for two hours. You were always the sensible one, now look at you, completely cuckoo.' He gave me a bear hug. 'I wish you all the luck in the world, Grover my boy.'

CHAPTER 24

I was down to my last £250 and had a plane to buy. The Heston air club put me in touch with a few people who knew what was on the market. I wanted something new, easy to fly and with a long range. For that I was politely informed, I would not get much change out of a couple of grand.

I went round all the dealers at the local aerodromes. I became increasingly desperate. My ambition was now merely to find something, anything, as long as it came with an engine and something resembling wings. Time was running short and winter was setting in. Then I chanced upon a dealer named Fellows, who operated near Hanworth. When he heard what I had to offer he grimaced, looked down his line of sparkling beauties, straight off the factory floor.

'I'm a bit out of your price range. Sorry,' he said. I thanked him for his trouble, and was about to leave, when he called after me, 'Hold on. I might have something for you in the back here.' He took me through to a dark and dusty hangar, where dried-up pots of paint, oil canisters and dirty rags fought each other for space on a grimy floor. There, in the centre of the room, half-covered by tarpaulin was what looked like a winged coffin on wheels.

'What was it you said you wanted it for?'

'Oh, just pottering about. Money's tight so – '

'Then this is just the job.' He pulled the tarpaulin back. 'The trusty Klemm Swallow. Not much to look at, I'll admit, but it does the job.'

I thought of the flight I was planning and it was hard to picture this rather fragile pile of wood and canvas, covered in dirt, paint flaking from the fuselage and rust creeping around the engine casing, being able to make it. Fellows saw my face and said, 'I've been meaning to get her souped up but haven't had the time. You know how it is.' Indeed I did.

I circled it, running my finger through the caked dust on the wings.

'Does it fly?'

'Does she fly?' Fellows was indignant on behalf of the plane. He slapped the body like an old friend. The frame shook with the impact and I imagined the wood splintering underneath its outer skin. 'She goes like a bomb, and she keeps going until you tell her to stop. We'll take her out. Once you climb inside, you'll wonder why you ever thought of anything else.'

He pulled the shutters up with a rattle and we took the plane on to his landing strip. 'See that over there?' He pointed to a low, grey building down one side of the field. 'The Hanworth factory. That's where they make these lovely creatures. And they're fifteen hundred quid straight off the production line so this little beauty is a bargain.'

He spun the prop. The engine spluttered uncertainly to life, faltered and ran down again. 'Listen to that purr. Five cylinder, 80 horsepower Popjoy engine, top speed 75 mph.'

210

'What's its capacity?' I asked.

'Oh, you can tank her up. She's had quite a history this old bird. It will do seven or eight hours at a time, if you push her.'

That was perfect.

'I'll take her,' I said suddenly.

He looked startled and not a little relieved, but quickly regained his composure. 'Two hundred seem reasonable?'

'One-fifty.'

He shook his head. 'One-eighty.'

'One-sixty.'

'I could get more than that for scrap.'

'And you've got six wives and ten children to feed, I know, I know. I'll give you one-seventy but that's it.'

I could see him ticking off the possibilities in his mind. Then he nodded. 'Done.'

We shook on it and I showed him my papers. 'I presume cash is acceptable,' I said to him, counting out the notes.

'Fine,' he said, and then grunted as though he wanted to add more. I looked up and held his gaze. 'I hope you don't mind me saying, but you seem in a bit of a hurry. What do you really want it for?'

'Let's just say, I'm going to visit an old friend.'

Over the next few days I reread all my books on air navigation and weather conditions. The more I looked into it, the more I understood Ray's final concerned look when I passed my test. He didn't know what I was going to do but, like Fellows, had sensed my urgency. Now, looking over the details of the project, it became apparent that I was nowhere near qualified to carry it through. It was one thing to fly circuits around the aerodrome, quite another to navigate my coffin from one continental airport to another. I was no good to Lena

if I ditched myself in the Channel a few hours after setting off.
I did a few financial calculations and thought I just had enough
to hire a professional pilot to take me as far as Stockholm.
From then on, I'd be on my own.

I put an advert in one of the air magazines and soon had a
partner, one Henry Mountjoy. He was experienced, lived for
flying and was the proud owner of a moustache so huge it was in
danger of stretching beyond the wing tips. He agreed to
accompany me for expenses only. I told him we were going over
for a business trip, and that I wanted to polish my skills.

'Super, super, super,' he said. 'Do a few whirls on the way, eh?'

'Well, I need to get straight there.'

'How about a few dives then?'

I was beginning to think he might not be such a sure bet, but I
really didn't have much choice. He took my second's hesitation as
a resounding affirmative.

'Super,' he said again. 'Can't wait.'

Frank had warned me that I would kill myself. Now it seemed
I might have help. But what the hell, if I was going to go down, it
didn't really matter who was at the controls.

So it was that on the 4th November 1938, just before
dawn, I arrived at Heston to find Henry with his head in the
Swallow's engine.

'Just caressing her arteries,' he said. He was wearing his goggles
already, moustache wings tucked up behind the straps. Within an
hour we were ready to go. We packed our kit in the hold. All I had
to my name was a spare shirt, a flask and a razor. It seemed a paltry
collection for my ultimate journey. Considering I was supposed to
be on a business trip, I was surprised my partner didn't remark
upon it but I don't think he could see anything beyond another
chance to fly. It was all he cared about.

In the changing rooms I donned my leathers and splashed my face with cold water to freshen up. I had aged. There were deep furrows on my brow, the odd wisp of grey above my ears. I wondered if Lena looked as weather-beaten as I did. We had both been through a lot. I wasn't sure which was worse, waiting for someone who never returned or trying forever to return but finding your path always blocked. Both took their toll.

We were given clearance to take off and Henry span the prop. The engine roared into life. For the trip over the Channel he would be sitting in the back cockpit with the main controls.

The runway sped underneath us until it was only a blur of grey. We soared over the outskirts of London, each little box house with its family still asleep, safe in their dreams. Conversation was nigh on impossible. Whenever I tried to say something to Henry he just shrugged and mouthed, 'What?' I had hoped I could learn from him, but it was pointless in the Swallow. The wind swept most words away and the whine of the engine drowned out the rest. Instead, I concentrated on going over the plans for my solo trip from Stockholm. I'd made it as easy as I could: set the right course and then fly in a straight line, pushing on until the fuel gauge dropped to empty. Then I would land in the nearest available field. By then the plane would have done its job so if she picked up a few scratches it wouldn't matter. I smiled. The same probably applied to me. I had no idea how I would be received by the Russian authorities and even if I got past them, how would things be between Lena and me? We were probably both imagining each other as we had been five years ago. Would we like the new us? There was no point in going down that road. Even reaching her seemed pretty unlikely. In my heart I knew this was probably little more than a reckless gesture but it was better than doing nothing. I decide that for once Ray's advice to think ahead was irrelevant. It would just be a matter of reacting to events as they arose.

We banked steeply to the left and most of Kent tipped into view 4,000 feet below us, a ribbon of the Rother winding through a patchwork of fields. Down there people were starting to go about their day, cows were being summoned to the milking shed, sheep were starting to graze, men were setting off for their offices, mothers were chivvying children to get ready for school. Everything was much as it had been the day before. From where I was sitting it seemed to be a world I'd only occasionally been a part of and was happy to leave behind. I thought briefly about my parents and wondered how they would react when they heard what I was doing. And what if I just disappeared never to be heard of again, missing presumed dead? Would they tell their friends, or just pretend I was still working away?

I gripped the sides of the cockpit as the compass swung violently. I heard Henry's laugh above the din of the propeller. So communication was possible - if you had lungs the size of an elephant. I felt as secure as a learner driver taking pole position at Monaco with all the engines revving behind me and Henry as the mechanic in the pits who'd loosened a wheel, 'just for fun mind you'. We headed south east, across the Channel, passing over the long shingle beaches of the Folkestone to Dover coastline. Waves chopped on the surface of the sea. It looked windy down there. But it was windier up here and a damn sight colder. Momentarily, I wished I'd tapped my father for the money to buy something a little more substantial. I buried myself in the cockpit, zipped my flying jacket as tight as it would go and thought of Lena and imagined us sitting on the veranda in Sochi, basking in the warm sun.

We'd been flying for about half an hour when we hit a thick

patch of fog. It seemed to cling to us, dense, cold. I turned to see how Henry was. He held a sandwich in one hand, a cup of coffee in another.

'Could have given me one,' I shouted.

Henry gulped down his last morsel. 'What?'

'I said I wouldn't mind a bite myself.'

'Can't hear you,' he mouthed.

Suddenly there was silence.

'Bugger!'

I heard that. The plane dipped nosewards and I felt my body leave my seat.

'What's happened?' I screamed.

'Engine's clogged up, must be the ice.'

We were losing altitude rapidly now, diving blind towards the sea. Henry tapped me on the shoulder, pointed his thumbs down. I knew what that meant.

Before we'd set off, he'd gone through different crisis scenarios. Ditching in the sea if the engine stalled had been described as one of the worst. 'Bloody cold, old boy, and not much chance of surviving.' Henry had explained that the idea in those circumstances was to pick up speed, nose downwards, pumping the throttle at the same time. With luck the propeller might start again. With a little less luck the plane would glide down and we'd float on the water for days waiting to be picked up. 'But most likely we'll be smashed to smithereens and never see the French coast!'

We broke through the fog and the dark sea hurtled towards us like an infinite wall. The altimeter span: 1000ft, 900, 800. In ten seconds, we'd be dead.

'Henry, pull back man! For Christ's sake! Pull back!'

When I turned round, there was an intense smile on his face.

'What will be, will be,' he cried and leaned back hard against his seat, ramming his feet against the elevator pedals and pumping the throttle for all his life. The Swallow jolted, then turned upwards as though a bomb had just exploded underneath it, and in the same motion the engine spluttered into life.

'Yes! Yes! Oh bloody yes!' he whooped.

We levelled out. The sea looked close enough to touch. I could see the crest of the waves frothing then slapping in on themselves. I realised that I'd held my breath for the last twenty seconds of my life and let it out in a harsh, relieved rasp. Although it was freezing, I could feel my body was clammy with sweat under my leathers.

We climbed steadily for the next hour and did a wide circle round the radio mast at Cherbourg which was the conventional signal to show we were all right. As the night wore on it began to rain. Soon the rain turned to hail that battered into the fuselage like tiny bullets. A storm was brewing, my face was stinging and yet I didn't care. I was just happy to be alive.

I fumbled around my bag for pen and paper. I wrote: 'How about an Irish coffee when we get to Hamburg?' and passed it over to Henry.

A minute later came the reply: 'How about a new plane?'

We sat in the airport lounge, our wet leathers squeaking when we moved. Several whisky coffees, topped generously with thick cream and crusted sugar, were consumed. I felt exhausted. The warmth of the whisky spread throughout my body, relaxing muscles that had ached with tension. And my brain, which had been racing for hours, slowed right down until thoughts drifted into one another, none of them quite complete. For once Henry had nothing to say, no adventures to relate. Even he'd had enough excitement for one day.

Later, after he'd gone to bed, I watched the night through the windows and wondered what Lena would be doing. The storm showed no signs of subsiding. The barman jolted every time gusts of wind slammed the panes of glass. I hardly noticed. My eyes felt heavy but I didn't want to go to sleep just yet. So I sat there mulling over all the things I had and hadn't done in my life and the ridiculous thing I was about to do. Eventually the barman made it clear that he couldn't keep the place open just for me. Anyway I was too tired even to hold my cup any more.

I looked in the direction of Moscow and saw only impenetrable darkness.

CHAPTER 25

The journey to Stockholm took four days in all but fortunately the rest of it passed off without further incident. Of course Henry felt he had to liven things up for me with the occasional loop and the even scarier hedgehop. I can't have been a lot of fun for him because it was obvious I didn't share his enthusiasm for *Boy's Own* capers, urging him at every opportunity just to get me to Sweden. He always looked hurt when I emphasised at every stop the need to fly straight and true and as fast as possible. His muttered apologies were worthless, because as soon as we were airborne again, he couldn't resist the odd stunt. I couldn't grumble too much. He knew his stuff and the day after the storm, he had spent several hours buried in the engine and, while it would be an exaggeration to say the plane was as good as new, it was certainly as good as she was ever going to be.

The weather was kind to us now: clear skies and calm seas. For the first few hours the sun was in our faces, providing fleeting fingers of warmth against the steady onslaught of cold winds sweeping down from the north. We left German airspace at midday on 6th November and started crossing the Baltic. Far to the left was Denmark, its island shadows rising faintly from the silver sea; ahead of us in Sweden we would fly over countless lakes already freezing up as winter set in. But my eyes kept being drawn back to that seemingly endless stretch of grey land that was between me and Moscow. It was just over a month since I'd received Lena's letter. It had been undated so I didn't have any idea how long ago she had written it. She had said she was returning to Moscow but the way things were, people could be moved without notice, without choice. She could be anywhere. I might never find her. If officials had any idea of the way she felt, of the kind of things she had said in the letter, she could be dead.

I quickly exorcised the thought from my mind. I had enough real problems to overcome without summoning up demons that could only make it harder for me to concentrate on the job in hand. I kept telling myself to focus on the things I could affect and forget the rest. God knows, I had little enough under my control, it would be complete folly to screw up by worrying about imagined obstacles. I always ended these pessimistic thoughts by laughing at myself. 'Why are you giving any thought to what happens when you reach Moscow? You will almost certainly be dead long before then.' In a strange way it was quite comforting.

When we arrived in Stockholm, I booked us into a hotel just out of the city. I felt restless, on edge, but forced myself to be organised and super efficient. I could go no further until the weather changed. I needed to fly above cloud cover because any sighting of a strange plane would guarantee my being turned back or forced down before I crossed the border. Inevitably the forecast was clear until the end of the week so I would have to use my time wisely. I spent the next few days ostensibly as a tourist. Each morning I would get up early, tell Henry I was off on a business meeting, then head into the city centre and shop. On the first outing I bought a haversack, a new pair of pyjamas, a toothbrush and a shaving kit. All essentials - if I ever finally got to see my wife, I wanted her to recognise me, not be repulsed by some hairy stray in sweaty clothes. The next day I picked up some gifts for Lena, and barter for the rest of the population: perfume, a couple of silk ties, handmade chocolates and the best brandy I could afford from the small amount of cash I had left. I returned to the hotel, arms bulging and piled them on to my bed. I was sorting them through when Henry entered the room. He let out a long whistle.

'You have been busy.' There was a glint in his eyes.

'Just presents for friends,' I explained, feeling the colour rising to my cheeks.

'I don't know if the old crate will be able to carry all that - with both of us flying that is.'

What was he getting at? Did he know I was going to leave without him? He couldn't. It was impossible. I was becoming paranoid, reading nuances into words that simply didn't exist.

'Don't worry,' I said after an unconvincing silence spent racking my brains for a reply. 'Most of them are going by post.'

He left the room. I collapsed on the bed, relieved that I hadn't yet bought the one item that would have given the game away completely - a set of luggage. When I sneaked away, I wanted to keep people off the scent for as long as possible. By leaving what looked like all my belongings in the room, it would appear, at least for a while, that I intended to come back.

Thankfully Henry asked no more questions and made no comments. Looking back, I felt a bit guilty that I didn't take him more into my confidence. I never really got to know him that well. For all his bravado he struck me as being a bit lonely and would probably have welcomed the chance to be involved in such a romantic venture. But he would also probably have insisted on coming along and I couldn't have coped with that, especially as he would certainly have nursed a desire to 'buzz' the Kremlin.

Although I was chaffing at not being on my way, I recognised that it was not entirely a negative thing. In my haste to get going, I'd let Henry do most of the flying to Stockholm so I was still not entirely up to speed with the Swallow. I used the delay to get some airtime in her, taking her up every day while the skies were clear, practising manoeuvres. Every plane has its own particular character. Henry and I had already learnt that she wasn't too partial to the cold. More troublesome, though, was the discovery that she refused to be rushed into anything. The Klemm Swallow was a pedal-operated model; the elevators and ailerons were all operated via low wooden poles at your feet: push down for lift, swing back to level out. The throttle was a little lever on the left wall of the cockpit. In theory, different combinations of the two meant you could make her do just about anything. In practice, she favoured Newton's first law of motion - once an object is on the move, it prefers to keep going in the same direction. The pedals were so heavy it was like trying to force a push-bike through thick, cloying mud. The throttle had a habit of sticking and the flaps were often a law unto themselves, paying no heed to the instructions sent from the cockpit. The first time I took her out of Stockholm it was an hour before I could get her back to the landing strip, though I did get a beautiful sightseeing tour of the city.

For once the forecasters were right. The skies remained dark but clear for over a week. Each day I filled my haversack full of kit and a thermos of hot coffee, stowing it in the Swallow's locker just in case. Every evening I topped up the fuel and oil tanks. I didn't know when I would be able to leave, but I had to be ready. No hitches, no delays.

Finally I awoke to the perfect day. I imagined that all over Stockholm people were quietly cursing a turn for the worse in the weather but I was delighted. Thick cloud stretched to the horizon. The rain fell near vertically. The odd car swished by on the main road leading into the centre, leaving orange trails from their rear lights, swirling in the darkness. Time to go.

I dressed quickly and checked my lists: fuel, oil, coffee, presents, gloves, luggage. I went over it again and again. When everything was packed I stood by the door and scanned the room. I felt sure something was wrong. But it was bare, I could see nothing incriminating. Just another hotel bedroom. I moved quickly down the corridor and slipped a note under Henry's door. The envelope contained thirty pounds, fulsome apologies but no explanations. I also begged him not to tell anyone about my disappearance. The money would be enough to cover the hotel bills and his passage home. I hoped he would understand.

I had just left the foyer when I stopped. The feeling that something was wrong had grown with each step. Now I felt sick. There was something. It lay on the fringes of my mind, nagging but not clear. I turned round and stared at the face of the building, searching for my room, hoping for some trigger. Then it hit me. I'd left the place clean. I'd been so careful to tuck the new luggage away at the back of the wardrobe so Henry wouldn't see it that I'd forgotten it myself. I rushed back upstairs, dragged it out and scattered it across the room.

There. Now it looked normal. I crept out again, and as I did so, saw Henry's door open. I hugged the wall as he wandered to the toilet, scratching himself. He walked straight over the envelope. I left before he returned.

There were few people around at the aerodrome so I reckoned it wouldn't be too difficult to slip away into the cloud without causing any commotion. I wheeled the Swallow out of the hangar, dipped my head in the engine to give it a final once-over, then angled her on to the runway.

I was in the cockpit ready to give myself contact when a man in blue overalls came running out of the control building waving his arms. I pretended not to notice him, flicked the ignition switch and jumped out to swing the prop.

He was shouting something, first in Swedish, which was impossible to understand even if I'd been able to hear it clearly, then in English. There was no mistaking that. 'NO... Stop... STOP!'

He reached me, breathless and red-faced. It was Ake, a voluntary traffic controller who I'd discovered over the last few days was meticulously efficient and took his job very seriously. I'd also noticed his annoying habit of saying many things twice. 'Mr Grover! Mr Grover! You must not fly today. Must not. Didn't you see the sign?'

I didn't want to admit to him that I hadn't looked. He would have been both shocked and hurt.

'Over there, I put it out first thing!'

I glanced at the control tower and saw nothing. 'Where?'

'It's in the window.'

And so it was, a small speck of white, almost invisible from 200 yards away.

'Ah, yes,' I said. 'What's the problem?'

'Bad weather. There are storms coming, big storms. No flying without radio. It is very dangerous.' Unfortunately, though voluntary, he had the authority to ground me. I guessed argument would receive a stony-faced silence. I decided the best chance was persuasion and bowing to his sense of self-importance.

I put on my humble, hard-done-by look. 'I only want to do a figure of eight. Keep my hand in. I'm just getting used to her.'

'It's out of the question. No flying without radio.'

'I'll be up and down within ten minutes, I promise. Surely you have the authority to allow me just that. I'll be back long before the storm hits.' There was a long pause. He looked over the shoulder the way people do when they're about to agree to something they shouldn't. There was nobody there.

'Please.'

Nothing.

'Please.'

Perhaps it was the repetition of the word that tipped it my way, I don't know, but he nodded solemnly. 'All right. Five minutes. Five minutes.'

'Heard you the first time,' I said and smiled. I swung the prop. The engine fired first time. I jumped into the cockpit and slipped on my goggles and earmuffs, immediately encased in a new world of muffled sound and vibration.

As the plane trundled down the tarmac, I looked back. The last I saw of Ake, he was standing chest out, overalls flapping in the slipstream of the Swallow, one hand held aloft, five fingers splayed.

Gradually the Swallow shook off her lethargy and started to pick up momentum. I eased the throttle to full power, pushing against the dead-weight pedals as she reached takeoff speed. I felt the lift in my chest, the freedom that all pilots experience when the wheels leave the earth. At that moment you know that gravity is too earthbound, too restraining. Perhaps man's greatest achievement is to shake off the restrictions imposed by gravity. Once you have defied it, the normal world of squabbling bosses and money worries and guilty consciences disappears. Soon there is nothing else except you and your plane. And the air, which miraculously holds you up.

My back pressed against the cockpit seat as I accelerated. The nose pointed straight for the cloud. At five hundred feet, a side wind picked up and the plane wobbled. I adjusted to level out and overcompensated. She wasn't being as stubborn as usual. Or maybe I was just inexperienced and nervous. I settled for the former.

We climbed, the Swallow and I, and the world grew insignificant. At 1,000 feet I entered cloud and it seemed I wasn't flying at all. There was no perspective. Everything was a dusty white. At any moment I expected a rock or a hill to loom out of the haze and hammer into me. Flying blind, even when you know there is nothing in front of you for miles, is a nervy experience. On more than one occasion I swerved objects only as solid as my imagination. When I reached 2,500 feet the cloud thinned into a transparent skin. The cockpit filled with pale yellow light and then I burst through, the sun smacking the fuselage so brightly I had to shield my eyes. I remembered Ray saying to me: 'The best thing about flying is that you see the sun every day.'

I could seldom remember being so exhilarated. I was on my way, at last. And sitting there with the engine of the Swallow ticking over perfectly, it was a magical world. I was in the land above the land. The place where as a child you imagine you can walk on air and pluck strands of white candyfloss off wisps of cloud. I blessed the cloud for hiding me and forgave it for being a little grey. It stretched beyond the horizon without breaking, like a huge comfortable, billowing bed, so real I wanted to step out and bounce up and down like an excited kid. When I looked up the sky was a pure blue canvas between earth and infinity. I could see both moon and sun in the same picture, the pale crescent descending, the bright orb climbing higher.

At 10,000 feet I levelled out, checked my watch, 8.10 am, and began to set my route. I had been unable to get hold of any aviation charts for the Soviet Union - that would have aroused suspicion more than anything else - so I had to make do with an old school map of Russia bought in a second-hand bookshop on Charing Cross Road. I reasoned anything more detailed would have been quite useless anyway. Above the clouds there were no landmarks to go by. The only way to determine my direction was to draw a straight line between Stockholm and Moscow. The angle between it and the meridian gave my compass bearing. Stick to that and hope for the best. I couldn't allow for drift because there were nothing to tell me the velocity of the wind. If the Swallow kept going, there was every chance I would miss Moscow by some miles, but I had calculated that I would run out of fuel before I got too far from where I wanted to be.

Once I'd set my route there was nothing more to do but sit back, concentrate on the dials and wait. But it's not easy to stop your mind wandering when you have nothing much to do. Henry would have read his note by now. He'd be sitting on the side of the bed, packing his things. No doubt he'd be cursing a lost opportunity. He'd also be glum - the way home was by boat and to a man like Henry that was purgatory. I chuckled, picturing Ake. He would be radioing other airfields to see where his 'figure-of-eight' beginner had got to. He'd be feeling important - Ake Kristensen at the centre of an international incident. But he'd be sweating in case he was in trouble for believing me. He knew now what he could do with his five fingers.

The cloud scudded by, the sun lay still in the sky, the needles on the dials remained constant. Gradually I noticed the cold. Insidious, creeping cold. At first my flying jacket and cap and five layers of vests and shirts kept it out. But slowly my fingers numbed, the joints stiffening despite my gloves. At 10,000 feet once something is cold, it stays that way. I concentrated on finding ways to get warm. I stuck my hands under my legs but the buckles from my gloves jabbed into me causing more discomfort than before. I stamped my feet on the floor of the cockpit even though I knew it would do no good. In films people always stamp their feet to get the circulation going but the simple truth is, it just wastes energy. I tried to find the warmest spot in the cockpit. My choices were limited. I leaned to the left. I leaned to the right. It was futile. Everywhere was cold and getting colder. I imagined myself on a beach in Trinidad sucking the juice out of a ripe mango as the sun beat down. That just highlighted how cold I was.

I pulled out the Thermos from under the seat and savoured a cup of steaming coffee. The heat of the liquid   blew into my face as I drank. Within seconds the coffee would be tepid. I gulped it down, my chest constricting in protest at the change in temperature. I checked the time. Ten-thirty. It could count as early elevenses.

Two minutes later I looked at my watch again. And then again. Shivering, I watched the second hand move, the gap between each tick an eternity. I started to think it was taunting me, that when I stared at it, the hand hesitated before moving on, but when I looked away it hurriedly caught up with itself.

My arms started to ache with the cold. My lips chapped and the desire to lick them better grew unbearable, like an itch, until I could stand it no longer. My tongue darted out against central command's strictest orders, and regretted it. The wind froze the spittle almost immediately - a blunt razor crisscrossing my face.

I put my head down and watched the seconds again. This time I challenged myself to count as high as possible between each movement of the hand. 'Onetwothree forfisisevehaynintenele –

228

' 'Onetothefufifsiseveghaynitelvutwelthirtinfor – '

I wanted to reach fifteen. Fifteen was the magic number to get to. Then I could stop the game and think of something else. I must have tried twenty times until my brain was as numb as my hands.

I looked up and my neck creaked with the effort. Not even three hours into the flight and I was longing for it to be over. The pleasure of the first hour was a forgotten memory. All my recollections now were grim. I thought of a time when I was a young child out for a walk with my parents. It couldn't have been more than two miles around the copse and back but it felt like a trek into the wilderness with no return. Mother gripped my hand and dragged me stumbling behind her. They grumbled amongst themselves, their grown-up words a mystery to a small boy. My mind slowly ignored everything except one all-consuming dread. I needed the toilet. Desperately. I wanted to go home, I just wanted to go home. But I couldn't say 'wee' or 'toilet' in front of Mother. If I did Father would be furious, he would roar at me. I counted each blade of grass that passed, agonised in case every step triggered the thing I feared most. By the time the house came into view I was about to explode. The sight of it was too much. I felt the release, and with all my effort stopped it. A tiny patch of wet appeared on my shorts.

'Mother?'

'What is it dear?'

'I need – '

'What, dear?'

'I need to go behind a bush.'

Mother's face dropped.

'Brian! We're nearly home. Be a gentleman.'

'But I have to.' Already I was edging towards an inviting tree. The trickle was coming back. I turned and ran and pulled down my shorts. Father pounded after me. 'Don't you dare, boy!' he shouted but there was nothing I could do. It streamed out in a long luxurious release. All the while Father harangued me, clipping my ear with the flat of his hand. 'A real man can control himself. You should be ashamed boy. We'll send you out in the wilds, is that what you want? To become a savage?'

I dragged my brain back to the matter in hand. No more clock-watching, I told myself. You can't dissect the journey into fragments of seconds and expect it to go quicker. I tried to keep alert, doing crosswords in my head, but none of the clues fitted. Several times I started a game of imaginary chess against an imaginary opponent. But within a few minutes, I couldn't remember where the pieces were on the board. My anxiety grew. I'd expected to be uncomfortable, factored in boredom, stiffness, even the possibility of a dicey landing and perhaps a bruise or two. Perhaps even worse. What I had never imagined was the possibility of being so frozen that I was unable to control the plane. Of being conscious but knowing that I was at 10,000 feet and helpless, unable to do anything. I didn't want my last moments to be as a frozen lump of meat racing helplessly towards impact with the ground.

I knew that if I went below the cloud layer it would be warmer, but I didn't dare risk that. Even the thought of descending a little way to try and find a few more degrees of heat was dismissed in case someone heard my engine.

An agonising hour passed. I checked my map and tried to work out my position. The Baltic was behind me now, so too Latvia. I calculated the speed of the plane, the time I had been flying and drew a dot just past Karsava.

I was in Russian airspace.

For a while I felt renewed energy at the thought. I was halfway there. I had crossed the border that had kept me out for five years. But the reality of my cramped cockpit soon closed back in and I was running on willpower again.

I felt dizzy, my head flopping from fatigue.

I blacked out.

CHAPTER 26

There were two women way off in the distance holding hands. Familiar, but too far away to make out their faces. They were calling but it faded in and out, like listening to a foreign station on the wireless.

Then I heard: 'I told you so, Brian. I warned you. You could have been a bank manager by now if you had listened to me. It's your own fault. Now down you go.'

It was Madeleine. She was laughing.

Then the other woman's voice reached me. My mother.

'Brian what did I tell you?'

'I can't remember.'

'Yes you can. Never...'

'Never... I can't remember, Mother. Please don't tell Father.'

'Oh, Brian, I despair of you. I only told you one thing. Never marry a woman without money. But you wouldn't listen. You were always stubborn. You ignored me, not once but twice. No wonder you are going down...'

A misfire from the engine jerked me out of my reverie. The sun was sinking below the clouds. The day was dying and so, I thought, was I. Ice had formed on my goggles, blurring everything. My mind cranked slowly, trying to send an order to my body to tighten my scarf but there was no response. I realised that I was not sitting properly. I had squirmed round, my left arm trapped beneath me, numb. My right arm was still stretched forward, holding the joystick, rigid. I was afraid to try to shift my position in case I found I'd lost all movement yet I knew I couldn't stay like this. Suddenly I found myself laughing – dry, hysterical, ironic laughter. If only Sirienko and Nikitich could see me now, two miles up, frozen like a carcass of beef on its way to Moscow. They would raise their glasses and toast each other. 'We won, at last.'

'I'm damned if you have,' I said out loud. With a monstrous effort I forced my neck to move first one way then another. Gingerly I sat back up straight and freed my arm. At first it hung limp then I heard myself whimper as the blood started to bring it back to life. I gradually, painfully, got all my body moving. It felt worse than when it had been dead. Every bit of me ached as though I had been kicked and beaten by a street gang. For a moment, I wished it would all just end. I was tempted to push the nose down and just let it go. Then I remembered the image of Madeleine and Mother and resolved not to give them the satisfaction of gloating in their grief.

'Come on! There's no time to feel sorry for yourself. How far have you gone? Where are you? If this old plane can keep going, so can you. Now, think!'

I checked my watch. Couldn't be right. I checked it a second time. 2 pm it insisted. My stomach contracted in panic. I had to go down. Had to go down now. I fumbled in my jacket and pulled out the compass. The glass was cracked, the fluid seeping out in a frozen film.

'Damn!' I threw it overboard.

I told myself it didn't matter. The only thing that counted was taking control again. I had to be in charge, not the Swallow and its rapidly emptying fuel tanks. 'What would Ray do? Think. What had Henry said?' Through the fog of memory I grasped the word altimeter.

'What's your height?'

'Six-foot two.'

'No, idiot. Altimeter! Altimeter!'

I was two people. One in a daze, every muscle screaming to be relieved of its duty. The other angry, clinging on to life, determined not to let go. They weren't getting on very well.

I looked down at the control panel.

'Too many dials. You might as well give up.'

'Middle top. That's it, what does it say?'

I leaned forward despite a complaining spine. The glass was frozen over. I peered at it, willing a needle to appear so I could tell where I was.

A solid, horizontal line of white underneath the sparkling grey. It read zero.

'Great, so you've landed. You can relax now. Get some sleep. Bloody great.'

I looked along the wings. They were covered in ice at least an inch thick and the tips were vibrating violently. But there was no sign of the ground.

'Never mind that, get some sleep. Oh what now?'

'A noise. Coughing. What was it?'

'Who cares!'

'The engine. Fuel.'

I rubbed the dial as awkwardly as an animal learning a new trick, my fingertips gathered together to provide more pressure. Nothing. I still couldn't see.

My weaker self started to meander off again, dreaming he was in Maisie's café with a nice pot of tea.

His rival pushed him aside but the image lingered and I remembered the Thermos. I couldn't make sense of the thought for some time but then the realisation of what it meant came to me and I fought to stop the idea fading away. I fumbled underneath the seat for my bag and cursed the straps as 1 tried to pull it open. They wouldn't budge so I yanked them and the flask tumbled to the floor. Leaning over, pain shooting through my legs, I retrieved it. Five minutes later I had the cap off and then wondered what I had intended in the first place.

'Ah, yes,' I said to no one and poured the coffee over the fuel gauge. For a few seconds the ice slid away in a cloud of steam to reveal the needle hovering in the red zone. The tank was almost empty.

On cue, the engine spluttered. The propeller juddered, missed a beat. Down to the last few dregs, the sludge that should never be used. The Swallow shook in protest, then recovered. But it could only be minutes before it happened again.

'Thank goodness for that. It will soon be over.'

I screamed as loud as I could. It hurt my throat but I had to drown out the other voice. If I was to survive there could only one person calling the shots. I needed my brain to recall every lesson I'd ever learned about survival and to remember every piece of advice Ray had given me. And to do it now.

'Most important of all before you land, even if you're just going up for a figure of eight, check everything works. It must become second nature, or one day you'll regret it.' Ray's final words the day before my exam came back.

I did the aileron pedals first: feet forward, up; feet back, level.

The plane responded wearily. Then I came to the tail fin. Left, the plane crabbed right, straightened out, just as it should.

Then it kept turning. I pushed the joystick left but it wouldn't go. I pushed all my weight behind it, but its will was stronger than mine. The plane continued to turn right in a slow circle. I checked the wings. One of the flaps was stuck. I looked over my shoulder, shuffled round to see better, then along the fuselage to the tail. The rudder was jammed full out to the right. Frozen.

Angrily, I hammered the joystick, relishing the groans of the pain that it caused.

Something snapped.

'Get a grip. You've covered this. Compensate, push the right flap up, level out then throttle down.' The whine of the engine lowered in pitch. The nose dipped and I felt my back pressing slightly against the seat.

But the plane, my trusty Swallow that had taken me so far, was still turning to the right. Like a horse that refuses at the final fence, it had had enough.

I looked down the wing again. The flap stayed put. The whole machine was freezing up.

Slowly, the Swallow descended in long circles, the tumble of clouds looming closer with each rotation. This was not how it was meant to be. Spiralling pathetically over God-knows-where in a shaky plane with only a few cups of petrol left in the tank. This was not how I'd planned it. I'd seen myself gliding smoothly into the outskirts of Moscow, finding a clear area and landing. I would stride purposefully from my machine, and to anyone who challenged me I would declare, 'I've come for my wife. Take me to the police.'

I grimaced at the thought now. How grandiose your plans

when you're cooped up in the safety of your home, maps spread on the table, the journey simple, a mere series of ruled lines from A to B to C until, *voila!* Moscow. With the gas fire hissing gently in the background, you don't think of fingers so numb you want to snap them off simply to stop the pain; or the agonizing cramp of sitting in a cockpit for endless hours with only your conscience for company. You don't consider the mental toll of trying to concentrate for such a long time, trying to stave off the overpowering wish to sleep.

I forced my eyes to stay open. The wheels of the Swallow sliced through the first wisps of cloud and I realised there was something I should have done before I set off. I slid down the zip of my leathers, unbuttoned a shirt pocket and brought out the silver case with Lena's portrait in it. I opened it up and kissed it. I had threaded a ribbon through the hole in the top and now I somehow managed to tie it to the rim of the windshield. She would be with me on the way down.

The cloud enveloped me. There was no resistance. It looked so thick but felt of nothing. This was the world I had entered on the way up, a world bent on confusing you. In cloud-country there was no direction. Just an endless expanse of cloying white.

I focussed on the picture of Lena. For minutes I saw nothing else. All I could feel was the vibration of the engine, taking me down smoothly to what I prayed would be a flat stretch of land.

The tone of the engine changed. It spluttered, coughed then screamed, a brain-curdling whine. Then it went silent.

It was the silence of death. It is what all pilots dread. The shudder through the fuselage, then the jerky deceleration of the propeller. Then nothing. A ton of metal and canvas and glue and wood, held up only by the insufficient pressure of air.

The Swallow tilted to the right. I gripped the joystick like a lifeline. But as the world swirled around the cockpit it felt like a straw.

My head jerked back with a snap, blood rushing to my cheeks, eyeballs slamming into the back of their sockets, and then I was nothing and nowhere.

'When a man has lost his bottle,

Give him a length of rope.

Show him how to pull, then throttle,

Sit back and watch him choke.'

Mother says this in a singsong voice, but there is no tune behind it. And then Madeleine and Father join in and the three of them dance to the rhythm. I look down at my feet. I'm on a revolving platform. It's going in the opposite direction to the dancers, their faces merge in streaks as 1 spin around and around.

'Choke,' they howl, 'choke, choke, chooooooooooke – '

My eyes snapped open. The Klemm was screaming. There was a crack to my right and I caught a glimpse of sheet ice flying off the wing, slicing into the side of the plane. Wood splintered on impact sending shards of debris tumbling in the slipstream. The Swallow veered violently, air trapped inside the fuselage.

'Choke! Flood the engine, prise out the last drops.'

I was still in cloud, with no bearings except down. I forced myself against gravity, reached for the throttle. My hand shook in triple image as I stretched, swiped at the handle, slammed it back then forward, back then forward.

'Come on! Come on!'

Nothing. Only the wind howling.

Then the cloud broke and it didn't seem to matter any more.

CHAPTER 27

I slipped in and out of consciousness. No longer afraid. Instead, I became fascinated by my mind's flickering switch between bright white light, flashes of blue, then darkness and between each, like a subliminal image, Lena smiling out of a silver frame. It was like a home movie as the spool runs out. But this film never quite reached the end.

They say a drowning man sees his whole life flash before him as he is dying but if my experience is anything to go by, it is different when you are plunging from the sky. The whole experience can't have lasted very long but somehow my brain managed to find time to rectify a few of the regrets of my life - this time I stayed in Moscow instead of going to Grozny, I turned the boat back when Ivan called, I took Lena home to England and sorted things out with her by my side. I told her I was sorry for hurting her.

In between there were moments when I was in the reality of my situation, when I was aware I was hurtling towards the ground, brief seconds when Ray and I had a silent dialogue, a final lesson.

241

'You still have some control. Use your feet...'

'I must clear the forest. Can't land there...'

'The elevator pedals. Push the pedals, raise the elevator, slow your descent.'

White, blue, black... silver. Lena's smile...

The miniature swung on its ribbon, tiny movements back and forward. The glass on the front of it was cracked. When I looked down there was a red smear on the instrument panel. I became aware of blood seeping from a gash in my scalp and coagulating down the side of my face.

Carefully, I lifted my body upright, waiting for the stabbing pain. It wasn't as sharp as I'd expected. I flexed my fingers. They responded to my commands. I leaned back in the cockpit, took in the surroundings. I was in a huge field, packed down with snow that shimmered in the low sun. Bits of stubble stuck through the snow defiantly. There was a hedgerow about half a mile away. It cast long shadows towards me. Beyond that was another field, then another, smooth and untouched since the snow had first fallen. I wanted to go there, to be the first person to mark that expanse with a trail of footprints, to prove that I was real. I looked behind me and saw the chaos the Swallow had left in its wake. That was certainly real.

I blacked out again.

'Wake up! Wake up! Why are you here?'

I felt fingers poke my cheek, tug at my eyelids. I was happy where I was. It had been a nice dream where the light was warm and welcoming. With consciousness came the cold and the pain and the questions. I opened my eyes and saw a young girl, probably around twelve years old, her cheeks pink with cold.

'Take me up in your plane,' she said.

I undid my safety strap and stood up in the cockpit. For a moment I swayed on my feet. Instinctively, unafraid, the girl held out her hand to steady me. She was wearing a goatskin coat and a cap to match, fur gloves and tall leather boots. She was smiling. There was a crowd of children behind her, all similarly wrapped up against the elements.

'Well?' she said.

'I can't. She crashed.' My Russian was a little creaky, but they didn't seem to notice. 'Perhaps tomorrow we'll get her fixed and I'll take you up then.'

At this there was a mêlée of voices crying, 'And me, me too, and me...'

I clambered out of the plane.

'Where'd you fly from?' a little boy asked.

'England.'

They all laughed. This silly man comes out of the sky in a rickety little plane and says he comes from England.

'Didn't your parents tell you it was bad to lie?' the girl asked.

'Stalin says it's wicked,' another voice piped up.

'I'm not lying.' They all giggled again.

I went over to check the damage at the back of the plane and the pack of children followed me. The tail had sheered off to one side. I looked back. A few hundred yards behind was the forest I must have passed over on the way down.

'What's your name?' I asked the girl.

'Petra,' she said proudly.

'And yours?' I nodded at a sallow-looking boy who stood slightly apart from the crowd.

'Traktor,' he mumbled.

'Speak up!' one of the others shouted. And then they all started jeering him. 'Traktor, Traktor, Traktor.'

'Quiet, quiet,' I shouted, as much for the sake of my own head as for the little boy's blushes. 'Where are the adults?'

'They're coming. Over there, see!'

Two men had appeared at the edge of the field. One was carrying a gun.

'They can't run as fast as us. They told us, "Come back," but we just kept going.' Petra peered up at me quizzically and said, 'Are you a bad man?'

That was debatable. I smiled at her and waited in the centre of the group of children just in case the man with the gun was trigger happy.

The pair stopped a few yards from me, warily. One of them gave me a shaky smile. I had prepared a little speech for this moment, but now it seemed faintly ridiculous. Yet there seemed no other way to put it.

'My name is Brian Grover. I have flown from England to meet my wife Ileana Petrovna because I have not seen her for five years. I know I have broken your laws but no offence is meant. You can arrest me and I won't struggle.'

There was quite a long silence. They looked at each other, unsure how to respond. Then one said: 'You're mad.'

'I'm desperate,' I replied.

The other one said accusingly, 'How do we know you are English?'

'I assure you I'm English.'

They weren't convinced.

The man with the gun motioned to the other who frisked me head to foot.

'Come with us,' he said.

'Where am I?'

'Glukhovo Collective.'

The two men shooed the children away as they milled round me, but they took no notice. We trudged away from the plane. The Pied Piper under arrest, I thought.

When we reached the beginning of the lane that led to Glukhovo, I turned round to look at the scene one final time. The evening had faded into night within minutes, leaving only the faint outline of the forest and the luminous glow of the ice-packed fields. I stood there for a while, breathing in the silence, and wondered where the light came from. It seemed to come up out of the snow. Then I realised my knees were buckling underneath me, that I should move to stop from falling, so I followed the men and the rest of the group down the lane. Everyone fired questions at me and I tried to answer, but the effort was finally too much. My words disappeared in a fog of freezing breath.

That evening I was introduced to the entire population of the Glukhovo Collective. For them, I was an eccentric curiosity, a welcome break from the endless drudgery of their lives. After an interview with the head man, in which I explained my story and urged him to contact the KGB immediately, I was posted with an old couple who had a mattress and a spare room. I would be leaving for Moscow tomorrow, the boss said. I didn't know whether to be elated or petrified. In the end I decided that it made perfect sense to be both.

'This is her,' I held out the miniature photo of Lena for the old woman, Ludmilla, to look at.

'Beautiful,' she said, 'so beautiful.' She stroked the silver frame lovingly and for a second I wasn't sure if she was referring to it or Lena. But then she said in an earnest voice, 'You've done the right thing by her.'

'You're one of the few people who believe my story.'

'It doesn't do to trust foreigners,' she said. 'Not in public

245

anyway.' She stared into the log fire as it spat out sparks from the damp wood. Her eyes rested on the flames and I felt she was remembering days when she was young and in love.

'You did all this,' she said, then turned to her husband and cackled. 'My sloth of a man. Look at him. Asleep and it's only seven. There is excitement in this village for the first time in a decade and he snores in tribute! Cah! He can't even be bothered to get up in the morning and pull turnips for me. Cross an ocean? For me? I'm an old woman with mousy hair. He'd rather have a heart attack. At least then he'd get a sniff of more vodka.'

As if hearing the word through his slumber, her husband sat bolt upright in his seat. 'We must celebrate, young man. I have one bottle left.' His knees cracked as he rose and staggered to the kitchen.

'You always have one bottle left,' Ludmilla called after him, but she smiled as she said it. 'I love him really. When he's able to complete his sentences without vomiting, he's quite a friend. We've been together so long, I would miss him if he wasn't here.'

We drank, crouched around the fire, and later Ludmilla brought in a pot of thick broth full of vegetables and chunks of beef. I asked if her food was always this good. Seeing the question behind the compliment, she replied: 'If you smile at the right people, the right people smile back at you. Remember that and you might be lucky.'

As I drifted off to sleep that night in a spare room cluttered with farming tools, I thought of her words and hoped that she was right.

CHAPTER 28

It had taken me eight hours to fly alone from Stockholm to Gluckovo. It took four policeman – Agan, Slava, Vitya, Arkady – and a regulation Soviet truck two days to go the one hundred miles to Moscow.

They came for me the next morning. The sun was not yet up when Ludmilla gently tapped my face to wake me. The room was crusted in shadows.

'They are here,' she said simply and thrust a bundle of damp cloths in my hand. 'Chicken,' she explained. 'You will be hungry, and so will they. You can share it on your way. They will like that.'

She paused, her eyes searching the spaces around me as though the room had been empty too long but was now filled with shadows of the past.

'They are good people, I know them. The young ones especially, tell them stories, make them smile. You will be all right.' Then she whispered, 'But watch Agan, he is bitter and small-minded. Do not make conversation with him; he will twist what you say.' She spoke as though from experience.

I dressed quickly, splashed cold water into my eyes from a tub Ludmilla had supplied the night before. Voices and the sound of feet stamping on packed ice filtered through the walls. I gathered my belongings, stuffed the chicken in the sack and went to meet them.

They were in line like a firing squad. Their green uniforms were crumpled, the brass buttons dull from lack of polishing. One stood slightly forward from the others. I presumed he was in command. He had decorations draped over his chest and the sure look of someone who knows he is unassailable and likes others to know it too. He hardly looked like a soldier. His face was pinched, his stomach jutted out like an expectant mother, his legs were a little too short for his torso. He had to be Agan. The others simply looked forlorn and bleary-eyed from getting up so early. They had already travelled a few miles from the nearest town and from the look of them I suspected they had spent last night drinking away the greyness of their lives, unaware they were going to be up before dawn to guard a stranger all the way to Moscow. They looked like actors from some second-rate theatre troupe. People were watching and I didn't want to get off to the wrong start so I suppressed a smile.

The whole collective had turned out to see me carted off. They stood silently, hands by their sides, just their eyes moving. The only sound was the first calls of birds in the woods and my feet clicking on the hard ground.

Agan gripped my wrists and slapped handcuffs on. 'Hurry,' he said, 'we have a long journey.'

'You don't need to do that. Really, I'm not going to run away.'

'You're not escaping while you are my prisoner,' he replied and shoved me into the back of the lorry. I caught a glimpse of little Petra as I fell forward on to the floor. She didn't look frightened and she didn't look sad. She was just fascinated, watching events with the detached eyes of the innocent. I wonder if today she tells her grandchildren my story. I wonder if they believe her.

At first there was silence. Agan and the driver were in front surveying the road for potholes, I was sandwiched between the two youngest men. Progress was tediously slow. Great piles of snow were piled up on either side of the road like replicas of mountains. It was a fantasy land that I had forgotten. A land of gnarled ice sculptures that produced rainbows at all angles as the sun came up. The landscape looked uninhabitable but at regular intervals along the way the horizon would clear to reveal farm complexes like the one I had just left: great grey buildings of corrugated iron. In the summer they would be centres of frenetic activity with tonnes of grain off-loaded into waiting trucks. But now they were still, and out in the flat fields, tractors, ploughs and combines lay stranded like cattle that had never been called home. Even the latest Five-Year Plan had to wait for the weather to ease.

We had travelled about twenty miles when Agan asked me suddenly, 'Do you think you are clever?'

'I'm sorry?'

'Some kind of a hero?'

'I just want to see my wife.'

He ignored me. 'You are not a hero. They are the heroes.' He waved vaguely towards imaginary peasants in the fields. I would have to watch him. A sentimental Stalinist. He obviously lapped up the propaganda, devoured it without question.

'If you knew where you were going now, you would shit yourself in fear.' He turned round, eagerness in his eyes. 'Do you know where you're going?'

'I hope Moscow,' I said politely.

249

'Oh yes, we're taking you there, but not to meet your pretty little wife. You're going to hell. You're going to *Lubyanka*.'

'But that's what I want.'

He paused, smiling at what he thought was bravado. Slowly, he shook his head. 'You obviously don't know much about *Lubyanka*. It is the tallest building in Russia - you can even see Siberia from inside its basement.' He laughed malevolently at his own joke.

We stopped overnight in a tavern at Staritza, which had been requisitioned by the army many years before and was now stripped bare of its character, the lights and the paintings pilfered over the years to leave only bare tables and uncomfortable chairs. I had made friends with Vitya and Slava, as Ludmilla predicted. We played billiards in the games room with ball bearings while Agan sat in the corner over a bottle of cognac. He had ended up being a man to pity rather than fear, a man who, Vitya confided in me, everyone mocked behind his back.

They laughed as I tried to play with my gloves on, my cue slipping everywhere. They reached five hundred while I was trying to make twenty. I asked for a rematch without the gloves.

'Agan, what do you say? Should we beat him again?' Slava asked, aware it was important to acknowledge who was in charge.

'The man gave us a chicken and he wants favours back. Typical of the Western bourgeoisie. They never do a thing without wanting reward.' Agan turned back to his bottle of brandy.

'It's worth another bottle of whatever you want,' I tried.

Agan flapped his approval and Slava set up the table. I lost the next game five hundred to forty. Agan was pleased.

We set off early the next morning and before noon found ourselves weaving through the Bulvar Ring, passing familiar churches, flats and factories. Despite my apprehension, I felt pleased to be back in Moscow. I liked its sense of familiarity.

'Not long now for the hero,' Agan said as the van pulled up, two wheels on the kerb.

'Take no notice of him,' Vitya whispered, 'you'll be fine. Be polite, tell them your story and I'm sure they'll let you go home.'

I shook my head. 'I don't want to go home. I want my wife back.'

Through the front windscreen I could see the *Lubyanka* building. It resembled a massive cake with layer upon layer of tiny windows separated by lines of yellowing crenellated bricks that stuck out like piped cream, and at the top, a round clock like a single eye. I guessed the inside would not be so attractive. For half an hour I was left with Vitya while the others went inside to bring news of their cargo. We sat without speaking, listening to trucks lumbering down the road, footsteps tapping by, the general hum of a city going about its business. For the first time since I'd landed I began to feel nerves gnawing at my thoughts. Without realising it, I started shivering, though it was warm in the van. Vitya put a hand on my shoulder. 'Slow down, breath deep. Everything is fine.'

I couldn't sort out my feelings. Lena was so close, less than five miles away, probably pressing her uniform right now, ready for her next shift. She had no idea I was here and might never find out, never realise how near we had come to being reunited. I thought of making a run for it but knew that Vitya's fear of the authorities would outweigh any newly formed friendship. He would have to shoot me.

My plan had seemed sensible back in London - even in Stockholm and Glukhovo for that matter - to be brought before the KGB and allowed to plead my case. But now sitting outside one of the most feared buildings in the Soviet Union, I wasn't so confident. What if they thought I was a lunatic, fit for nothing more than being locked away forever in a grim sanatorium with the truly insane and the dispossessed? What if they dismissed my story out of hand? Violation of their sovereign territory was potentially a capital crime. They could cast me away in some cell and let me rot. They could execute me without a squeak from the outside world. The British Embassy might never be contacted and even if questions were raised, the Russians would shrug and suggest that anyone foolish enough to try such an exploit was probably at the bottom of the Baltic. And if they let me off with exile, how would Lena be treated?

What had I unleashed?

My mouth filled with saliva. I felt my stomach churn. I wanted to be sick. When I told Vitya, he edged away, then dug in his pockets and brought out a paper bag.

'Almonds. Suck on one. The feeling will pass.'

I did. Bile rose in my throat. I forced it back and the queasiness subsided a little.

'What have I done?' I said quietly. 'I've been a fool, a terrible fool.'

'Sometimes, there is no other option,' he whispered back. 'Sometimes the fool plays an ace and wins the hand.'

The back doors opened and I gulped in fresh air. I stumbled out into the arms of a burly guard. While Agan oversaw the exchange of handcuffs, I said goodbye to my three unlikely friends. 'Good luck,' Arkady mumbled under his breath so Agan would not hear and I smiled at him so Agan would not see.

I was marched past Diaghilev's Monument, a forbidding black statue of another Soviet hero gone to the ground, then under the dark marble entrance and up to a set of glass double doors. Here, my papers were handed to an armed sentry who demanded that each of us in turn state our names in his ear before he would let

252

us pass. It didn't matter that the guard who was taking me probably drank with the sentry after work. Orders were there to be obeyed.

This procedure happened three times, each set of doors sturdier than before. The guard I was cuffed to said nothing, looked at no one. Eventually we came to a lift. I was pushed forward into a separate compartment where I was shut in alone. The ancient lift creaked to a halt at the seventh floor. We entered a deserted passageway, carpeted edge to edge. Utter silence. We took a right turn into a corridor with a single door at the end. The guard knocked and we waited. For a long time nothing happened. I avoided his eyes, stared at the wall and tried to compose myself. Then a voice cried: 'Enter.'

I was led into what looked like a room in a Victorian gentlemen's club. It was huge with wood-panelled walls decorated with imposing portraits of Lenin and Stalin. There were a few, smaller spaces where the wood was lighter – all that remained to mark the life of former prominent officials who had become non-people and had their portraits removed. In the centre of the room, flat on a polished slatted floor, was a priceless Kashan rug. On top of the rug was a twelve-man mahogany dining table. Around it sat twelve men, each of them with a telephone in front of him.

I hovered by the door, unsure what my next move should be. All the men wore black suits, white shirts and black ties, except for the man at the centre. His suit was grey. I presumed it was a deliberate move to make him stand out. The chair he sat in was different too, an old pre-revolution piece with a high back and carved arms. Their faces were lit from below by concealed lamps. There were no windows in the room.

The man in the centre spoke: 'Step forward.' I did so, reluctantly.

I felt completely out of my depth, like a small boy in the headmaster's study, with the whole teaching staff in attendance.

'Take a chair. Any one will do. Though I suggest you pick the one opposite me.'

I did as he said, and as I sat I got a closer look at his features. His hair was lank, thinning at the top, his eyes were small behind tight lids, but it was his chin that was most noticeable. It jutted out a full two inches from the rest of his face. It was so prominent in the eerie light that I felt a strange compulsion to reach out and touch it just to make sure it was real.

'Why have you flown into Soviet territory without permission?' he snapped.

'I haven't seen my wife for five years. I tried everything to get back here but was refused a visa each time. It was a last resort.'

I pulled out an envelope full of official letters from the Soviet Embassy in London that proved my case and realised suddenly that I was still wearing my flying jacket. It was all I had brought with me, but it seemed inappropriate somehow. I hadn't shaved since leaving Stockholm and had only had time for a quick rinse in cold water. I wondered what this man saw before him. A mad tramp? Or perhaps something more sinister.

He gave the documents a cursory glance and passed them down the line. They were unimportant, not what he wanted.

He leaned forward. 'Tell me, Mr...'

'Grover.'

'...Mr Grover. What did you notice during your flight?'

'Not very much. I flew above the cloud the whole way.'

He nodded. It was a fact that could be verified, and probably already had been. 'Let me put it another way. What were you looking for?'

'My wife.'

'It is a long way from Stockholm to Moscow. What did you do to pass the time?'

'Nothing. I blacked out.'

There was a collective murmur from the others, glances exchanged. They discussed me in snatched whispers as though I wasn't there.

'Pardon?' the man in the grey suit said.

'I was delirious for most of the way. From the cold.'

'How convenient. And your friend. Did he not try to revive you?'

'Sorry?'

'I think you heard me, Mr Grover.'

'Nobody revived me. I flew alone.'

Without a word, he got up and left the room. The other men stared at me, a line of impassive eyes, questions in their expressions but nothing coming out of their mouths. The man in the grey suit returned a few minutes later and started the interrogation again, almost as though the earlier exchanges had not taken place.

'My name is Feodorov and these are my assistants. You brought another man in with you from Stockholm, did you not?'

'No, sir,' I replied.

'It's no good you saying "No sir," to me. This isn't a dressing down in a public school. I have it in black and white in the next room.'

'That's not true. If you want proof, you have only to ask at Stockholm airport.'

Feodorov smiled. 'We did. They said you arrived with a man named Henry Mountjoy.'

'That is true.'

'And now he cannot be found.'

'I left him money to go home, back to England.' He made me

feel like I was lying. Where was Henry? He must have left immediately. Surely, if they checked out my story, they would see all the facts tallied.

'And you also left clothes all over your room. To make the authorities believe you were returning.'

I nodded.

'You brought this man Mountjoy into Russia to spy on us. What is your position?'

'Do I look like a spy?' I said desperately.

Feodorov leaned back in his armchair and swept a hand through his thinning hair.

'If you looked like a spy, you wouldn't be one.' His eyes were unnerving. I wondered how he looked at his wife and his children if he had any. Were those eyes capable of a tender look? I felt he knew things about me that even I didn't know: what my first words were, whether I snored in my sleep, perhaps what I would be doing in five years' time. Maybe he knew that all too well.

'You are in very serious trouble,' he said and rapped the table with his knuckles.

On cue, the guard appeared and escorted me to the lower depths of *Lubyanka* where all my personal belongings were taken off me and listed. I was shown to a shower room where the water went on automatically as I entered. It was freezing and smelled strongly of disinfectant. I was given a pair of coarse grey overalls to change into and then, like a dog on a leash, I was led down brightly-lit corridors, all painted off-white. I passed door after door, all closed. Left then right, then a U-turn, then a T-junction. I wondered if it was a disorientation process to unnerve me further, as if it were needed. Eventually we reached the jails. I was shoved into a cell and left with my thoughts.

The room was featureless except for an iron bed, a tiny

washbasin and a bare bulb hanging from the ceiling. The brick wall was whitewashed. I sat on the bed, feeling the stiff springs through the thin mattress. I went back over the interview in my mind, searching for hopeful signs. I couldn't think of any.

Apart from serving me barely edible food they ignored me for three days. Then, the following day before breakfast, a new face appeared at the door, a blond man with a centre parting and a slightly raffish look. He strode in offering his hand and speaking at the same time, 'Sorry to barge in so early. The name's Maclean, from the embassy.'

'Good to see a friendly face.'

His smile lasted a quarter of a second. Everything about him said, this is a formality, let's get it over with. 'How've they been treating you?'

'They think I'm a spy.'

'That doesn't answer my question.'

'Is this another interrogation?'

'Play the game man. I'm here to help.'

'Then inform them, diplomatically of course, that I'm not a spy and you want action at the highest level taken on my behalf as soon as possible.'

'It doesn't work like that. You broke their laws. We can plead your case but we can't order.'

'I see.'

'Actually, I'm not sure you do.' He perched on the bed, looking distinctly out of place. 'I should warn you, they can do what they like with you. If they want to make you a spy, they will.'

'But it's obvious. They just have to check out my story.'

The expression on his face changed and it sent fear through me. He felt pity. 'You should know by now that truth doesn't matter here,' he said.

'I came to see Lena,' I said feebly.

'I know. You've caused quite a splash.' He pulled out a pile of papers from his briefcase and threw them on the bed. 'The *Times, Telegraph, Mail* ...They love a love story. A good old British hero. One in the eye for the commies, just in time for Christmas.'

They'd dug up a photo of me in all my finery at my graduation, mortar board slightly askew, broad smile, eyes that anticipated nothing but a life of adventure. Well, I'd achieved that but to what end? I looked so much younger. I looked innocent.

'How did they get hold of this?'

'That little air traffic controller chap you tricked in Stockholm. A local reporter prised the story out of him, so I'm told.'

His eyes shifted away from mine. 'You've landed yourself in a bit of a pickle, haven't you?'

I stared at the photo. They must have got it from my mother's paltry collection.

'We're doing all we can.' He was up again, close to the door now, eager to leave. 'Our boys will liase with the relevant authorities. We'll keep you informed of developments.'

It trotted off his tongue so glibly that I realised he'd made the same speech several times before. Officialspeak, meaningless but meant to comfort. This was just a social call, really, the embassy doing the decent thing. If only I'd had tea and biscuits we could have talked about cricket or rugger.

'You'll get a few months here, perhaps a fine. Most likely a fine, they need the currency.'

'But what about my wife?'

'I'm not sure on that score, Grover. She really isn't any of our business.'

Maclean shook my hand vigorously and knocked on the door

for the guard. 'Cheer up,' he said with false good humour. 'It's my job to paint the worst picture. Just in case,' he assured me. 'You'll probably be home in no time. Your wife is a different matter. That will be very difficult.'

I couldn't look at him. I'd been home for five years and to me, it had been no better than this cell. There was a pause as Maclean hovered, then the cell door slammed behind him. I felt empty, certain that when a man from an embassy says something is difficult, he means it is impossible.

Time dragged past. I did my best to fill it but there is a limit to the number of times you can shave without bleeding, especially in cold water, and I found that I was too out of condition to do many sit-ups. Most of the time I just paced up and down, or lay on my bed staring sightlessly at the blank wall. The bare bulb was kept on all the time. I slept fitfully. The only clue to the difference between night and day was the appearance of the meal they dumped under my door. I counted to a thousand then started again. I tried to count backwards from a thousand in Russian. One day, as the food was brought in, a bowl of green liquid and a damp roll, I asked the guard for a book to read.

'What kind?'

'Anything, I just need something to do.' An unwise reply. He returned with a farming manual. *Fertilization, machine maintenance, and grain storage*. I found several mistakes in the machine maintenance section and wondered if the rest was equally flawed. I read it anyway. Twice.

Every few days I was taken up to the eleventh floor. I'd been isolated from the other prisoners but I could guess what happened to them. Sometimes, on the way up to my interrogation, I heard muffled shouts. The rooms were soundproofed but that didn't stop the thuds and the bumps, the vibrations of an inanimate object meeting a nearly inanimate object, drifting into the corridors.

The men who questioned me only hinted at physical harm. They were content to wear me down mentally. One officer would play the friend, offering coffee and mouth-watering snacks. He would invite me to a table in a warmly lit corner of the room. Sometimes I would play a game of cards with him and he would jokingly say, 'If you win, you're free,' and proceed to deal me the best hand. It was to soften me up, to make the little man feel grateful. Then Feodorov would come in. The enemy. He would stick his jaw in my face, spit rapid-fire accusations at me, twist my answers as he had on the first day, and wait for me to break, to confess to something which did not exist. I reasoned that if I stuck to the truth, they couldn't trap me.

'I have told you everything,' I said. 'I know nothing more. All I want is to see my wife.'

'We have evidence to the contrary,' he snapped. 'You work for British Intelligence. We have a report from an operative in London. He saw your name in their files.'

'It's impossible. You know that's not true, so why do you say it?'

'I ask the questions,' he would shout, 'you answer!' Then softly, 'Is that all right with you, Mr Grover?'

And I had to bite back the frustration, play humble. 'I'm sorry.'

'That is not an answer, Grover.'

'Yes, of course it is all right.'

'That's better. Now...'

And it would go on and on and on, his voice nibbling away at my strength. All my questions about Lena were ignored. I held fast to my story and they held fast to their lies. It was a game of chess that never ended although I was suspicious that Feodorov secretly knew how to trap my king the moment he tired of toying with me.

CHAPTER 29

Feodorov was in his favourite armchair. There was a grey folder on his desk labelled BG1027. He bent the corner back with his thumbnail and released it with a click. I was not asked to sit.

We were alone. I had lost count of the times I'd been up here but each time there'd usually been at least one other person in the room. I wasn't sure what it meant.

'There has been a new development,' he said.

My heart thumped at the words. At last, they believed me. They had finally admitted I was telling the truth. I sighed, and I shouldn't have. Feodorov took it as a sign of capitulation.

He looked at me sharply. 'You may well sigh, Grover. Your wife has been brought in. She told us some interesting stories.'

'Where is she?'

'Don't interrupt me, Grover, it's rude. Now, you tell me what I want to know and I will answer your question.'

'Tell you what?'

He ran his finger along the desk and inspected it. He shook his head at it. 'Tell me what Ileana told us.'

'I don't understand.'

'Ignorance is no defence even in English law, isn't that right?'

'I don't know what you want me to say.'

'I don't "want" you to say anything. I want you to tell the truth. Finally, once and for all. Then perhaps we can make a little progress and see what can be done with you. You are lucky we are being so patient. You should thank your friend Maclean. He might be junior but he knows his stuff. He has – how do you English quaintly put it? – "saved your bacon" many times. Somebody up there must like you. After all, you're still in Hotel Lubyanka. But remember, it is people like me who will eventually decide your fate and people like me don't like people like you. You are a nuisance. You clog up the works. You take up too much time. So, please, tell the truth and put an end to all this.'

I opened my mouth, hesitated – was it worth it? – then went through the same story yet again. Feodorov started to tap his fingers after about the second sentence and his eyes glazed over. He was bored too. About halfway through, he waved a hand. 'Enough. You think you can mock me but your darling little Lena has confessed everything. You wrote to her saying you wanted revenge for the way you were pushed out of this country before. You were going to apply for citizenship here then work on the wells again. Sabotage was your aim.'

'With respect,' I said, though my voice held none at all, 'I have never heard anything so ridiculous in my life.'

'Well, it's up to you. You have twenty-four hours to tell me. Go away and think about it, think about your wife. My office is always open.'

I made to leave, but as soon as my back was turned he screamed, 'Here! Now!'

Slowly I returned to my position, wondering what could be next.

'You think you have it worked out don't you, Grover. Your story tallies, you've covered your tracks.'

'There are no tracks to cover.'

'No? We all have a past we'd rather forget.'

'Dig away.'

'Oh we have, we have.' He opened the folder now and slid a large, grainy photograph across the desk. I caught my breath. It was me in a long trench coat, scarf around the lower half of my face. I was handing a package to another man outside the door of an indistinguishable block of flats. He looked vaguely familiar and very nervous. 'Do you know this man?' Feodorov asked.

It had obviously been taken during the time Frank and I were delivering documents for Talbot but there were thousands of them. I couldn't single out a name or a time or a date.

'No,' I stumbled, 'I must have met him at some point but I've no idea who he is.'

'An acquaintance of Stephen Talbot. You know him, surely.'

'I knew him, but I haven't seen him for years.'

My brain was racing. What was this?

'He left the country two years ago.'

I shrugged. 'And?'

'And, in his absence, he was found guilty of currency speculation. This gentleman, here,' he stabbed the photo with his forefinger, 'is serving five years as his accomplice. Does that interest you?'

I felt sick. Currency speculation! How could Talbot do this? I'd considered him a friend. He'd got me the job in the oilfields, helped Lena to Grozny. He'd always been there. I'd owed him a lot and I'd been grateful. I'd told him so, many times. I thought back to the night of our wedding, the feast he'd laid on. Lena called him our guardian angel. He'd smiled an embarrassed smile and said, 'You'd do the same for me in times of need.' And now I realised I already had.

'You were in league with him.'

'No.'

'You helped exchange millions of roubles for dollars. You acted as his go-between.'

'That's not true.'

'Then how do you explain this photograph?'

'He hired Frank Brown and me as runners. He set up contracts between your government and British businesses. We delivered documents, proposals, that's all.'

Slowly, Feodorov shook his head, incredulous. 'You didn't notice some packages were fatter than others? You didn't notice how many "documents" you were handling? You expect me to believe that?'

'He knew everybody. He dined with your ministers for God's sake. Important people. Who was I to question what he was up to? I came here to work on the oil rigs. Talbot said if we helped him, he'd set us up with a representative of Soyuz and that's what happened.'

'A favour for a favour.'

'Yes... No, not in the way you mean.'

'You obviously did him a big favour. He arranged your wife's transfer, did he not?'

'Yes.'

'And you didn't wonder why he was so good to you?'

'He was a friend. We were grateful.'

'So it seems.' Feodorov smiled slyly. 'And is he a friend now?'

'What do you think?'

I'd been used. We all had. Frank, Lena, me, probably everyone who'd been in contact with Talbot.

When the guards came this time they grabbed my arms and pushed them behind my back. 'You're going to jail for a very long time,' Feodorov said as I was hauled out of the room.

That night, no meal came and when I called for something to drink the guards looked past me as though I wasn't there. What seemed like weeks passed and nothing happened. I wasn't called up again; no one came to see me. I began to think they'd forgotten me. I became concerned in case my file had been lost in some dusty pile; perhaps Feodorov had been moved on and not told anyone about me; maybe I would be left to rot here forever. I knew the guards would never question why I was just growing old and sick. They probably wouldn't even notice. Time dragged by. I tried to figure how long I'd been there. I couldn't. Occasionally the silence was interrupted by the tap of footsteps down the corridor. Mostly there was nothing but the sound of my heart pumping. Pointlessly.

Sometimes I dreamed of Lena. It was always the same dream - we were picnicking in the shade of tall trees beside a cool clear stream, the sun dappling against her bare legs. She was completely relaxed and smiling. 'It's over, Brian.' she said. 'It's over... over... over...

'Grover?' It was Maclean. He wasn't happy. 'Wake up, man. We need to talk. You didn't mention Talbot. How are we meant to help you if you don't tell us what's going on?'

'I didn't know what was going on. Feodorov showed me a photo and said "There you are handing over illegal currency. Do you plead guilty or guilty?" I didn't know what he was going on about. It was five years ago, anyway.'

Maclean was unsympathetic. 'I should be at home now,' he said. 'I haven't been back for eight months. I was looking forward to a nice Christmas with my friends and then you crash land on my bloody head and they tell me I have to stay over and deal with the case. Now I find out not only are you a romantic idiot, you're also a petty thief stealing from the great Soviet state.'

'Sorry for making you do your job,' I said and immediately regretted it. He was pompous and he was arrogant but he was the only friend I had. In a softer voice, I said, 'Really, I didn't knowingly do it.'

'Well, guilty or not, luck might be on your side. You've become an international incident. The papers are clamouring for your release. And that puts pressure on the boys upstairs. If His Majesty's Government doesn't do anything, it makes them look bad. If the Soviets are lenient with you, it might make them look good in the eyes of the outside world.'

'Last time you said you were doing everything in your power.'

'Well, we are.'

'You implied that it wouldn't amount to very much. You said you didn't have much influence over events.'

'You've got a lot to learn about diplomacy, Grover. "Doing everything possible" can mean anything from coming round for a chat and making you feel better to threatening sanctions unless we secure your immediate release. It all depends how important you are. I think you'll find things start moving quite quickly from now on.'

Sure enough I was summoned to Feodorov's office the next day. He looked disappointed. There was a document on his desk. He shoved it across to me. 'Sign it.'

I hesitated. 'What am I signing?'

'It is your indictment. You're going to trial. You must sign to show you understand the charges.'

I read it through. It contained a summary of the evidence against me: illegal violation of sovereign territory, flying over forbidden frontier zones and damage to a field belonging to Glukhovo Soviet Collective. No mention of currency. I read it again to be sure.

'The charges for spying and racketeering have been dropped, Grover, but rest assured I will be pressing for the maximum sentence. You have two defence solicitors to choose from, both top men. Pick one.'

The names meant nothing to me so I chose the first on the list, a Mr Komodov. Feodorov grunted and filled in the necessary form. I waited for him to excuse me, but nothing was said. So I asked him if I could leave. He looked up at me, hatred in his eyes, and said, 'You'll never see your wife again.'

I had misjudged Maclean. He really had done all that was possible. Anyone who could disappoint Feodorov was OK in my book. At last I could put my case before a judge, plead guilty with mitigating circumstances. I had a chance. And if Feodorov had been wrong about me going to jail for a very long time, which now seemed to be the case, then he might also be wrong about Lena. If there was pressure from all sides to see a diplomatic resolution to the problems I'd caused then maybe they'd let Lena come with me too. After all, as Maclean had said, it would be a massive propaganda coup. Whatever they claimed, even Bolsheviks wanted the world to like them. Anyway, what use was a scared, unhappy nurse to them? And what harm could it do?

For the first time in months, I felt hopeful.

The trial date was set for New Year's Eve. I had a week of waiting and wondering to get through. Komodov came to visit me on Boxing Day. He bought me a box of Belgian Chocolates. 'You can spend the day getting fat like everyone else in England,' he told me. They must have cost him a fortune and I thanked him profusely. I had nothing to give back except problems. He sat down beside me on the bed, which creaked under our combined weight. Thumbing through a folder, he explained that the situation was relatively simple. Since I was pleading guilty, his job was to try for as light a sentence as possible. The rest, he said, was dependent on how lenient the judges were feeling on that particular day.

I asked him if he knew anything about Lena. He had done his homework. As far as he knew, she had been brought in, and been given the heavy treatment. Nothing physical, but they had bombarded her with questions, trying to frighten and confuse her. But she must have stood up to it quite well because they didn't seem to have much against me.

'They don't like the mix,' Komodov said simply. 'She is fine Russian stock, she should marry a man of her own type and produce good Russian children, not hook up with a capitalist who brings nothing but trouble. There are some outside of this room who will do everything to keep you apart.'

'Do you believe it is wrong?'

Komodov stood up and said stiffly, 'I am a solicitor not a philosopher.'

'I'm sorry. Stupid question.' Just by asking him, I could jeopardise his career. It just took one guard, one official to overhear and elaborate. Even bringing the chocolates had been risky.

I needed him on my side, there was no doubt about that. After all, I knew that there was a only a slim chance of getting a sympathetic Russian judge.

CHAPTER 30

Maclean and Komodov were waiting for me on the steps of Moscow City Court as I was bundled out of the police van. It was my first taste of fresh air in seven weeks and even handcuffed to a grim-faced guard, it was sweet. I shuffled through the snow.

'How do I look?'

Maclean gave me a wry smile. 'You'll do.'

The trial had been moved forward a couple of hours at the last minute, giving me scant time to prepare myself. Under my leather flying coat was the shirt I had flown in, still crumpled and filthy. They'd boxed my clothes away in the prisoner's personal effects room and they'd lain there all this time, unwashed and un-ironed. I'd managed to reclaim one of the silk ties I'd bought in Stockholm but it was stuck around my neck like an afterthought.

'I'm a mess.'

'Heroes often look like rogues,' Maclean said. 'The world's press is in there. You can't lose.'

Komodov gave him a sharp look and stepped in, a reassuring

hand on my arm. He was not given to such sentimental predictions. 'Soviet judges don't go by appearances. However, you won't make a good impression if you keep them waiting. Let's go in.'

Like the town hall in Grozny, this court was a beautiful throwback to pre-revolution days. The central hall had a floor of polished marble that echoed each footstep high into the arched ceiling. I had been expecting almost a secret trial but when I was led into the courtroom, the place was more like a theatre. The gallery was packed with reporters, embassy officials and a few people who were merely curious. Maclean had said the case was getting attention but I hadn't expected this. I felt suddenly sure that it was going to be all right. There was certainly no danger that they could secretly bundle me off to some far away destination and forget me.

The handcuffs were removed and I made my way to the dock, Komodov by my side at all times. The bench was deserted, and for a while I stood there not really knowing what to do. I looked around, smiled at some of the correspondents. A flash bulb went off as a photographer sneaked a quick shot but he was immediately escorted out of the court by a couple of burly security guards, minus his camera. I reflected on the contrast from my court appearance in Grozny when photographers were encouraged to snap away, ensuring the maximum coverage for a Hero of the Soviet Union.

Then a bell rang announcing the arrival of the judges, one woman and two men. Everyone stood as they filed into their places on the bench. Komodov whispered. 'The woman is the head judge here. She is renowned for her fairness. Make the most of your story, it might sway her.'

She sat in the centre, her well-groomed assistants beside her, and motioned for the court to do likewise. When the charges were read there was a cheer from the gallery. This was the first official sign that I was no longer considered a spy. The judge cast a weary eye upwards and said in a deliberate voice, 'I will have no rowdiness in this court. This is a serious case and will be dealt with as such. Any person who participates in premature celebrations is both foolish,' she cast a glance at a correspondent who had bellowed particularly loudly, 'and in danger of being extricated from this court. I hope that is understood.' Then she turned to me.

'Brian Grover, you have been informed of and understand the charges brought against you. How do you plead?'

'Guilty, your honour.'

She smiled. 'There is no need to call me that. This is not England. Just answer the questions simply.'

'My apologies.'

'They are not needed either.'

To this I just shrugged my shoulders, which seemed to amuse the court, though I had no idea why.

She continued, 'There are no witnesses to be called in this case, either for the defence or the prosecution so this should not take up much of our time. You took off from Stockholm aerodrome on the morning of 14th November 1938, and landed at Glukhovo at around 3.00 pm the same day. Correct?'

I cleared my throat. 'That is correct.'

'You immediately asked to be arrested and taken to Moscow.'

'Yes.'

For the next quarter of an hour the questions followed almost exactly the ones I had first been asked by Feodorov and his team. The judge, as Komodov had said, seemed fair in her questioning, interrogating for facts, not searching for nuances that she could twist to mean something else. However, when she was finished she gave way to her two assistants who were keener to unearth the 'real' motivation behind my actions.

'You say you came back to be with your wife.'

'She is all I care about now.'

'If that is the case, why did you leave in the first place?' The prosecution counsel's eyes were eager. He was aiming for the jugular and had found it.

The question took me aback. I hadn't prepared for it. Frantically I searched for a plausible answer. If I mentioned Madeleine any hope I had of portraying myself as a romantic figure would disappear. If I said that I felt I was being hounded out of Grozny or was unhappy at my situation in Moscow, then the trial would take on a political slant, something which had to be avoided at all costs.

'Well?'

I became aware of the whole court watching me, waiting on my answer. My heart thumped.

'I... I heard that my old employers might be taking on staff again, for exploration work in Iran. It was only a rumour on the grapevine, but I thought I should follow it up. I told Lena I had to return to London – '

'So you were prepared to abandon your wife, the woman you now say you would die for, in order to make money? What sort of a romantic are you?'

The twisting had started in earnest. How could I get him off my back?

'We arranged for her to follow me later when her exit visa was processed. I thought it would be a formality, since we were married... But the visa never came. And I was not allowed back into the country.'

272

'And is that unreasonable?' the prosecutor asked. 'You decide you can find better work elsewhere, perhaps taking trade secrets with you?'

'It wasn't like that…' I was floundering for words. I looked in desperation at Komodov, who stood up immediately.

'If I may intervene, I think we are straying from the point. Mr Grover has admitted all charges, he freely gave himself up. His motives are clear for all to see.'

The judge nodded, and said to the prosecutor, 'I think your line of questioning has gone far enough. Do you have any more queries?'

He shook his head. A few moments glory were clearly not worth risking the wrath of his superior.

'Defence? Your mitigation.'

Komodov had warned me his speech would be short. 'They don't like us to go on,' he had said. Now he stepped forward, addressing the court as a whole rather than just the judge: 'The Soviet Government prides itself on its security,' he said gravely. 'The guarding of our frontiers against the intrusion of spics from foreign countries is of paramount importance, and rightly so. My client, Brian Montague Grover, was ingenious and resolute in his deception, but he broke one of our most sacred laws. Clearly, as he himself confesses, he is guilty. However, close examination of his case reveals no political motives. On the contrary, he came at great personal risk and expense to draw attention to his domestic affairs. He chanced everything to be with the wife he hasn't seen for five years. He knew the dangers and was prepared to face them. While we rightly frown upon frivolous attachments between foreigners and Russian women, nevertheless we greatly respect and approve the genuine devotion of a committed couple. Here is a young man who became dissatisfied with capitalism, who entered the Soviet Union to engage in work that aided the First Five-Year Plan. His record was exemplary.'

He paused and turned in a graceful sweep to address the judge directly. 'In summation, he must be made to understand that the Soviet frontier cannot be violated with impunity, nevertheless he has a right to expect a just verdict from a Proletarian Court.'

The judges acknowledged the end of his speech then retired to consider their verdict. Komodov and I were taken to a bare antechamber where we sat down on a hard wooden bench and stared in silence at the walls. There was nothing left now but to wait. Komodov was in no mood to speak. He hadn't been pleased with the way I'd answered some of the questions. I tried to put on a brave face and thanked him for his excellent final speech.

When he looked at me his eyes were dull. 'I've had a lot of practice. This was not a difficult case. I defended in the show trials.'

'Who?'

'It doesn't matter who. They were all nobodies by the time they were dragged before the prosecutors.' He looked suddenly forlorn. His life had been devoted to defending clients who were condemned before they even knew they were going to be charged. The Great Purge was over in the courts but it clearly still lived with him every day, a memory that could never be expunged. I found myself consoling him, rather than he me.

'The cards were stacked against you. You could have done no more.'

'I could,' he said fiercely but under his breath so no one could hear. 'I could have told the truth.'

'And found yourself in the dock.'

He sighed. 'You are right, of course. There is only so much any one person can do. But is that an excuse? You did more. That is why there are so many hounds out there, baying for your story.'

'They may be helping me. World opinion. Extra pressure.'

'Don't count on it.'

There was a rap on the door and we jumped up. 'We'll soon see if you're right,' I said, worried by his gloomy prognosis.

I gripped the dock as the judge stood up to deliver her verdict.

'After careful consideration, the court finds you guilty on all counts. However, the reasons behind your crimes cannot be overlooked. We consider it an established fact that the defendant is sincerely in love with a Soviet woman. Their love has passed the test of time and separation and is therefore to be respected. For this reason, and this reason alone you will not be sentenced to imprisonment as would normally be the case. You are fined £60 sterling, your plane is to be confiscated and you are exiled from the Soviet Union for five years. You have four days in which to lodge an appeal if you so wish, during which time you will be required to stay in Lubyanka jail. That is all.'

There was muted applause from the gallery. As soon as the judges left, reporters started to yell questions, I saw embassy officials shaking hands on good work done. Maclean was smiling. But, like me, they all realised it was a hollow victory. I turned to Komodov, who had his head sunk low.

'They won't let me see her! I want to appeal, Komodov. I have to!'

'I would advise strongly against it.'

'But – '

He shook his head. 'You're a free man, Brian. That is a great concession. I am sorry, but you must accept it.' The courtroom blurred as tears filled my eyes. As the press closed in, firing questions, security guards manhandled me down the steps and through a pack of photographers on the pavement outside the court to the waiting van. I had never felt more alone.

CHAPTER 31

The harsh clanking of steel against steel woke me. At first it seemed just another day. Then I remembered - I had been to trial. Many considered me lucky. I was not going to jail for the next few years of my life. I would stay here for a while until they sorted out the paperwork and processed the payment of my fine. Then they would put me on a plane to London. After all that, it had come to nothing. I'd nearly killed myself for no reason at all. I would return to England to face reporters desperate for my story and parents equally keen to play it down.

In five years, when the term of my exile had elapsed, I could try again. But so much could happen to Lena in that time. In a few months when the fuss had died down, it would be so easy for them to quietly imprison her on some trumped-up charge. They had her marked now. She was on the list, no chance of being anonymous. She had been involved with a currency cheat, embarrassed the Soviet by her marriage to an English dissident, and before that been married to an abortionist on the run.

Anyway, by then it would be ten years since we had been with one another. She probably wouldn't want to see me again. I wondered if she knew I'd even managed to get here. My antics wouldn't have been reported in *Isvestia* or *Pravda* and I didn't think Feodorov would have told her that I was just a few corridors away when he dragged her in for questioning. He would have wanted her to worry. Why was she being brought in after all this time? What was going on? I wouldn't have blamed her if she wished she had never met me.

The cell door opened and a guard barked 'Dress, Mr Grover.' He threw my clothes on the bed. They were clean and newly pressed.

'But I'm not leaving until tomorrow?' I said.

His face remained impassive. 'Dress please,' he said again.

We walked along the corridors I had gone down so many times over the past few weeks. I was joined by another guard. They pressed in on either side. I asked where I was going but was met with silence. Soon I was in a part of the building I'd never seen before. Door after door passed by, each decorated with a polished brass number placed neatly in exactly the same place. Occasionally someone would shuffle out of a room clutching a sheaf of papers and sneak a quick glance at me. The Englishman, the madman. Our eyes would meet and there would be an instantaneous shift in their expression, a sharp momentary question smothered immediately by the realisation that any interest at all might be frowned upon.

We walked for five minutes and I wondered about the thousands of people employed in this place, each with their own room, their own desk, and their own typewriter, all filling out forms in triplicate, confirming decisions that changed unseen lives forever. This was the heart of the Soviet machine, where the sticky-tape to catch the flies was painstakingly manufactured.

Somewhere here was the person who had scrutinised all my applications for visas and then tossed them into a bin. What did they think of their job when they got home at night?

We stopped. One of the guards turned and knocked at a door and I heard a voice call 'enter'.

The room was large. A hazy light streamed in from two barred windows casting faint shadows over a thick rug that spread across a meticulously polished marble floor. At the far end of the room was an ornate ebony fireplace and mantelpiece, on top of which stood various antique statues and ornaments. I recognised some of the paintings on the wall as works I'd seen in art books. But for the obligatory picture of Lenin casting his eye over the proceedings, the place looked more like the living room of a very wealthy aristocrat.

Before me was a mahogany table, inlaid with brown leather, and the back of someone who must be extremely powerful. At first there was silence and I was not sure what to do. Then I heard a rustle of paper and Lavrenty Pavlovich Beria swivelled round in his chair. He smiled immediately. A wide affable smile.

The second most powerful man in the Soviet Union had aged. There were bags under his eyes and his hair had receded. What little remained was going grey.

'So Mr Grover, a reunion.' His handshake was firm. 'Please, sit down.' He gestured to a chair. I took it gratefully, my legs weak with anticipation.

Beria looked down at the file on his desk. He doodled a circle on a spare piece of paper and delicately filled it in. Without lifting his head he said:

'So, Mr Grover. You are probably wondering what you're doing here?'

I nodded, and felt suddenly stupid because obviously he wasn't

279

looking at me. But he didn't seem concerned that he got no answer, and carried on. 'It's quite simple really. I wanted to see in person the man who violated our international borders with the aid of a second-rate map, a cheap compass and a rusty-engined light aircraft.'

He leaned back and the leather chair squeaked with the movement. 'The very same man to whom I presented a medal and some fine vodka - how long ago was it? Six years? You're a remarkable man, Brian. I don't forget men like you. I make it my business to know all about them. We could do with many more citizens with such courage and the desire to do the right thing.'

The use of my first name put me off-balance. He sounded sincere. I felt myself warming to him but warned myself this could be the final attempt at a trap. Languidly tapping his pen against his knuckles, he stared right at me, his dark eyes searching mine.

'But you are not a comrade, are you, Brian? So you have caused us a bit of trouble.'

There it was. The crunch. And now the punishment. Nobody gets off easily here. Komodov was right. To walk away free was a great concession. Now I'd done something to make them change their minds.

'And if I may say so,' he continued, 'your attitude has surprised us all.'

He could tell I was hanging on every word he said. He was enjoying it, this 'hero' cowering before him, every muscle in my body rigid.

'Do you think you are a brave man, Mr Grover?' He paused, just long enough for me to open my mouth in response, then continued, 'or a foolish one?' Each word was clipped now, the syllables precisely pronounced.

He was leaving it open to me. It was time to make my final plea.

'With respect, your Excellency, I think it is neither foolish nor brave to want to live with my wife. I have to live with Ileana. Nothing else matters.'

It seemed so simple to me, so obvious. But I wasn't sure that Beria would see it that way.

'I like it Brian,' he said. 'But do you really think we should allow our people to be contaminated by Western values? What would happen to this great nation of ours which we have rebuilt with such toil, such diligence? Should we let all this progress crumble because of the hopes and self-seeking actions of individuals?'

I had gone too far. By stating plainly what I thought, I had put him on the defensive. I wanted to tell him that I loved my time in Russia, had learned much from its people, had spent some of the best years of my life here and never regretted it once. But now it would as if I was only saying it to flatter him.

Then he started laughing. 'Do I live up to expectations? Good little speech, eh?' He learned forward, switching back to serious in an instant. 'Do you imagine that your words might sway whatever decision it is I am about to make? Do you think you have that much influence? I must applaud your belief in the power of the individual, however naïve. But individuals are such malleable beings, cluttered with emotions and personal desires. No, Brian. Facts, plans, logic, consequences, they are the only things to believe in. The truth is that cases like yours need careful consideration. Collective consideration. They must be discussed at the highest levels and weighed up until a course of action is agreed upon.' He nodded at the ceiling, raising his eyebrows in respect for some higher deity. 'If you see what I mean.'

'I think so.'

'I'm sure you do. I have spoken to Ileana myself.'

'You've seen her! How is she?'

'I have spoken to Ileana,' he repeated calmly, 'and she is fine. She's a good woman, a credit to herself and her country. You needn't worry about anything Feodorov said. It's all a ploy to get at the truth. She was brought in for routine questioning and released. It may surprise you to hear but we do not punish our citizens out of spite or unnecessarily. We are only harsh on those who stand in the way of the greater good by their own selfishness.' He snapped another brief smile and I remembered him shaking my hand on the podium. The thin gesture, the dead eyes.

'I remember your heroics at Grozny. You did us a good turn, so...' He paused, savouring the moment, the power. 'You both seem to be honest people.'

He was going to let me see her! I knew that now. He might have said it in a roundabout way, but that's what he meant. We might even be allowed to leave together, start our life again. I wondered if there was anything I could or should say to make sure it happened. I decided silence was safest.

Beria leaned forward until his face was only a few inches from mine. His breath smelt sweet.

'You have three days to leave the country. Together.'

I closed my eyes. 'Thank you,' I said.

When I opened them, he was looking at his watch. 'I have twenty minutes before my next meeting. Would you care for a vodka? A little celebration. I don't get a lot of time when I'm not meant to be doing anything. Seems as good a reason as any to drink to, don't you think?' He turned to a beautifully polished cabinet in the corner and opened the lid to reveal a gramophone. 'The best drink is even better when accompanied by the most sublime music,' he said and put on Prokofiev's first symphony, the Classical, with its homage to Mozart and Haydn. He poured me a hefty measure. We sipped together as the sound of violins and flutes filled that exquisite room.

With all that has happened to me in my life, I have to confess that those few minutes were amongst the most surreal. I was desperate to leave but knew I had to wait to be dismissed. I was also aware that I was being allowed a moment that few others had ever experienced - one of the most powerful men in the world momentarily off duty. We chatted for a while. He still asked the questions and I still answered them. Some habits can't be overturned even by magnificent music and the best vodka. But these were questions based on real curiosity and for once he was interested in the answers without seeking a hidden meaning. He wanted to know about my parents, did I have any brothers and sisters? And what were they like? What was it like growing up in England?

The last chord ended abruptly as Beria downed the remnants of his drink, timing our meeting to the last drop. He stood up and took an envelope from the file. 'Inside here is the rest of your life. Her exit visa, enough roubles to get both of you to England and her address. She should be there now. Get off at Yaroslavsky station, a pleasant ramble for two miles and you find yourself in Bolshevo. She doesn't know you're in Russia. So be gentle. You don't want her to have a heart attack after all this.' It was his little joke. 'Here, Brian. Take it.'

I reached out, and he whisked it away from my hand.

'What?' I thought.

'Before you go I have one more question. Where do you intend to make your home?'

'In England. Why?'

He shook his head slowly. 'Don't live in England. It's not safe.'

'What do you mean?'

'War. It will happen soon. Your country will be attacked and I fear she will be overpowered. None of us in Europe will be unaffected, maybe none in the world.' He meant every word. 'Take your wife somewhere far away where you can enjoy your life together in peace.'

He handed me the envelope again and this time let me take it.

We shook hands. As I was at the door, about to leave, he said, 'It has been good to meet you but I don't want to see you again. Now, hurry home before I change my mind.'

CHAPTER 32

I grabbed my belongings from the release office, waving my papers like a man who'd just won a lottery. I ran through the sets of double doors, my haversack banging against my back, and out into the streets of Moscow.

It was pitch black and snowing heavily. No cars passed, no people walked by me as I made my way to the station. A biting wind blew into my face, whipped snow like dust from the pavements. Under a street lamp I stopped, collar up and back to the onslaught, to rip open the envelope Beria had given me. I pulled out the address. The words were scrawled in an almost illegible handwriting. I held it away from me to see it in stronger light, and made out the word Bolshevo. I looked at my watch - 11.58. I didn't know if there were any trains this late. I ran until my lungs felt they would explode.

Panting, I asked for a train to Yaroslavsky. The porter waved towards a platform where a train was pulling out. I followed it all the way up the platform, gauging its speed, and leapt onto the foot rail under a door on the second last carriage. Angling myself to the side, I swung it open and collapsed into the nearest seat. For a few moments I just sat there, catching my breath, wheezing like an old man. I leaned against the window and watched the white-capped trees flitting by faster and faster as the train picked up speed, and I prayed to God that I could find Lena's house. It was an area I didn't know well.

Half an hour later, I stepped on to Yaroslavsky platform. Thick dark clouds loomed overhead, the moon hidden behind them. Beyond the confines of the station buildings there was no light to guide me, only the faint outlines of a track leading into open countryside. This was the outermost edge of Moscow, where the suburbs dissolved into an endless expanse of flat land. Two miles, Beria had told me. A pleasant ramble, he had said. Who said the Russians had no sense of humour?

The weather was getting worse. I pulled my cap tight around my ears, bent my head into the wind and ploughed on. The further I went, the deeper the drifts got until I found myself wading at times knee-deep in the darkness. Beria had also said something else, and it began to plague me. 'Before I change my mind.' The man had enjoyed playing me along. Would he do it again?

There was no point in worrying about that. Just keep moving before you freeze to death. I imagined Lena walking this way the next morning and finding a frozen statue that looked very familiar, and I pressed on. The track climbed the only hill for miles around. I slipped and fell in my haste and at times I was on all fours, crawling to get to the top. When I finally made it, I sank down in the drifts, desperate for a rest.

I looked down the other side of the hill. There was a yellow dot swaying below me, no more than a few hundred yards away. At first I thought it was someone swinging a lamp as they walked.

Then I realised it was my head not the light that was moving. With all my will I held it still, and stared harder. There were vague shapes, deeper black than the background. Houses. It must be Bolshevo. With renewed strength I picked myself up, and tried to run down the slope towards the light. My legs wouldn't obey and I stumbled like a drunk. I fell on my backside half way down, scrambled forward and fell again. I must have looked like something out of a Buster Keaton film. Finally the track levelled off and the light became brighter. As I got closer, I saw that it came from the first building in the group. I looked for a street sign but it could have been anywhere, covered under the drifts. I stumbled up to the old oak door.

I hesitated. My hand hovered over the knocker. The light had come from an oil lamp in the window, a diffuse glow through faded curtains. I went over to it, peered inside, but could make nothing out. I had to knock. This was the only place that showed any sign of life. Everyone knew everyone else in these sorts of places. They might know where Lena lived, if not they could direct me to her street. That's if they didn't slam the door in my face as soon as they saw me.

I pulled off my cap and patted down my hair. I stuffed my gloves in my pockets and rubbed my face. Coarse stubble like sandpaper grated my skin. Nothing I could do about that. I banged on the door. I waited, stamped my feet and was reaching for the knocker again, when I heard the shuffle of feet behind the door. A scraping as the latch chain was put on. A thin headscarfed face peeked out, covered in shadow. The eyes looked frightened. I stepped back to try to reassure her and said, 'I am sorry to bother you so late but I'm looking for Ileana Petrovna. I got lost in the snow, but I know she lives somewhere round here. Can you help me?'

The woman tried to close the door but I stuck my foot in the way. 'Please,' I begged. 'I mean her no harm. She is my wife. I have come from England to find her.'

A moment's hesitation. 'She is from Moscow?' The thin voice was hardly audible.

'Yes, that's right.'

'Two streets down, the third house on the right side.'

I gasped my thanks and set off, elated and nervous.

I had to knock several times before a light came on. I just hoped I'd got the right house in the darkness. The door cracked open and I glimpsed a small brown mark on a pale cheek. I couldn't speak.

Then the voice inside whispered: 'Brian? No, it can't be. *Brian!*' She yanked at the latch, ripped it from its hold. The door swung open and snowflakes danced into her house. We stared at each other like strangers. She was thin and frail, her eyes dark. But it was Lena.

Five years older. Five years more beautiful.

The ship's horn sounded as we entered Harwich harbour.

'Looks like we stopped the traffic,' I said.

'There are so many people!' Lena cried. 'Why are they here?'

'You're famous. You'll be the talk of the society columns.'

'Brian, I'm scared.'

I squeezed her hand. 'Relax,' I said. 'Enjoy it while it lasts.'

We smiled and we smiled again as photographers called from different sides and questions were fired at us from every angle. Someone threw confetti as we descended the steps of the great liner. Cheering crowds strained against a thin line of policemen. There must have been over a thousand people jostling for position, some with flowers, some with 'welcome home' banners, some just wanting to be part of an occasion they had read about. Lena slipped her arm around my back and rested her head on my shoulder. She held me urgently, bewildered but excited.

'Brian?' There was a tremor in her voice as she stared at the rows of outstretched hands. I turned her face away from them and kissed her.

'It'll be all right,' I whispered.

We searched the sea of faces. 'Look!' she squealed and pointed. 'There's Frank!'

He was right at the back, pushing his way through. As we got closer, he saw we were watching him. He lifted a banner above his head.

YOU LOST YOUR BET. YOU OWE ME.

'What does it say? What does it say?' Lena asked. Before I could answer, there was a loud pop above us. We turned to see the ship's captain merrily shaking a huge bottle. Champagne shot up in a frothy fountain and cascaded all over us.

Lena shrieked, then licked her lips. 'Tastes good.'

'As good as in the Metropol?' I shouted.

'Better.'

I picked her up and swung her round as the champagne drenched us from head to toe. The cameras clicked, bulbs popped and the world watched us spin.

We became freeze-frames, dancers caught in a flash of light.

When the furore eventually died down, I took Lena to the old house in Monmouth where I'd lived as a child. We went there on a blustery afternoon in late January. I wanted to show her round the grounds, the little pond where the tadpoles had hatched and the tunnel through the copse. I grabbed her hand and started running. She stumbled behind me, laughing and slipping on patches of frost.

'What are you doing?' she cried.

'I want you to see something,' I called back.

We reached the grove and I was struck once again, after all that time, by the stillness of the place. It was untouched, wilder than when I had played in it as a child. Ferns spilled out over the old pathway, branches broken in autumn gales hung limply from lopsided tree trunks. It had been abandoned, Alex no longer there to tend it; it had become its own little wilderness.

It was hard work fighting our way through but eventually I found the spot I was looking for, the clearing and there, to the left surrounded by long wisps of dark green grass, was the tree stump from my childhood.

'I told you I would bring you here one day,' I said.

'And will we live here?'

I sighed. As appealing as that thought was, I had decided to take Beria's advice. 'No, I have been offered a job in South Africa. We can start completely fresh. But I wanted you to see it before we left. Is that OK?'

'As long as we are together, I don't mind where we go.'

EPILOGUE

For many weeks she had been frail, though still just as headstrong. The body winding down but the spirit not wanting to accept it. She refused her food, told me to stop fussing. I think she knew.

We lay together, her head on my chest. The air was dry and hot and still. Outside the sounds of the South African night that we had become accustomed to over the last 50 years - the constant whirr of the cicadas, the occasional distant bark of a hyena and low growl of a lion - were reassuring. We spoke in whispers.

'Brian. You know I wouldn't change a thing, don't you?'

'Really? Despite all the hassle?'

'Despite it all.'

I buried my head in her neck, not wanting her to see my tears. She drew back. 'You could at least have shaved,' she said.

'I'm sorry.'

'Too late for that now,' she rasped. Her chest heaved as she struggled for breath. I drew back to give her space. Her hand gripped mine with ferocious strength and her eyes sparkled. Suddenly I realised she was laughing.

'Get back here. I'm not finished yet,' she ordered. I tightened the sheets around us and curled my arms behind her shoulders. She looked up at me, teasing.

'Will you remember me?'

'Don't say things like that.' I turned away.

'But will you?'

'Lens, how could I not? You are everything to me. You have been since I first met you.'

She shuffled under the blankets, rearranging her body with difficulty until her head was back on my chest. In a quiet, wicked voice she said, 'All right Mr Grover,' and bit my nipple with all her might. I yelped. 'You'll remember me now,' she said.

Quietly, she turned on to her back.

'I need to sleep. I'm so tired. Will you stay with me, Brian?'

'Of course.'

'Cross your heart?'

'Cross my heart.'